T0305226

Political Institutions and Development

GLOBAL DEVELOPMENT NETWORK SERIES

Series editors: Natalia Dinello, *Principal Political Scientist, Global Development Network*

Meeting the challenge of development in the contemporary age of globalization demands greater empirical knowledge. While most research emanates from the developed world, the Global Development Network series is designed to give voice to researchers from the developing and transition world – those experiencing first-hand the promises and pitfalls of development. This series presents the best examples of innovative and policy-relevant research from such diverse countries as Nigeria and China, India and Argentina, Russia and Egypt. It encompasses all major development topics ranging from the details of privatization and social safety nets to broad strategies to realize the Millennium Development Goals and achieve the greatest possible progress in developing countries.

Titles in the series include:

Testing Global Interdependence
Issues on Trade, Aid, Migration and Development
Ernest Aryeetey and Natalia Dinello

Political Institutions and Development
Failed Expectations and Renewed Hopes
Edited by Natalia Dinello and Vladimir Popov

Political Institutions and Development

Failed Expectations and Renewed Hopes

Edited by

Natalia Dinello

Principal Political Scientist,
Global Development Network, New Delhi, India

Vladimir Popov

Professor,
New Economic School and Academy of the National Economy,
Moscow, Russia

GLOBAL DEVELOPMENT NETWORK

Edward Elgar
Cheltenham, UK • Northampton, MA, USA

Published by
Edward Elgar Publishing Limited
Glensanda House
Montpellier Parade
Cheltenham
Glos GL50 1UA
UK

Edward Elgar Publishing, Inc.
William Pratt House
9 Dewey Court
Northampton
Massachusetts 01060
USA

A catalogue record for this book
is available from the British Library

Library of Congress Cataloguing in Publication Data
Political institutions and development : failed expectations and renewed
hopes / edited by Natalia Dinello, Vladimir Popov.
    p. cm.
  "Global Development Network."
Includes bibliographical references and index.
  1. Economic development—Political aspects. 2. Institution building. 3.
Democracy. 4. Developing countries—Economic policy. I. Dinello, Natalia
E. II. Popov, Vladimir, 1954–

  HD82.P55 2007
  338.9—dc22

                                                                2007029855

ISBN 978 1 84720 224 6

Printed and bound in Great Britain by MPG Books Ltd, Bodmin, Cornwall

Contents

Notes on the Contributors

ARILD ANGELSEN is an Associate Professor at the Norwegian University of Life Sciences and a Senior Associate of the Center for International Forestry Research. He has worked and published extensively on deforestation, environmental income, local resource management and poverty, with a geographical focus on Eastern/Southern Africa (Uganda, Malawi) and Indonesia, where he has lived for over four years. He is currently coordinator of CIFOR's Poverty Environment Network, that collects comprehensive socioeconomic and environmental data from 5,000–6,000 households in more than 20 countries.

LUCA BARBONE is the World Bank director for poverty reduction – PREM Network. He joined the World Bank in 1988 and has held a number of positions in the Latin American and Caribbean, European, Central Asian and African regions of the bank. From 2000 to 2004 he was World Bank director for Ukraine, Moldova and Belarus. He holds a doctorate in economics from the Massachusetts Institute of Technology.

BHAGIRATH BEHERA is currently working at the Indian Institute of Technology, Kharagpur. He holds a doctorate in environmental and natural resource economics from the University of Bonn, Germany. He holds a master's and M.Phil. degree in economics and environmental economics, respectively, from the University of Hyderabad, India. His research interests are environmental and resource economics, New Institutional Economics and its application to natural resource management, political economy, and public policy and governance. He has had several scientific papers on these areas published in both national and international journals such as *Ecological Economics* and *Forest Policy and Economics* and in edited books.

LOUISE CORD is the sector manager for the Poverty Reduction Group (PRMPR) in the Poverty Reduction and Economic Management Network (PREM) of the World Bank. Prior to holding that position, she led a multi-donor program examining the how the micro underpinnings of economic development strategies affect the ability of poor households to participate in and contribute to growth. Prior to joining the World Bank, she held a variety of jobs in development, including working for USAID on a livestock project in rural Niger, interning for the State Department in Burundi and consulting with the Development Assistance Committee of the OECD in Paris. She received her Ph.D. from the Fletcher School of Law Diplomacy.

NATALIA DINELLO has earned doctoral degrees from the University of Pittsburgh and the Soviet Academy of Science. As Principal Political Scientist at the Secretariat of the Global Development Network, she designs and implements strategies and programs for building research capacity in developing and transition economies. She also has an extensive publication record for her own research and is executive editor of the *Global Development Network Series*, designed to give voice to researchers from the developing and transition world.

STEFANIE ENGEL is Professor of Environmental Policy and Economics at the Swiss Federal Institute of Technology in Zurich, Switzerland. She holds a doctorate in agricultural and resource economics from the University of Maryland. During and upon completion of her Ph.D., she spent two and a half years in Colombia, South America, where she was lecturer and research fellow at the Universidad de Los Andes and at the economic research institute Fedesarrollo. From 2000 to 2006, she was senior researcher at the Center for Development Research of the University of Bonn, Germany.

RUBEN ENIKOLOPOV is a doctoral candidate in economics at Harvard University. Before going to Harvard, he received an M.A. in economics from the New Economic School in Moscow and M.Sc. in physics from Moscow State University. His research interests include the effect of political institutions on the results of fiscal decentralization and comparison of elected and appointed public officials. In 2006, his paper won first prize in the Global Development Research Medals competition.

IGNACIO FRANCESCHELLI obtained his B.A. in economics in 2004 from Universidad de San Andrés, Argentina. His research interests include public opinion, mass media and social mobilization. He is currently a doctoral student in economics at Northwestern University.

FRANCIS FUKUYAMA is Bernard L. Schwartz Professor of International Political Economy at the Paul H. Nitze School of Advanced International Studies (SAIS) of Johns Hopkins University, and the director of the SAIS International Development program. He has written widely on issues relating to questions concerning political and economic development. His 1992 book, *The End of History and the Last Man*, has appeared in over twenty foreign editions and made the bestseller lists in the United States, France, Japan and Chile.

KATY HULL works in the Poverty Reduction Group of the World Bank, where she has researched the relationships between democracy, institutions and poverty reduction. She has an E.M.A. in human rights and democratization and an M.A. in international relations from Johns Hopkins School of Advanced International Studies.

CHARLES B.L. JUMBE holds a doctorate in economics from the Norwegian University of Life Sciences. He spent 11 years working as a Research Fellow at the Centre for Agricultural Research and Development in Lilongwe, Malawi, and six years as an economist in various government ministries, including the Ministries of Economic Planning and Development, Energy and Mining, and Agriculture. His research interests focus on assessing institutional and economic outcomes of development policies and programs by applying both qualitative and rigorous quantitative econometric tools. He has published a number of articles in international journals, written book chapters and compiled research reports for completed assignments.

VICTOR POLTEROVICH is Head of Laboratory at the Central Economics and Mathematics Institute (TsEMI) of the Russian Academy of Sciences and Chairman of the Academic Committee at the New Economic School in Moscow. He holds degrees in engineering, mathematics and economics, including a doctorate in economics from TsEMI.

VLADIMIR POPOV is a Professor at the New Economic School in Moscow, a sector head at the Academy of the National Economy in Moscow and Visiting Professor at Carleton University in Ottawa. In 1996–98 he was a Senior Research Fellow at the World Institute for Development Economics Research of the United Nations University (WIDER/UNU) in Helsinki, Finland, co-directing a project 'Transition Strategies, Alternatives and Outcomes'. His publications include: *Three Drops of Water: Notes on China by a Non-Sinologist, Transition and Institutions: The Experience of Late Reformers* and *The Asian Crisis Turns Global*.

LUCAS RONCONI is a doctoral candidate in public policy at the University of California, Berkeley. He is also a lecturer at Universidad de San Andrés in Argentina and holds a master's degree in development economics from Yale

University. His research focuses on labor and social policy in Latin America. He is currently completing his dissertation, that investigates the causes and consequences of labor informality.

JUSTIN SANDEFUR is a doctoral candidate in economics at Oxford University. He has worked as a consultant to the World Bank Poverty Reduction Group and a research assistant at the Centre for the Study of African Economics at Oxford.

SHAOGUANG WANG is Professor of Political Science at the Chinese University of Hong Kong and the chief editor of the *China Review*, an interdisciplinary journal on greater China. He studied for his LL.B. at Peking University and his Ph.D. at Cornell University. He taught at Tijiao High School in Wuhan from 1972 to 1977 and Yale University from 1990 to 2000. He has authored and co-authored about 20 books and numerous journal articles in Chinese and English.

EKATERINA ZHURAVSKAYA earned a doctorate from Harvard University and currently is an Associate Professor of Economics at the New Economic School and the academic director of the Center for Economic and Financial Research in Moscow, Russia. Her academic writings focus on estimating the effect of political and economic institutions on development and transition. Zhuravskaya won the Young Economists Competition of the fifth Nobel Symposium in Economics in 1999 and was named a Global Leader for Tomorrow by the World Economic Forum in Davos in 2001. She was awarded the Best Economist prize by the President of the Russian Academy of Sciences in both 2002 and 2003. In 2006 her paper won first prize in the Global Development Research Medals competition.

Acknowledgments

This book is the result of the Global Development Network's efforts to promote policy-relevant social science research on development. Published as part of the GDN Series, it assembles papers from the 2006 Global Development Research Medals competition and the Seventh Annual Global Development Conference held under the theme *Institutions and Development: At the Nexus of Global Change* (St. Petersburg, Russia, January 2006). The editors and contributors to the book owe their gratitude to GDN President Lyn Squire as both reviewer and adviser and to the GDN Secretariat staff for general support. Their thanks also go to Ann Robertson, who was invaluable in supervising the copyediting process and preparing the text for publication. Finally, they are indebted to the staff of Edward Elgar Publishing Ltd, whose extraordinary receptivity and tactful advice make preparation of the GDN Series a continually rewarding experience.

Introduction

What Matters for Institutions' Effect on Development: Conditions and Qualifications

Natalia Dinello and Vladimir Popov

Most social scientists agree that 'institutions matter'. But there are variations in the interpretation of this thesis. Some consider the recent advances in institutional analysis to be a breakthrough, claiming that 'neoclassical economics was dismissive of institutions' (Williamson 2000, 595). Others contend that no socioeconomic inquiry – including research stemming from the teachings of Adam Smith – is absolutely institution-free, even though the 'weight' attributed to institutions as a factor of development varies depending on the school of thought. Not challenging the postulate that 'institutions matter' and building on previous research, this book explores how much political institutions matter and seeks to identify exactly what matters if institutions are to affect development.

In the opening chapter, Francis Fukuyama defines an institution as 'a rule constraining human choice and which permits collective action among a group of people' (21). His description is very similar to Douglass North's definition of institutions as rules and norms which constrain human behavior (1990b). Both Fukuyama and North make a distinction between formal and informal institutions,[1] although Fukuyama is more emphatic in asserting the critical importance of this distinction, preferring that the term 'institution' be confined to formal rules established by states (21). In the same vein, Bhagirath Behera and Stefanie Engel (Chapter 7) define institutions as 'formal and informal rules of a society. They [institutions] set the limits of individual action and crucially determine the incentives faced by individual resource users' (200). Serving as instruments for overcoming imperfections of individual rationality and for decreasing transaction costs, institutions improve the effectiveness of decisions and, as a result, stimulate investment, economic growth and social advancement.

Learning from the research on economic institutions, including constraints

1

pertaining to the production, allocation and distribution of goods and services as well as markets, this book focuses instead on political institutions. This type of institution generally refers to the rules and norms guiding elections, operation of a particular form of political system and government, checks and balances in governance and political accountability and stability (Jütting 2003, 14). Highlighting the link between political and economic institutions, Luca Barbone and his coauthors indicate in their contribution to this volume, 'Political institutions reflect the allocation of power in society; those with power will in turn determine the shape of economic institutions, influencing who has power ...' (50, refering to Acemoglu, Johnson and Robinson 2005).

Specifically, the book chapters explore governance at the national and subnational levels, including democracy versus authoritarianism, forms of democratic rule (e.g., presidential versus parliamentary) and different levels of governance ranging from the regional to the community level, in order to understand the intricate interplay between political institutions and development.

Which macro- and micropolitical institutions are most conducive to development? And how are political institutions themselves shaped by successful versus ineffective development? The goal of this book is to discuss these questions and also to shed light on how political institutions interact with other institutions and when, where and under what conditions this interaction produces optimal development outcomes. It thus intends to qualify the imperative that institutions matter.

The book is divided in two parts. The first five chapters examine macropolitical institutions, such as authoritarianism and democracy, electoral systems, the state apparatus, political parties and federalism as well as their impact on economic growth and development in general. The second part contains three meticulous case studies of the operation of local institutions in developing countries – success stories as well as failures which analyze why allegedly well-designed political arrangements may produce unexpected outcomes in terms of socioeconomic advancement and poverty reduction. Each case spells out the exact conditions needed to reap the benefits of democratic political institutions.

It is widely believed that many existing macropolitical institutions serve to maintain a status quo marked by enormous inequalities and injustices to the impoverished layers of the population, while micropolitical institutions often help organize, empower and mobilize various groups within the developing world to change the status quo and to improve their condition. Going beyond theory and cross-country studies, it is essential to understand 'what improving institutional quality means on the ground' (Rodrik, Subramanian and Trebbi 2002, 23). Complementing the discussion of macropolitical institutions with an analysis of norms and rules governing human behavior in indigenous communities, the book attempts to further the 'ground level' understanding of those micro-level institutions in the developing world which involve the participation of less-privileged groups.

This collection of articles builds on the previous research and confirms the consensus that 'institutions matter' for development. However, these chapters start from this assumption and present new evidence that the most 'advanced' and well-designed political institutions which may work successfully in Western countries often fail to promote economic growth, equity and stability in the developing world. In particular, democratization and decentralization are not always associated with better economic performance. Without administrative capabilities and a strong commitment to the rule of law, they can lead to the outright deterioration of economic and social performance indicators.

This book seeks to correct a common misperception in the institutionalist literature. Similar to the criticism of the Washington Consensus for its 'one size fits all' policy, the authors here argue that one institutional form is not appropriate for every situation. Instead, institutions must be tailored to local conditions, and the best people to explain context are the local experts themselves. With its commitment to incorporating local knowledge into rigorous research, the Global Development Network (GDN) is ideally suited for this task. In this volume GDN-affiliated scholars from developing countries not only expose the exceptions to the common expectations about institutions, but they also share their unique knowledge of how to reshape institutions to accommodate local circumstances.

Following *Testing Global Interdependence: Issues on Trade, Aid, Migration and Development* (Aryeetey and Dinello 2007), this is the second volume within the *Global Development Network Series* designed to present empirical knowledge on the forces driving global development and to give voice to researchers from the developing and transition world – individuals experiencing first hand the promises and pitfalls of development. The articles included in this book were presented at the Seventh Annual Global Development Conference that took place in St. Petersburg, Russia, in January 2006. Most of the authors here represent GDN's network partners in the developing world; some of them were finalists in the annual Global Development Research Medals competition.

'INSTITUTIONS RULE'

The emphasis on the institutional explanation of development is often interpreted as a reaction to the inadequacy of the Washington Consensus, with its neoliberal emphasis on a minimal state. In response, the New Institutional Economics (NIE) emerged as a school of thought based on two major propositions: 'institutions do matter' and 'the determinants of institutions are susceptible to analysis by the tools of economic theory' (Matthews as quoted in Williamson 2000, 595). The incorporation of institutional analysis into economics has been complemented by the new institutionalism in sociology (Powell and DiMaggio 1991) and in political science (Hall and Taylor 1996). Regardless of the brand of institutionalism, most of its proponents believe that institutions are the product of 'visible hands' and attribute much importance to an active and efficient state.

Reflecting a view of institutions as embracing all domains of life, North (2000, 7) insisted that 'there is no such thing as *laissez-faire*'.[2] Rather, institutions operate in ways that either reduce or increase the costs of market transactions. Moreover, the originator of the *laissez-faire* principle, Adam Smith, has been occasionally presented as a misunderstood institutionalist. Note that Dani Rodrik and his coauthors used a quote from Smith on the importance of the administration of justice, protection of property rights, enforcement of contracts and payments of debt as an epigraph to their now famous article, 'Institutions Rule'. Further strengthening the 'institutions matter' thesis, they showed that when giving a 'fair chance' to geography and trade openness to compete with the institutions variable, 'the quality of institutions trumps everything else. Once institutions are controlled for, integration has no direct effect on incomes, while geography has at best weak direct effects' (Rodrik, Subramanian and Trebbi 2002, 4). A number of studies have also demonstrated a robust and significant indirect relationship between the quality of institutions and growth via institutions' effect on the volume of investment (Knack and Keefer 1995; Aron 2000).

Given an impetus by the writings of North, NIE authors and Rodrik, authors outside of economics have also placed high expectations on institutions as a clue to unlock many conundrums of development. Focusing on political arrangements, Robert Bates and his coauthors (Bates et al. 2004) have confirmed the importance of institutions for growth. Studies focused on various types of democratic regimes have corroborated predictions that particular institutions correlate with many aspects of socioeconomic development (Persson, Roland and Tabellini 2000; Persson, 2002; Persson and Tabellini 2003, 2004; Alesina, Ardagna and Trebbi 2006). Some of the studies have also provided empirical evidence that particular political institutions are associated with greater economic growth and equality (Persson 2005; Burkhart and Lewis-Beck 1994).

The contributors to this book share the emerging consensus that institutional quality is important for development. Fukuyama, for example, takes for granted the assumption that 'institutions matter' (21). Barbone and his coauthors empirically test this assumption and discover a relationship between macro-level institutions and poverty reduction. Their case studies of four countries which experienced significant poverty reduction in the 1990s under a variety of political regimes (Bangladesh, Ghana, Tunisia and Uganda) have produced evidence suggesting that democratic accountability can increase the provision of basic public services. Furthermore, their cross-country empirical results reveal a robust statistical association between democracy and reductions in child mortality. These findings corroborate observations from previous research; namely, that democracy may favorably influence various indicators of socioeconomic development (Olson 1996; Fidrmuc 2003; Quinn and Wooley 2001; Fish 1999).

Using data from 75 developing and transition countries, Ruben Enikolopov and Ekaterina Zhuravskaya conclude that institutions play an important role in determining the results of fiscal decentralization. In particular, they find that a strong national party system is a very effective way to align the political incentives of local politicians with national objectives, while preserving their accountability to local constituencies, a necessary combination for efficient decentralization. They also find that in developing and transition countries, older and more stable party systems as well as lower fractionalization of government parties are associated with fiscal decentralization's better effects on economic growth, government quality and public goods. Well-grounded in previous research on federalism and centralization, these findings confirm William Riker's (1964) theory stating that the results of fiscal decentralization depend on the level of a country's political centralization.

The same sentiment about the role of institutions is expressed in respect to their operation at the micro level. Writing about local institutions in forest management, Charles Jumbe and Arild Angelsen use the following metaphor: 'Forests "grow" on institutions as much as they grow on the soil. The soil provides nutrients for trees to grow and generate different environmental goods and services for use by mankind, while institutions shape the behavior of forest users to ensure sustainable forest utilization and management' (171). Jumbe and Angelsen explain that after many years of strict government control over forest resources which constrained the flow of benefits to the surrounding communities, many governments worldwide have developed policies to devolve responsibility for forest management to local bodies. The devolution of forest management is seen as a rural development strategy to enhance the contribution of forests to poverty reduction and promote village-level economic development and biodiversity conservation. By showing the significance of local institutions for managing and protecting forests, Jumbe and Angelsen advance the knowledge about community systems of governance in the developing world gathered by previous studies on access to and use of such resources as forests, land, soil and water (Dustin Becker 2003; Lanjouw and Levy 2002; Nemarundwe and Kozanayi 2002; Mazzucato and Neimeijer 2000).

The consensus on institutional quality and development is, however, not the pinnacle of this book. It is rather its prerequisite, highlighting the relevance of institutional analysis. As suggested by the book title, a dose of skepticism regarding the power of institutions is necessary in order to draw an accurate picture of their impact on development.

FAILED EXPECTATIONS

Even though recent studies have confirmed that institutions do indeed matter, many of them have also cooled the euphoria about institutions as an ultimate explanation for the outcomes of comparative development. Furthermore, they have challenged the expectation that there exists some 'perfect' set of institutions most conducive to growth and prosperity, suggesting that very strong claims about the link between institutions and development need to be critically assessed and moderated. This book learns from previous observations regarding the limited impact of institutions on development and corroborates some of them. It also rejects unconditional institutional determinism and provides new evidence that some allegedly 'good' institutions have failed to universally generate positive development outcomes.

The historical analysis performed by Stanley Engerman and Kenneth Sokoloff (1994; 2003) has shown that economic differences have both institutional and non-institutional explanations, and that no particular institution, narrowly defined, is indispensable for growth: there can be reasonable substitutes. Moreover, the empirical analysis of the relationship between institutions and development has produced mixed results and often runs against intuition and widely held political beliefs. For example, even though Bates and his coauthors demonstrated the benefits of political accountability for growth, their message on the worth of competitive elections is rather ambivalent: the shift to competitive politics appears to heighten the level of political disorder, thus highlighting the costs of 'good governance' (Bates et al. 2004, 50–51). This finding contrasts with the conventional focus on the costs of 'bad governance' and disputes absolute truths about 'good' versus 'bad'.

In the same vein, many studies have questioned the common belief that 'democracy is good for equality and growth'. Although democratic regimes may be expected to mitigate income inequalities via redistribution and, if successful, may finally arrive at a point of stable equilibrium with high economic growth, the actual record of democracies in this respect is not that clear. But even if a democracy generates greater income equality, this does not necessarily entail economic growth. Building on the assumption that redistribution is more pronounced under democracy than under an authoritarian regime, that can easier ignore concerns of the poor, Alesina and Rodrik (1994) present a model demonstrating that a stronger pressure toward redistribution of incomes in favor of the poor in democracies could negatively affect stimuli for economic growth.

Consistent with the authors quoted above, the contributors to this book question the narrowly conceived institutional determinism in relation to development. The key thesis of Fukuyama's chapter is 'There is no such thing as an optimal formal political institution'. Not denying the role of institutions, he highlights the false expectation that some optimal institutional design exists which can be effectively imported to any country and produce the desired outcomes. Although institutions are important, he argues, there are limits to their importance, and their operation is contingent on many factors: 'Institutions are only enabling devices; those that facilitate or encourage strong and decisive political decision making are only as good as the policies being pursued' (34).

Similarly, the empirical study by Barbone and his colleagues suggests that the relationship between institutions and development is neither simple nor straightforward: researchers have failed to support the hypothesis that improved governance leads to broad-based income growth and have obtained mixed results on the impact of democratization on poverty reduction. These new findings further corroborate the results of the extensive literature attempting to link quantitative measures of institutions (such as civil liberties and property rights) with GDP across countries and over time (Aron 2000), which have revealed that the relationship between the quality of institutions and investment and growth is by no means robust. For example, the review concludes that 'democracy, acting through various channels, may have both positive and negative implications for growth' (Aron 2000, 124). Moreover, in many cases when correlations between institutional variables and growth were established, a relationship was suggested but not the direction of causality.

Writing about micropolitical institutions in forest management, Behera and Engel also draw a complex and equivocal picture of the development effect of programs devolving rights and responsibilities over natural resources to local user groups. Theoretically, they claim, the stronger involvement of village-level organizations can lead to micro-level institutions which promote sustainable development and enhance local livelihoods. But assuming that the success of the devolution programs is largely dependent on the active participation of a broad segment of local communities, including poor and marginalized groups, they find only partial evidence that genuine participation has been achieved. Contrary to theoretical expectations and the findings of past studies, Jumbe and

Angelsen reach quite contradictory conclusions from their study on a similar topic: although there is some evidence that local participation in the forest co-management program had positive effects on household income in one setting, it had negative effects on household income in another setting.

Moreover, because of the endogeneity problem – factors other than political institutions influence performance, and they are in turn influenced by performance and non-political institutions – the search for an 'optimal' set of political institutions conducive to development may be misleading. Since institutions are not cast in stone, it is more appropriate to ask why political arrangements which become entrenched and function well in some countries do not work in other countries and are in fact abandoned again and again, despite numerous attempts to introduce or transplant them. The expectations of universally 'good' institutions which magically make everyone prosperous and happy have indeed failed. But this does not mean that institutions do not affect development. Rather, it calls for a more nuanced and guarded approach to the institutional analysis.

RENEWED HOPES

Since generalizations about the impact of institutions on development are not consistently supported by data, it may be more productive to think in terms of particular conditions under which the imperatives of development could materialize. This is congruent with the idea of institutions being embedded in a local setting influenced by historical trajectories and culture. Having observed that 'The history of institutions in high-performing societies is one of change over time in response to changing circumstances', Engerman and Sokoloff defined 'good institutions' as those 'well adapted for economic performance in ... specific settings' (2003, 29). Since no single institution is universally effective at promoting growth, the question becomes which specific conditions and factors of institutional change would be most conducive to sustainable development. Similarly, Rodrik and his coauthors stated, 'Desirable institutional arrangements have a large element of context specificity, arising from differences in historical trajectories, geography and political economy or other initial conditions' (2002, 22).

Contemplating conditions under which institutions can generate best development outcomes will advance the conventional wisdom about the importance of institutions to the next level – qualifying what exactly matters if institutions are to affect development. For example, Robert Barro (1999) finds that the preference for democracy rises with per capita GDP, primary schooling, middle-class share of income and lower reliance on natural resources. In a slightly different variation of the same argument, Adam Przeworski and his coauthors (2000) have shown that any country, even a poor one, can become democratic, but in order to *stay* democratic a certain level of income and other conditions need to be in place.

The renewed hopes that institutions indeed affect development refer to meeting particular conditions which trigger this effect. Writing about macro-level arrangements, Victor Polterovich and Vladimir Popov connect political institutions with legal institutions and identify order based on legal rules as a condition of successful economic development under democracy. They demonstrate that in countries where law and order is strong enough, democratization stimulates economic growth, whereas in countries with poor law and order, democratization undermines growth. If the condition of initial law and order is not met, illiberal democracy emerges – the shadow economy expands, the quality of governance worsens and the macroeconomic policy becomes less prudent, with negative consequences for growth. Similarly, Shaoguang Wang argues in his chapter that an effective state is a precondition of high-quality and sustainable democracy, while Barbone and his coauthors confirm, based on their empirical estimations, that initial conditions – namely poverty, income inequality and ethnic fractionalization – undermine democracy's positive effects on the poor.

The studies at the micro level also highlight conditions under which political institutions can affect development. According to Jumbe and Angelsen, the relative success of the forest management program in one area of Malawi – Chimaliro (as contrasted with another area, Liwonde) – is contingent on such local circumstances as the greater social and cultural homogeneity of this community, the active participation of the tribal chiefs in the program and the population's lesser dependence on forests and therefore lesser pressure on their resources). Investigating why various groups participate in forest management in India, Behera and Engel conclude that local institutions can be most effective if they do not suffer from a lack of acceptance and compliance, that requires the empowerment of poor and marginalized groups in the community.

As suggested by these studies, there are renewed hopes that under certain conditions – strong law and order, an effective state apparatus, mediation of ethnic tensions through accountability, a supporting political culture or people's civil rights and opportunities for participation in decision making – political institutions can positively impact development. Also, the failed expectations of a single optimal institutional design do not mean that we cannot extract any lessons from the performance of existing institutions. Fukuyama affirms, 'A number of institutional reforms, like central bank or judicial independence, have a clear logic and are broadly accepted as being desirable' (35). The hopes for the effectiveness of these and other reforms can, however, materialize only if the pattern of their implementation is appropriate and conditions for development (some of which are indicated above) are met.

IMPORTANT QUALIFICATIONS: WHAT REALLY MATTERS

This book challenges the high expectations of unqualified institutional powers, including the conventional wisdom that democratization and decentralization of decision making at national, regional and local levels are always good for development. Rather, there are reasons to believe that both vicious and virtuous paths exist in the process of democratization and, more generally, in the dynamics of political institutions and economic performance. It is therefore important to reveal the prerequisites of the virtuous trajectory. Addressing the question of what exactly matters if institutions are to affect development, this book suggests at least three major lessons. First, the context matters. Second, the interplay of formal and informal institutions matters. And third, improving existing institutions may produce better results than overhauling the fundamentals of political systems. These lessons emanate from both macro- and micro-level studies and thus contribute to the existing knowledge on development.

Context

As noted by Fukuyama in the opening chapter, 'the full specification of a good set of institutions will be highly context-dependent [and] will change over time ...' (21). This statement echoes the earlier quoted view of Rodrik and his coauthors (2002, 22) on the context-specificity of desirable institutional arrangements. Fukuyama explains that optimality in the design of political systems (similar to Pareto optimality in economics) is not feasible because 'Political systems seek conflicting social goods between which there is often a continuous tradeoff' (32). The end results 'depend on a host of contextual factors like the society's historical traditions and political culture, the external environment and economic conditions' (32). Illustrations of the importance of context are abundant: industrialized nations with well-established democracies (including the United States and Great Britain) have very different political systems, largely due to their different historical experiences, and the countries of Latin America have displayed very different outcomes from rather similar reforms, due to circumstances specific to particular settings.

Other research on macropolitical institutions included in this book confirms the relevance of context and provides additional illustrations. Barbone and his coauthors emphasize that, of all of their findings, they are most confident of the 'importance of country specificity, since historical patterns of inclusion and exclusion and traditions of accountability, among many other factors, will influence the extent to which democracy helps the poor' (67). As demonstrated by Polterovich and Popov, out of all countries in the World Development Indicators database, democratization is associated with economic growth only in a subset of countries with strong law and order. According to Wang, the quality of democracy tends to be higher in countries where the state possesses strong assimilative, regulatory and steering capacity. As revealed by Enikolopov and Zhuravskaya's analysis of 75 countries, the outcomes of fiscal decentralization, such as economic growth, quality of government and public goods provision, are better in countries with strong national parties.

The same message on context specificity is derived from the analysis of micropolitical institutions. Writing about a new social movement popularly known as *Piqueteros* (people who block roads), Lucas Ronconi and Ignacio Franceschelli connect its emergence with specific conditions in Argentina at the turn of the twenty-first century. Asking why the democratic system failed to channel popular discontent and grievance into more conventional, formally institutionalized types of political opposition, the authors find answers in the peculiar implementation of temporary public works programs. The Argentine government's attempt to silence the initial protests by channeling workfare benefits through *Piqueteros* in fact provided the resources for the movement's growth, empowering these organizations and allowing them to become the leading social actor in the country. Since only *Piqueteros* members who actively participated in road blockades received workfare benefits, state funds actually further fueled dissent.

Analyzing local institutions for forest management in Malawi, Jumbe and Angelsen also highlight the crucial role of context: while in Chimaliro (a remote area with underdeveloped forest markets and a relatively homogeneous community) the program raised forest income for participants, it reduced revenue for participants in Liwonde (an area closer to cities with a more dense and more ethnically diverse population). The authors' explanation of the divergence in the impact of the program has much to do with the local conditions of its implementation, in particular the ability of non-participants in the program in Liwonde 'to free ride on the benefits of the program (better forest management)' (187).

Interplay of Formal and Informal Institutions

Attributing much importance to informal rules, Fukuyama stresses that the effectiveness of formal institutions depends heavily on informal norms, political culture and intangible factors like political leadership. His thesis can be interpreted as a further qualification of the understanding that 'context matters': the same formal institutions can work more or less well depending on their informal context. It is similar to North's position: 'Economies that adopt the formal rules of another economy will have very different performance characteristics than the first economy because of different informal norms and enforcement' (North 1994, 366).

The implication of this interplay between formal and informal institutions is that although formal institutions matter, they 'probably matter less than some of the current academic literature suggests ... [since they] are embedded in the matrix of informal norms, values, traditions and historical path-dependencies' (39). Consistent with Fukuyama's perception, Jumbe and Angelsen's research implies that the greater success of the local forest management program in one of the settings analyzed (Chimaliro) may be due to its better integration into traditional institutions through active participation of the local chiefs, that makes 'non-participation and non-compliance ... more socially costly' (194). Tracing the history of forest policies and institutions in Malawi, they show their evolution from unwritten codes to formal arrangements which both compete with and are complemented by informal institutions.

Ronconi and Franceschelli shed light on another angle in the formal–informal interplay. They depict how a newly emerged informal institution (*Piqueteros*) 'trumps' established formal structures – at least temporarily – due to the miscalculations and missteps of the establishment. Their story also demonstrates that whenever trust in formal state institutions is diminished, alternative channels for passing social security benefits can emerge, that eventually undermine the power of the government.

Adjustment versus Radicalism

Considering the delicate business of adjusting formal institutions to the context and informal norms, values and traditions, the studies in this book also caution against radical institutional changes: 'It is sometimes preferable to work within the context of imperfect existing institutions than to spend political capital on long-term institutional reforms' (39). This point is consistent with the views of some other scholars who advocate a less costly and more rapid reform to enact efficient rules to be administered by less-than-efficient institutions, rather than wholesale, expensive and time-consuming reforms of the institutions themselves (Hay, Schleifer and Vishny 1996). Building on both macro- and micro-level observations, this book reinforces the argument that the marginal efficiency of efforts to replace one (allegedly less advanced) political institution with another (supposedly more advanced) may be lower, compared with efforts to improve the efficiency of the government without changing basic political arrangements. This latter improvement may be the best way to use limited resources – not only would it contribute to growth and reduce inequality and poverty, but it also could open the way for the evolutionary transformation of political institutions themselves. In turn, a transformation based on efficient government would enhance overall economic performance.

Having demonstrated that institutional and poverty outcomes are heavily affected by the nature and objectives of the political regime and how it interacts with informal institutions and power divisions in society, Barbone and his coauthors reckon that 'good' institutions which are capable of delivering faster growth and poverty reduction are those better adjusted to the informal rules of the game. This is consistent with the other authors' interpretation of 'good' institutions as being well adapted to particular settings (Engerman and Sokoloff 2003, 29; Rodrik, Subramanian and Trebbi 2002, 22). One of the concrete empirical findings of Barbone and his coauthors is that 'ethnic fractionalization undermines the material benefits of democracy' (64). The policy implication of this finding is that addressing fractionalization and mediating ethnic tensions, rather than overhauling basic political institutions, may be the better means to promote human development. They refer to Ghana's gradual transition to multiparty democracy as well as Uganda's 'no-party democracy' as divergent ways to build institutions of accountability, increase political inclusion in different contexts and ultimately contribute to poverty reduction and income equality.

Enikolopov and Zhuravskaya also advocate a non-radical way to address poor governance – namely, through building strong national political parties. They explain, 'Strong parties help to provide elected local officials with efficient political incentives, because their chances of reelection depend both on national party support and the satisfaction of the local constituency. This allows leaders to strike a balance between national objectives and local accountability' (127).

Presenting additional support for the strategy of adjustment, Wang's careful cross-country investigation of state effectiveness can be interpreted as a response to the radical experimentation with 'shrinking the state' and as confirmation of the critical importance of a capable state, not just a minimal state, if democracy were to perform well. The policy implication of his research is that reformers' efforts should be focused on the routine, hardly glamorous work of improving state infrastructure and operations, that may be less costly and more productive than a complete dismantling of existing institutions and establishing new ones. In a similar spirit, Polterovich and Popov argue that 'introducing democracy overnight may not be the best way to transform authoritarian regimes. Democracy building, like market-type reforms, should be gradual, rather than shock therapy, and should go hand in hand with the strengthening of law and order' (95).

Offering empirical ground-level insights into what is needed to move development forward, the studies of micropolitical institutions included in this book also endorse gradualism and mutual accommodation between formal and informal institutions. Faced with the puzzle of the relative success of the forest co-management program involving participation of the local bodies in one Malawi setting but its failure in another setting, Jumbe. and Angelsen propose addressing widespread free riding as a remedial action. This would require, they contend, better integration of the formal program into informal institutions. Analyzing similar local forest management in India, Behera and Engel also abstain from questioning the set-up and benefits of this micro-level institution, even though they show that marginalized segments of local communities have very limited influence on management decisions. Their proposal for change is anything but radical: they encourage improved access to education for poor and marginalized groups as the best means to increase their influence.

The study of road blockades in Argentina by Ronconi and Franceschelli also demonstrates the power of accommodation: despite the radical nature of social protest through Piqueteros, the genesis of this movement – due to the selectivity of social benefits, which ironically were rewarding participation in pickets – reflected pragmatic adjustment to the social security system. Furthermore, the measures taken by the Argentine government to decrease road blockades – by making workfare benefits virtually universal – also manifested a pragmatic and modest amendment of the social security system.

CONCLUSION

In the opening chapter, Fukuyama poses a key question: 'What is the optimal political system for a developing country which seeks rapid economic growth?' Based on the studies in this book, a simple response to this question would be: 'It depends.' Indeed, effective operation of formal institutions depends on 'local social context, tradition and history' (35). Political arrangements which work in some countries, regions and localities often do not work when transplanted into a different environment. There are important pre-conditions which pertain to political accountability and civic participation, to law and order in general and to the efficiency of the government apparatus at different levels in particular. When these conditions are absent, the best and most advanced political institutions, that are perfectly effective in other places, fail to meet expectations – to promote growth, reduce inequality and poverty, ensure a fair provision of public goods and encourage real participation of all groups without leaving some behind. Conversely, when these conditions are present, they give renewed hope that development will go forward.

The non-existence of a universal recipe for success may be disappointing: grand, widely applicable designs have unquestionable appeal. But the sweeping general messages are rarely useful for our unruly and complicated world, that calls for humble accommodation. The lack of an 'optimal' pattern and a single scenario of development for all countries does not mean that the analysis of existing institutions is futile. To the contrary, creative, imaginative reinterpretation of successful political models in particular contexts is both desirable and possible, and learning about factors and conditions of relative success as opposed to failure can guide the replication of similar practices in different settings. In this spirit, the following chapters offer insights into the local settings, the relationship between formal and informal institutions and the art of adjustment and moderate reforms, aiming to advance our understanding of the link between political institutions and development.

NOTES

1. Formal institutions include mostly written rules, such as constitutions, laws and property rights. Informal institutions are typically unwritten codes of conduct (sanctions, taboos, customs and traditions) that either supplement or substitute formal rules and norms (North 1991, 97).
2. *Laissez-faire* is short for 'laissez faire, laissez aller, laissez passer,' a French phrase meaning 'let do, let go, let pass'.

BIBLIOGRAPHY

Acemoglu, Daron, Simon Johnson and James A. Robinson (2005), 'Institutions as the Fundamental Cause of Long-Run Growth', in Philippe Aghion and Steven N. Durlauf (eds), *The Handbook of Economic Growth*, San Diego: Elsevier, pp. 385–473.

Alesina, Alberto and Dani Rodrik (1994), 'Distributive Politics and Economic Growth', *Quarterly Journal of Economics*, **109** (2), 465–90.

Alesina, Alberto, Silvia Ardagna and Francesco Trebbi (2006), 'Who Adjusts and When? The Political Economy of Reforms', *IMF Staff Papers*, **53** (Special Issue).

Aron, Janine (February 2000), 'Growth and Institutions: A Review of the Evidence', *World Bank Research Observer*, **15** (1), 99–135.

Barro, Robert J. (1999), 'Determinants of Democracy', *Journal of Political Economy*, 107 (6), 158–83.

Bates, Robert, Avner Grief, Macartan Humphreys and Smita Singh (2004), 'Institutions and Development', Cambridge, MA, Harvard University Center for International Development Working Paper No. 107.

Burkhart, Ross E. and Michael S. Lewis-Beck (1994), 'Comparative Democracy: The Economic Development Thesis', *American Political Science Review*, **88** (4), 903–10.

Dustin Becker, Constance (2003), 'Grassroots to Grassroots: Why Forest Preservation Was Rapid in Loma Alta, Ecuador', *World Development*, **31** (1), 162–76.

Engerman, Stanley L. and Kenneth L. Sokoloff (1994), 'Factor Endowments, Institutions and Differential Paths of Growth Among New World Economies: A View from Economic Historians of the United States', Cambridge, MA, National Bureau of Economic Research Historical Paper No. 66.

—— (2003), 'Institutional and Non-institutional Explanations of Economic Differences', Cambridge, MA, National Bureau of Economic Research, Working Paper No. 9989.

Fidrmuc, Jan (2003), 'Economic Reform, Democracy and Growth during the Post-Communist Transition', *European Journal of Political Economy*, **19** (3), 583–604.

Fish, M. Steven (1999), 'Post-Communist Subversion: Social Science and Democratization in East Europe and Eurasia', *Slavic Review*, **58** (4), 794–823.

Hall, Peter A. and Rosemary C.R. Taylor (1996), 'Political Science and the Three New Institutionalisms', *Political Studies*, **44** (5), 936–57.

Hay, Jonathan, Andrei Schleifer and Robert W. Vishny (1996), 'Privatization in Transition Economies: Towards a Theory of Legal Reform', *European Economic Review*, **40** (315), 559–68.

Jütting, Johannes (2003), 'Institutions and Development: A Critical Review', Paris, OECD Development Centre Working Paper No. 210.

Knack, Stephen and Philip Keefer (1995), 'Institutions and Economic Performance: Cross-Country Tests Using Alternative Institutional Measures', *Economics and Politics*, **7** (3), 207–27.

Lanjouw, Jean O. and Philip I. Levy (2002), 'Untitled: A Study of Formal and Informal Property Rights in Urban Ecuador', *Economic Journal*, **112** (482), 986–1019.

Mazzucato, Valentina and David Niemeijer (2000), 'The Cultural Economy of Soil and Water Conservation: Market Principles and Social Networks in Eastern Burkina Faso', *Development and Change*, **31** (4), 831–55.

Nemarundwe, Nontokozo and Witness Kozanayi (2002), 'The Use of Informal Institutions and Social Networks to Access and Manage Water Resources in a Semi-Arid Area in Zimbabwe', Stockholm, Beijer International Institute of Ecological Economics, Ecological and Environmental Economics Program Working Paper No. 2.

North, Douglass C. (1990a), 'Institutions', *Journal of Economic Perspectives*, **5** (1), 97–112.

——(1990b), *Institutions, Institutional Change, and Economic Performance*, New York: Cambridge University Press.

——(1991), 'Institutions', *Journal of Economic Perspectives*, **5** (1), 97–112.

——(1994), 'Economic Performance through Time', *American Economic Review*, **84** (3), 359–68.

—— (2000), 'Understanding Institutions', in Claude Ménard (ed.), *Institutions, Contracts and Organizations: Perspectives from the New Institutional Economics*, Northampton, MA: Edward Elgar, pp. 7–11.

Olson, Mancur with Martin C. McGuire (1996), 'The Economics of Autocracy and Majority Rule: The Invisible Hand and the Use of Force', *Journal of Economic Literature*, **34** (1), 72–96.

Persson, Torsten (2002), 'Do Political Institutions Shape Economic Policy?', *Econometrica*, **70** (3), 883–905.

—— (2005), 'Forms of Democracy, Policy and Economic Development', Cambridge, MA, National Bureau of Economic Research Working Paper No. 11171.

Persson, Torsten and Guido Tabellini (2003), *The Economic Effects of Constitutions*, Cambridge, MA: MIT Press.

Persson, Torsten, Gerard Roland and Guido Tabellini (2000), 'Comparative Politics and Public Finance', *Journal of Political Economy*, **108** (6), 1121–61.

—— (2004), 'Constitutional Rules and Fiscal Policy Outcome', *American Economic Review*, **94** (1), 25–46.

Powell, Walter W. and Paul J. DiMaggio (1991), 'Introduction', in Walter W. Powell and Paul J. DiMaggio (eds), *The New Institutionalism in Organizational Analysis*, Chicago: University of Chicago Press, pp. 1–40.

Przeworski, Adam, Michael E. Alvarez, José Antonio Cheibub and Fernando Limongi (2000), *Democracy and Development: Political Institutions and Well-Being in the World, 1950–1990*, New York: Cambridge University Press.

Quinn, Dennis P. and John T. Wooley (2001), 'Democracy and National Economic Performance: The Preference for Stability', *American Journal of Political Science*, **45** (3), 634–57.

Riker, William (1964), *Federalism: Origins, Operation, Significance*, Boston, MA: Little, Brown and Co.

Rodrik, Dani, Arvind Subramanian and Francesco Trebbi (2002), 'Institutions Rule: The Primacy of Institutions over Geography and Integration in Economic Development', Harvard University, Department of Economics, unpublished paper.

Williamson, Oliver E. (September 2000), 'The New Institutional Economics: Taking Stock, Looking Ahead', *Journal of Economic Literature*, **38** (3), 595–613.

PART ONE

Macropolitical Institutions: Democracy,
Federalism, Decentralization and Economic
Performance

1. Development and the Limits of Institutional Design

Francis Fukuyama

While institutions apparently matter for economic development, there is no such thing as an optimal formal political institution. There is a body of knowledge concerning how such institutions relate to outcomes, yet the full specification of a good set of institutions will be highly context-dependent, will change over time and will interact with the informal norms, values and traditions of the society in which they are embedded. Therefore it is quite possible to overestimate the importance of certain kinds of formal institutions and to seek institutional reforms in conditions where imperfect institutions can actually be made to work quite adequately.

INSTITUTIONS MATTER – DON'T THEY?

There is by now a huge empirical literature making the case that 'institutions matter' for economic growth (Knack and Keefer 1995; Acemoglu, Johnson and Robinson 2000, 2002; Rodrik and Subramanian 2003; Kaufmann, Kraay and Mastruzzi 2005; Chhibber, Peters and Hale 2006). In this discourse, an institution is usually understood to be a rule constraining human choice and which permits collective action among a group of people. These rules need to be persistent over time, rather than not linked to the individuals who promulgate them. By the broadest definition of an institution, these rules can be formal (i.e., written or codified as law) or informal (a norm or inherited social practice). The distinction between formal and informal rules is a critical one, and it is better to confine the term 'institution' to formal rules established by states. A state, following the Weberian definition, is a political hierarchy which can legitimately enforce rules across a certain territory.[1]

In recent years, the only systematic counterargument to the institutionalist school has been made by Jared Diamond, Jeffrey Sachs and their followers (see Diamond 1997; Sachs and Warner 1995; Sachs and McArthur 2001), who have pointed to the importance of material factors such as resource endowments, disease burdens, climate and geographical location as determinants of economic growth. I believe the institutionalists have won this argument hands down. Easterly and Levine (2002) and Acemoglu, Johnson and Robinson (2002) have shown, for example, that resource endowments are important only as mediated through institutions, e.g., by providing more or less favorable conditions for the emergence or survival of certain types of institutions. The institutions themselves remain the proximate causes of growth, and in many cases they are exogenous to the material conditions under which a given society develops.

Going back further in history, however, there is a different kind of anti-institutional argument which was much more popular in the years immediately following World War II, but which has not been articulated so clearly in recent years. American political science in the pre-war period focused heavily on legal studies and formal political institutions. But the collapse of democracy in the 1930s in the face of the twin totalitarian challenges of communism and fascism convinced many observers that the exact specifications of formal institutions mattered much less than underlying structural conditions not conducive to democracy.

This type of anti-institutionalism was the long-standing position of most Marxists, who maintained that in a capitalist democracy the state was simply the 'executive committee of the bourgeoisie', reflecting underlying social forces and not an autonomous agent shaping outcomes. In a curious way this belief in state as superstructure jibed with a certain U.S. anti-statist penchant (see Lipset 1995) which saw the state simply as a mechanical processor of societal demands, without interests or a logic of its own. Much of the post-World War II research agenda focused not on the design of formal institutions, but on subjects like political culture or value systems (McClelland 1961; Almond and Verba 1963); in modernization theory, sociology and anthropology played as important a role as political science in explaining development outcomes.

Institutions and the autonomous state were re-inserted into the research agenda only in the 1970s and 1980s, partly in response to the recognition of the importance of state-directed development in regions like East Asia which could not simply be accounted for by structural or cultural models (Nettl 1968; Mann 1984; Evans, Rueschemeyer and Skocpol 1985). In addition, the rise of Douglass North's new institutional economics gave a new legitimacy to the study of institutions in economics and provided a powerful set of new conceptual tools. These converging streams produced a large body of literature not just on the general question of state autonomy, but also a rich and contextualized literature on institutional design which continues up to the present. The debate on presidentialism started by Linz (1990), discussed in much greater depth below, was one important example of the new focus on institutions and institutional design.

The new institutional economics muddied the waters in one important way, leading to confusion in subsequent thinking about institutions. North (1990) defines institutions as 'the humanly devised constraints that shape human interaction', whether formal or informal. The eliding of formal and informal institutions made North's definition conceptually robust and useful as a means of attacking the institution-less premises of neoclassical economics. But the older anti-institutionalist position had been built around the distinction between formal and informal institutions: it argued that formal–legal structures at best depended on – and at worst were undermined by – factors like political culture, discordant value systems or social structures which gave rise to political preferences at odds with the institutional structure.

There was also a very important practical difference between formal and informal institutions. Formal institutions can be established, abolished or changed with the stroke of a pen. They were thus the typical objects of public policy to be manipulated at will. But informal institutions reflect embedded social practices which were often hard to perceive and measure, and even harder to manipulate through the usual levers provided by public policy. It is one thing, for example, to mandate certain terms and appointment rules for Supreme Court justices, but if politicians routinely fail to follow them because packing the Supreme Court with sympathetic justices has become a normative behavior for an entire political elite, then the issue has left the realm of conventional public policy. The new institutionalism recognized the importance of informal institutions but often failed to clearly label them as a distinct conceptual category subject to very different evolutionary dynamics.

Today, there are relatively few scholars who continue to insist on the importance of the distinction between formal and informal institutions, and the priority of informal over formal.[2] One exception is Samuel Huntington, who in recent years has been making a larger argument in favor of the centrality of culture in shaping political outcomes. His book *Who Are We?* (2004) points to the importance of culture in the shaping of U.S. national identity and in the success of U.S. democracy. There are few clearer statements of the older anti-institutionalist position than this:

> Would America be the America it is today if in the seventeenth and eighteenth centuries it had been settled not by British Protestants but by French, Spanish, or Portuguese Catholics? The answer is no. It would not be America; it would be Quebec, Mexico, or Brazil. (59)

Huntington has been severely criticized for his policy prescriptions regarding Mexican immigration. But his broader point – that U.S. national identity has not simply been a political one defined by institutions like the Constitution

and system of laws but also rooted in certain religious and cultural traditions
– would seem to be incontrovertible as an *historical* fact. It is an interpretation
of U.S. society which was shared by observers from Tocqueville to Bryce
to Lipset, and constitutes one long-standing answer to the question of why
Latin America, after achieving independence from Spain or Portugal, modeled
many political institutions explicitly on those of the United States, but failed to
achieve North American levels of either growth or political stability.

Political culture does not determine political or economic outcomes.
Culture changes over time and is shaped by formal institutions even as it shapes
them. Formal institutions matter; they change incentives, mold preferences
and ideally solve collective action problems. On the other hand, the informal
matrix of norms, beliefs, values, traditions and habits which constitute a
society are critical for the proper functioning of formal institutions, and a
political science which pays attention only to the design of formal institutions
and fails to understand the accompanying normative and cultural factors will
fail. A large cultural variable like Catholicism may not be very helpful in
explaining or predicting political behavior or institutional development, but
a norm which assumes that bureaucratic appointments ought to favor friends
and relatives over people with formal credentials might. Therefore we must
look to both formal and informal institutions when explaining the difference
in development outcomes among different societies, taking each side of the
equation seriously, as well as the importance of their interaction.

THE PERILS OF PRESIDENTIALISM RECONSIDERED

The two-decade debate over institutional design illustrates the complexity
of the problem of specifying the nature of good formal political institutions.
This debate was initiated by Juan Linz in his 1990 article 'The Perils of
Presidentialism'.[3] Linz argued that political instability in Latin America was
due to the fact that many of the democracies there were presidential rather than
parliamentary, based on an imported North American model which did not
work well in other parts of the hemisphere.

Linz identified four basic problems with presidential systems. First,
presidential systems are inherently majoritarian, allowing for the possibility
that a president would be elected by a slim plurality of the population and
therefore lack legitimacy. Second, presidential systems have rigid terms and do
not provide easy mechanisms for removing a president who has lost legitimacy
after being elected. Parliamentary systems deal with this problem through
no-confidence votes; impeachment is the messy alternative in presidential
ones. Moreover, term-limited presidents often spend a great deal of time and

political capital figuring out how to extend their tenure. Third, in a presidential system both the executive and the legislature are directly elected and thus have separate sources of legitimacy; since they survive separately, there is always the possibility of gridlock and political paralysis when the two branches are controlled by different parties. And finally, presidential systems tend to personalize politics, emphasizing the character and foibles of the president rather than the broad program of a political party.

Although he did not address this issue explicitly, Linz was concerned with two separate and often conflicting goals. First, he was concerned with the effectiveness of democratic decision making and worried that the dual legitimacy of presidential systems would lead to executive–legislative deadlock. Effectiveness in this context usually means the speed of political decision making, although in some cases it may mean the ability to make a decision at all.[4] He was also concerned with legitimacy and the possibility that an executive would receive support from a relatively small minority of the population. One can see immediately that the mutual checking of the two branches is actually an advantage with respect to legitimacy, while the plurality election of a president may be an advantage with regard to effectiveness. What is difficult is to optimize *both* effectiveness and legitimacy simultaneously.

In many respects, Linz's concerns about presidentialism remain well-founded. Many of the new democracies in Asia, for example, are presidential, and they have experienced many of the problems Linz predicted (see Fukuyama, Dressel and Chang 2005). Indonesia, the Philippines, South Korea and Taiwan have all initiated impeachment proceedings against sitting presidents. Presidents Abdurrahman Wahid and Joseph Estrada were actually removed from power (in the latter case, through means many deemed illegal), while Presidents Chen Shui-bian and Roh Moo Hyun survived the campaigns against them. In all four cases, however, presidents found themselves facing legitimacy crises, commanding minority parties or coalitions in the legislature and often unable to get their agendas enacted into law. Politics in each of these countries has been highly personalized, focusing on charges of corruption, nepotism or the glamour surrounding particular candidates.

Linz's critique of presidentialism was immediately challenged by Lijphart (1991), Horowitz (1990), Shugart and Carey (1992) and a variety of other authors. These critics pointed out that parliamentary systems could be as weak and illegitimate as presidential ones; indeed, some like the interwar Weimar Republic or the French Fourth Republic became illegitimate *because* of their weakness. Parliamentary systems required strong political parties; while party discipline could to some extent be engineered, party fragmentation mirrored the religious, ethnic, class and geographical structure of the underlying society. Presidentialism had certain advantages: voters knew exactly whom they were

Figure 1.1   Executive Systems versus Electoral Systems

	Plurality	Proportional representation
Presidential	United States, Philippines	Latin America
Parliamentary	Westminster	Continental Europe

Note: A classical Westminster system is (1) parliamentary; (2) has a single member plurality electoral system; (3) has no written constitution and therefore no judicial review; (4) has no other form of separated powers like bicameralism or federalism. In a plurality electoral system, the candidate receiving the highest number of votes is elected. In this kind of system, a simple majority in parliament can change any law without constraint.

Proportional representation systems allocate legislative seats in proportion to the popular vote, by various rules that make the proportionality more or less strict. In a closed-list PR system, political parties determine the rank-order of candidate lists, giving parties a high degree of control over their legislative delegations; in an open-list PR system voters are allowed to choose individual candidates from the list provided by parties. In some PR systems, there are minimum thresholds of the popular vote that parties must achieve before they can be represented in the legislature.

electing and that official remained directly accountable to voters, while in parliamentary systems parties or coalitions could remove chief executives without any change in the popular mandate. The inherent majoritarianism of presidential systems could, moreover, be tempered by requirements for second-round runoffs or, as in Nigeria or Sri Lanka, requirements that the president receive pluralities in multiple electoral districts.

Lijphart (1991) early on argued that a single design axis like the nature of executive power could not be understood in isolation from other aspects of the political system; electoral systems, in particular, were critical in determining the overall effectiveness of a political system. He suggested the matrix in Figure 1.1 for characterizing combinations of executive and electoral systems.

For Lijphart, presidential systems coupled with single-member plurality systems like that of the United States tended to produce two relatively strong and cohesive parties (Duverger 1950). While the possibility of different parties gaining control of the executive and legislative branches has in fact been a reality for much of recent U.S. history, this has not led necessarily to gridlock because politics was still organized around two relatively coherent competing

Figure 1.2   Participation versus Speed of Decision Making

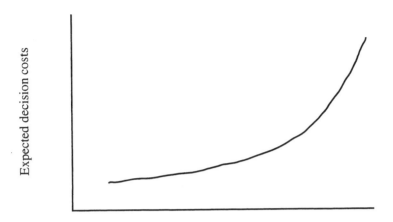

Percentage of population required to make a decision

ideological points of view. From his standpoint, the worst combination was presidentialism together with proportional representation in the legislature, that he argued characterized many political systems in Latin America. This led not just to gridlock, but to presidents having to bargain with disorganized and fragmented parties – the worst features of both parliamentary and presidential systems.

A MORE GENERAL FRAMEWORK FOR CATEGORIZING POLITICAL SYSTEMS

It soon became clear that presidentialism interacted not just with the electoral system, but with virtually all other aspects of the political system. Cox and McCubbins (in Haggard and McCubbins 2001) introduced the general concept of veto gates – actors within the political system which have the power to stop or modify legislation or policy. All political systems can be arrayed on a continuum from perfect authoritarianism with one veto gate (the dictator's will) to a perfect consensual democracy in which all citizens have to agree to a policy. The concept of veto gates in a sense reprises the conceptual framework laid out by Buchanan and Tullock (1962) to explain the principle of majority voting, where they posited a clear tradeoff between legitimacy and effectiveness (see Figure 1.2).

As more members of a society participate in a decision, the expected decision costs rise; for large societies the costs rise exponentially as consensus approaches. Buchanan and Tullock argued that the principle of majority voting had no inherent normative logic; any point on the curve in Figure 1.2 could be an appropriate tradeoff between effectiveness and legitimacy and, in the case of constitutional law, supermajorities were indeed often required. But with monetary policy, by contrast, many democracies delegated decision rights to an independent central bank with a very small number of decision makers.

The concept of veto gates as used by Cox and McCubbins does not refer to individual voters, but to organized institutions within the political system which, through delegation, acquire veto rights. Legislatures and the rules under which they are elected are only one of several possible veto gates. Others include:

1.   The electoral system: Proportional representation (PR) usually increases the number of veto gates over plurality systems because it leads to a more fragmented party system. Small district size (especially when combined with PR) tends to increase fragmentation, as do electoral cycles not synchronized with presidential ones. PR systems with thresholds reduce fragmentation.
2.   Party discipline: Strong parties (e.g., those operating under closed-list systems) are better able to make decisions than ones with weak discipline.
3.   Bicameralism: An upper house adds another veto gate, often based on territorial criteria and/or electoral rules different from those in the lower house.
4.   Federalism and decentralization: Federalism delegates important decision rights to subunits like states which can further delegate to even smaller subunits like municipalities and districts.
5.   Independent judiciaries: If courts are truly independent and have powers of constitutional review, as in the United States, they can constitute a major check on the powers of the other two branches. Courts can intervene in different ways as well, from merely interpreting legislative intent to initiating policies on their own.

This range of options reveals that political systems need to be categorized not by Lijphart's 2x2 matrix, but by an *n*-dimensional matrix which would array all of these design axes against one another. It is possible to come up with a very large number of combinations of design features which will add or subtract veto gates from the political system, thus shifting the balance between effectiveness and legitimacy.

Since it is not practical to graphically portray an n-dimensional matrix, I will have to substitute a continuum like that on the x-axis of Figure 1.2 as a means of ranking different political systems. Political systems with different types of veto gates are hard to compare in the abstract: Is a system with weak party discipline but no federalism and an independent constitutional court stronger or weaker than one with federalism, cohesive parties and a somewhat politicized court? Is the premier-presidential system of the French Fifth Republic,[5] whose president does not appoint the cabinet but has clear reserved powers in foreign and defense policy and does not have to devolve powers to federal subunits, stronger or weaker than the U.S. presidential system whose president appoints the cabinet and shares powers in foreign affairs?

Taking these complexities into account, it is nonetheless possible to do a rough rank-ordering of different political systems in terms of their aggregate number of veto players:

1. Classical Westminster (New Zealand before 1994).
2. Parliamentary/PR with cohesive parties, no federalism (Austria, Belgium, Netherlands, Thailand).
3. Premier-presidential, no federalism (French Fifth Republic, Finland).
4. Presidential with plurality voting and federalism (United States, Philippines).
5. Parliamentary with fragmented parties (French Fourth Republic, Italy pre-1994).
6. Presidential with PR and fragmented parties (Colombia, Brazil).

If one thinks about political systems generically in terms of veto gates, there is no reason to confine the classification system to democratic political systems. Authoritarian political systems can also be categorized in terms of veto gates. A perfect dictatorship has only one veto gate; the will of the dictator. In reality, most authoritarian systems also have multiple veto gates, such as the head of the intelligence service, the head of the army or of the different service branches, different actors within the dominant political party (e.g., members of the Politburo in the former Soviet Union), etc. In a relatively institutionalized authoritarian system like that of China, there are multiple hierarchies of veto gates which, while not democratic in the usual sense of the term, prevent those at the top of the party hierarchy from acting arbitrarily.

There is also a rather new regime type which has emerged since the end of the Cold War which might be classified as quasi-democratic or quasi-authoritarian (see Krastev 2006). Iran, Venezuela and Russia all hold democratic elections and have some degree of democratic accountability. And yet these systems have authoritarian characteristics insofar as the executive can limit or manipulate press freedom, control opposition political parties and otherwise escape a host of horizontal accountability mechanisms like courts and civil society. It is hard to know whether these are democratic systems in transition to more familiar authoritarian ones, or whether they represent a stable equilibrium. In any event, they also can be characterized in terms of veto gates presented by various institutional actors (e.g., the Revolutionary Guards and Basij in Iran or civil society actors which continue to operate in Venezuela).

Of all democratic systems, the classical Westminster system has by far the fewest veto gates and is capable of the most decisive action. Such a system, in its pure form,[6] is parliamentary with a plurality voting system and party discipline, leading to exaggerated majorities in parliament. There is no federalism or decentralization, no written constitution and therefore no requirements for supermajority voting and no judicial review. A simple majority in parliament (which, given the electoral system, can represent less than a majority of the popular vote) is sufficient to change any law in the land and leads to what some have described as a democratic dictatorship. In the 2001 British general election, for example, the Labour Party received only 42 per cent of the popular vote, and yet received 62.5 per cent of the seats in Parliament, while the Liberal Democrats received almost 19 per cent of the popular vote and got only 8 per cent of the seats.

In contrast, the U.S. system is a relatively weak one. It is deliberately designed to place many more veto gates – checks and balances – in front of executive decision making, by adding separated powers, bicameralism, federalism, weak party discipline and judicial review. The only important feature of the U.S. political system which increases rather than decreases decisiveness is its single-member plurality voting system. A British prime minister's budget is approved within days of its being submitted to parliament; a U.S. budget takes the better part of a year to pass and never survives in the form proposed by the president.

While there are clear differences between the Westminster and U.S. systems, and between either of them and those which prevail in Argentina or Peru, the actual behavior of political systems may not correspond to a simple quantitative tabulation of veto gates. As will be seen below, even the notional ranking of systems outlined above can be very misleading. Within the broad categories of veto gates there are countless other rules which affect the ability of political systems to generate decisions or enforce policies. Sometimes these rules are formal, but are so specialized that they escape the notice of even informed outside observers (e.g., World Bank country directors or North American academic specialists). At other times they are informal and intrude into the realm of political culture, as will be explored below. But first, let me give an example concerning legislative coherence.

Legislative coherence is the ability of parliaments to pass legislation, hopefully, which is public-regarding rather than patronage-based and/or clientelistic. Legislative coherence is the product of the interplay of various institutional design features, such as the electoral system (usually held to be the prime determinant), party discipline, rules concerning executive–legislative interaction (i.e., presidentialism and which branch controls the legislative agenda) and the party system which reflects the underlying structural conditions of the society.

Political scientists associate legislative incoherence with PR systems, particularly those with open-list voting and no minimum thresholds, weak party discipline and party systems which are not firmly anchored in important social groups or cleavages. By this account, Colombia and Brazil have traditionally been put forth as examples of weak legislative systems. Colombia has coherent parties but very weak party discipline, in which the parties have been unable to control the use of their own party labels (Archer and Shugart 1997); Brazil has open-list PR, a traditionally weak party system and supposedly weak party discipline (Mainwaring and Scully 1995; Mainwaring 1997). Argentina, by contrast, should have much greater legislative coherence, since it has a closed-list PR system and relatively coherent parties (Corrales 2002).

But reality is rather different. Colombian presidents have in fact had to work with incoherent legislatures which have demanded particularistic payoffs in return for votes, as the theory predicts. Colombian presidents have resorted either to emergency powers or to maneuvers of questionable legality to implement major reforms.[7] The Brazilian Congress, however, has actually been able to pass a large volume of legislation since ratification of the 1988 Constitution. While Brazilian presidents have never had legislative majorities of their own party, they have nonetheless been able to put together coalitions of parties with relatively strong party discipline in support of far-reaching reforms like the Fiscal Responsibility Law of 2000, that restricted the ability of Brazilian states to run budget deficits (Limongi and Figueiredo 2000). Yet Argentina has suffered from legislative incoherence despite the fact that presidents from both the Partido Justicialista (Peronist party) and the Allianza have had strong legislative majorities or pluralities in Congress.

The reason for this has to do with the fact that legislative coherence is the product of the interplay of many more rules than the usual ones of open- or closed-list PR. Brazilian presidents, for example, have been able to discipline legislators and enforce party-line voting through their control over fiscal policy and bureaucratic appointments. That Presidents Fernando Cardoso and Luiz Inácio Lula have used this power not to build clientelistic bases but to enact public-regarding reforms of fiscal federalism or the social security system may reflect changing political culture rather than formal institutional constraints.

Nonetheless, the result is contrary to the expectations of many political scientists and at odds with simple models of how formal rules correlate with policy outcomes.

Legislative coherence in Argentina was undermined by the way that the electoral system interacted with federalism. While the national electoral system was closed-list PR, voting was done by province and it was not the national party but the provincial party chiefs which determined the voting lists. The national party was in fact not a cohesive bloc but an alliance of provincial fiefdoms (Tommasi 2004). In the years leading up to the economic crisis of 2001, the Argentine government could not maintain fiscal discipline because the Partido Justicialista leader, President Carlos Menem, succumbed to a spending duel with Eduardo Duhalde, governor of Buenos Aires province and Menem's leading rival in the Partido Justicialista party. The entrenched power of provincial party bosses is also the reason why this system will be extremely difficult to reform. The coherence of the Argentine legislature, then, was more apparent than real, and goes far in explaining why Menem continued to rule by decree even when his party possessed a majority in Congress.

WHY THERE IS NO OPTIMAL POLITICAL SYSTEM

The groundwork has already been laid in the search for an explanation of why there can be no such thing as optimality in the design of political systems, unlike Pareto optimality in economics. Political systems seek conflicting social goods between which there is often a continuous tradeoff. The balance of goods which the system seeks to achieve will depend on a host of contextual factors like the society's historical traditions and political culture, the external environment and economic conditions.

Cox and McCubbins describe this tradeoff as one between decisiveness and resoluteness. Systems with fewer veto gates produce more decisive political decisions. However, decisions which have to be vetted by more actors within the political system generally produce more lasting results, because there are fewer players interested in overturning the initial decision: hence greater resoluteness. It should be clear that the Cox–McCubbins tradeoff between decisiveness and resoluteness largely corresponds to the tradeoff between effectiveness and legitimacy described earlier. That is, the more members of a society who participate in a decision, the more legitimate it is (with perfect legitimacy being perfect consensus). Legitimate decisions are resolute because there are fewer interest groups or sectors of society opposed to the decision.

To complicate things a bit further, excessive resoluteness or legitimacy can sometimes undermine itself, while decisiveness on occasion becomes self-legitimating. That is, a democratic political system with excessive decision costs often fails to produce policies of any sort, leading to voter disillusionment not just with the current administration, but with democracy as a whole. Societies may actually express a preference for the decisiveness of authoritarian governments which can cut through the miasma of ordinary politics and get things done.

What is the optimal political system for a developing country which seeks rapid economic growth? For a long time a segment of the academic and policy communities held a strong bias in favor of decisive over resolute/legitimate systems. One version of this was the 'authoritarian transition', advocated four decades ago by Samuel Huntington (1968) and re-articulated more recently by Huntington's student Fareed Zakaria (2003). They argued not simply that authoritarian modernizers were more decisive, but that in many developing countries liberal autocracy alone was capable of supplying basic public goods like physical security and public order which were preconditions of development of any sort.

But even among those committed to development under democratic conditions, there was a pronounced bias in favor of decisiveness (Sachs 1994). According to this argument, a typical developing country needs liberalizing economic reform, usually in the form of tariff reductions, deregulation, privatization and reductions in consumer subsidies (i.e., the famous Washington Consensus). Often these policy reforms needed to be undertaken in the context of an economic crisis, such as a current account deficit leading to currency devaluation and high interest rates. While these reforms were expected to bring stability and long-term economic growth, they also produced a great deal of transitional pain, as workers were laid off or consumers lost subsidies. Technocratic experts could see the long-term logic of these policies, but ordinary voters and politicians might not. Therefore, a developing country in this position needed a decisive political system which would shield technocratic experts from populist demands and push through long-term public-regarding policies. A decisive system which implemented successful reforms would then become self-legitimating as it produced long-term stability and economic growth. This was the path followed by Chile under General Augusto Pinochet in the 1970s and 1980s.

Political systems with excessive checks and balances tend to slow down decision making and impose many other decision costs as interest groups are paid off. What Geddes (1996) refers to as the 'politician's dilemma' is the phenomenon that reformist governments often need to pay such a high price to get reform that they end up undermining the goals of the reform which they seek to achieve. This price would presumably be lower in a more decisive political system.

In the end, it is not clear that decisive political systems are preferable to resolute/legitimate ones from the standpoint of long-term development. Constitutional rules which amplify executive power by reducing veto gates can produce policies which come to be regarded as illegitimate over time. Without a broader underlying social consensus, reforms are likely to be undermined over time. For example, the liberalizing reforms undertaken by Venezuelan President Carlos Andres Perez in 1989–90 provoked opposition not just within the broader Venezuelan society, but within Perez's own Accion Democratica Party (Corrales 2002). Even though the reforms produced economic growth, they were immediately undermined not just within the political system, but outside it as well (in the form of military coups launched by Hugo Chavez). Similarly, the Russian Federation under Boris Yeltsin had a strong presidential system biased toward decisiveness, and many important reforms were issued by decree. The privatizations of the 1990s were undertaken by a weak state with weak legitimacy; while they may have made economic sense, they provoked strong popular opposition and were thus easily undone by President Vladimir Putin a decade later.

The preference for decisive political systems, moreover, reflects a moment in history stretching from the mid-1980s through the late 1990s in which the development problem was seen as excessive state scope which could be solved with liberalizing economic reforms. In the early twenty-first century, the political agenda has already begun to shift: left-leaning or outright populist presidents have come to power in Russia, Brazil, Ecuador, Argentina, Uruguay, Venezuela, Bolivia, Taiwan and South Korea. In many cases their agenda is the reassertion of state power, re-regulation of the economy and re-nationalization of certain economic sectors, control over the media and civil society or else dramatic changes in foreign policy. Decisive political systems will only enhance the ability of populist presidents to enact bad economic policies and return their countries to state control and closed markets.

Institutions are only enabling devices; those which facilitate or encourage strong and decisive political decision making are only as good as the policies being pursued. What inhibits the ambitions of a liberalizing reformer also checks the power of a would-be populist dictator. If decisive government were always preferable, then the ideal would be Westminster-type systems with their largely unchecked executive powers. But since the founding of their republic U.S. citizens have expressed a strong preference for a system of checks and balances which limits government power. This relatively weak political system reflects the preferences of the U.S. political culture, that has always been distrustful of state power (Lipset 1995). Checks and balances make large-scale reform much more difficult, but in the long run they also reduce the risks of the government being captured by politicians advocating policies which would not receive the support of the broader society. The preference for resolute or legitimate political systems over decisive ones can thus be seen as a preference for lower long-term political risk.

There is no optimal level of long-term political risk, and thus no optimal balance between decisiveness and resoluteness or legitimacy. The United States and Great Britain are among the world's oldest and best-established democracies, and yet they have completely different political systems arising out of very different historical experiences. The largely unchecked Westminster system is a high-risk institutional arrangement which has worked reasonably well in the English-speaking world. Margaret Thatcher's reforms of the late 1970s and early 1980s could not have been carried out without the exaggerated parliamentary majorities then held by the Conservative Party. Similarly, in the mid-1980s the liberalizing reforms of Roger Douglas benefited from New Zealand's even purer Westminster system.[8] Both stand in sharp contrast to the situation faced by Chancellor Angela Merkel under Germany's far less decisive institutional rules, that have forced her into a coalition and will sharply limit the kinds of liberalizing policies she will be able to put into place.

But a Westminster system would likely produce disastrous results if transported to a country with a different social structure and political culture (e.g., an ethnically fragmented society with a dominant ethnic group). Where it has been copied, it has been heavily modified to meet local conditions, as in the case of India, where the success of democracy would scarcely be conceivable in the absence of thoroughgoing federalism. The U.S. presidential system, that is much less decisive than the Westminster system, has nonetheless been capable of achieving decisive action at certain critical junctures in U.S. history. But when U.S. presidentialism was transplanted to Latin American countries, it worked only indifferently well. How each formal set of institutional rules plays out in practice is thus highly dependent on local social context, tradition and history.

The fact that analysts cannot specify an optimal set of formal institutions does not mean that they have no knowledge of the likely impact of changes to formal institutional rules. A number of institutional reforms, like central bank or judicial independence,[9] have a clear logic and are broadly accepted as being desirable. Changes in electoral rules have broadly predictable effects, and there are a number of recent cases where electoral reform has produced desired results:

• Chile, that always had a coherent party system, since 1988 has been operating under an electoral system designed to force the country's four or five large parties into two broad left–right coalitions, this has in fact happened.

- Japan changed its single non-transferable vote (SNV) system to a mixture of single-member constituencies and PR in 1994. The SNV system forced parties to run multiple candidates in the same electoral district, that many observers blamed for the factionalism within the ruling Liberal Democratic Party. While it took over ten years to produce the desired effect, Prime Minister Junichiro Koizumi's electoral victory in 2005 marked the demise of the faction system.
- Italy modified its low-threshold PR system, that had produced notoriously weak coalition governments, to a mixed single-member/PR system in 1994. As hoped, this move forced parties into broad left–right coalitions. Italian politicians gamed the system, however, to ensure the survival of the smaller parties, and the system reverted back to a modified form of PR in 2006.
- New Zealand, with a classical Westminster-style single-member plurality voting system in its parliament, changed to a mixed-member proportional system in 1994. The result has been broader representation of smaller parties, together with relatively weak coalition governments in place of the two-and-a-half party system which had prevailed earlier.
- Thailand's 1997 Constitution changed the electoral system from a PR system which had produced weak coalitions to a mixed system of 400 single-member constituencies and 100 PR seats. The reform gave Prime Minister Thakskin Shinawatra an absolute legislative majority.

In addition, there is accumulating knowledge about the design of federal systems. Federalism has posed a problem for many large states in Latin America like Argentina, Brazil and Mexico, because the subunits were delegated too much budgetary discretion and could run fiscal deficits. This differed from the situation in the United States, where most states are constitutionally prohibited from running budget deficits and face hard budget constraints based on their own ability to raise revenues. But in Argentina and Brazil states could run deficits which would have to be covered by the federal government, a form of fiscal federalism which undermined overall budget discipline. In Argentina, the rules were particularly problematic, because they were constantly being renegotiated; governors would spend more time politicking in Buenos Aires than raising their own tax revenues (Tommasi and Saiegh 1999). The solution to this problem – putting states and other subunits under hard budget constraints – is relatively straightforward conceptually; what is hard is implementation, since such a reform means a de facto shift in power from the states to the federal government. Brazil, despite its supposedly weak political parties and strong federalism, moved in this direction with passage of the 2000 Fiscal

Responsibility Law, while Argentina has failed to deal with this problem due to the entrenched power of state-level politicians (Stein et al. 2005).

POLITICAL CULTURE

Most conventional analyses of the formal structure of political institutions would conclude that Brazil should produce weaker government than Argentina, given its open-list PR system, weak political parties and entrenched federalism. And yet, Brazil weathered the period from 1990–2005 better than Argentina, avoiding the latter's severe economic crisis in 2001–2002 and moving ahead with a series of structural reforms and public policies. And neither country has done as well as neighboring Chile, not just over the past 15 years but for the preceding 15 as well. What accounts for these differences?

One factor is clearly leadership. Economists generally do not like to talk about independent variables like leadership because it amounts to throwing a massive random-number generator into their models. They prefer modeling institutions and hierarchy endogenously, as the result of strategic interactions of individual agents who cannot achieve collective action without leadership. But leadership is more often than not exogenous. It was simply Argentina's bad luck that Carlos Menem chose to throw away the positive legacy of his first term as president by seeking not just a second but a third term as well, leading him into a spending competition with challenger Eduardo Duhalde. President Cardoso, by contrast, chose not to waste his political capital seeking ways to remain in office, but instead tried to solve some long-standing public policy problems. Many good development outcomes are thus attributable not to the structure of formal institutions, but rather to the emergence of the right leader at the right time: Park Chung Hee replacing Syngman Rhee as president of South Korea in 1961; Yowery Museveni coming to power in Uganda after a period of misrule by Idi Amin and Milton Obote; Botswana discovering diamonds on its territory while Seretse Khama was president. These shifts were totally unpredictable ex ante and thus something about which social scientists have little to say.

The only way leadership may become a more tractable variable is when a certain leadership style is not simply the outgrowth of the foibles of a particular individual, but reflective of a broader political culture. Menem was widely blamed for packing the Argentine Supreme Court with his political cronies, but he was neither the first nor the last Argentine president to do so. Argentine elites have been notorious for avoiding or manipulating rules they find inconvenient, a behavioral tendency which shows up not just in Supreme Court appointments but in rates of tax compliance and ordinary corruption.

These phenomena exist in Brazil and Chile as well, but the degree of disregard of law and rules seems simply to be lower, particularly in the latter case. A well-functioning rule of law is not simply a set of visible formal institutions like courts, bar associations, police and judges. No formal arrangement or incentives will make such a system operate properly unless the participants share a certain normative respect for law and rules.

One early critique of institutionalism argued that formal institutions mattered less than variables like political culture and social structure in explaining political and development outcomes. This critique remains valid, but only if culture is understood properly. To say that political culture is important is not necessarily to affirm the importance of certain large cultural categories like 'Catholicism' or 'Anglo-Protestantism'. Chile, Argentina, Ecuador and Costa Rica are all predominantly Latin Catholic countries and former colonies of Spain, and yet they all have distinctive political cultures with respect to rule of law. Political culture varies among groups and regions within societies and over time; it is shaped not only by large symbolic forces like religion, but by shared historical experience like war or economic crisis. And it is clearly key to understanding why certain formal political institutions do or do not work.

CONCLUSION

The scholarly work done on the subject of macropolitical institutions over the past generation has generated a considerable body of knowledge about how institutions work and how certain types of institutional reforms will yield certain kinds of results. We know how to design electoral systems to increase or decrease the number of political parties in a party system; how to increase or decrease party discipline; or how to change the rules of federalism to promote greater fiscal responsibility on the part of states. We also know that there are certain types of institutions which are in virtually all circumstances undesirable, for example overly politicized judicial systems. Yet that is not the last word on the subject. Rather, the discussion above revealed six key points.

First, there is no such thing as an optimal political institution or universally valid design criteria. Changes in design parameters often shift the balance between competing social goods. Whether a particular balance of goods is appropriate will depend on the particular circumstances of a society at a particular point in time. A society's needs or environment can change over time, necessitating different types of institutions.

Second, institutions often come as complex, interdependent packages. Thus it often is not possible to achieve one particular outcome without adjusting several dimensions of institutional design simultaneously. Understanding the interplay of different aspects of institutional design requires a highly detailed knowledge of how those institutions work on a micro level, encompassing both formal and informal rules.

Third, good institutions are heavily dependent on local context, traditions, habits and political culture. People without this local knowledge often do not understand how even existing institutions actually work, much less how to reform them. While comparative knowledge of foreign models helps expand the universe of alternative design possibilities, local knowledge is necessary to understand the possibilities available to a given society.

Fourth, we need to invest more in regional or area studies which focus on local knowledge. Large cross-country regressions which seek to uncover general causal relationships are much less useful at this point. People with the best access to local knowledge are academics or practitioners who live in the societies being studied. Such a cadre exists in more developed regions like Asia, South Asia and Latin America, but is much weaker in Africa.

Fifth, leadership matters. While this reduces the ability to predict behavior or influence outcomes, it is a fact of political life.

Finally, formal institutions matter, but they probably matter less than some of the current academic literature suggests. Formal institutions are embedded in the matrix of informal norms, values, traditions and historical path-dependencies known as 'political culture'. Without a supportive political culture, even the best institutions will not work well. Alternatively, formal institutions which seem less than optimal can often be made to work with the right leadership, judgment and political will. It is sometimes preferable to work within the context of imperfect existing institutions than to spend political capital on long-term institutional reforms.

This chapter has mainly focused on the supply side of institutions. But institutional reform will not take place in the absence of demand for good institutions, and this must be generated within the society itself. If reform is to happen, demand for good institutions must be translated into political power; however, international donors have only limited influence over this process.

NOTES

1. These definitions, of course, beg other questions, such as what legitimacy is, what it means for a rule to be formalized, and what it means for a rule to be enforceable.
2. One important source for thinking about informal institutions is the large literature on social capital.
3. This article, published in the *Journal of Democracy* in 1990, circulated for several years prior to that as a mimeo.
4. In some cases, speedy decisions are poor ones; a decision which is vetted by more institutional actors may not simply be more legitimate, but they may be of higher quality as well.

5. The French Fifth Republic was established in 1958 and continues to the present. It replaced the parliamentary-PR system of the Fourth Republic with a weak presidential system, in which the president appoints the prime minister but not the cabinet, and has reserved powers in defense and foreign affairs.
6. The British system is no longer a pure Westminster system; there is a bicameral legislature with increasing devolution of powers to different regions in Britain. In addition, courts, including European courts, have increasingly been able to limit the discretion of the British Parliament.
7. An example of this was President César Augusto Gavaria's bypassing of the legislature in the constitutional reform of 1991.
8. New Zealand ceased to have a pure Westminster system when its electoral system was changed from single-member first-past-the-post to mixed-member proportional in 1994.
9. Though even there, judiciaries that are too independent of public opinion have become highly controversial in the United States and other developed democracies that can take basic judicial independence for granted.

BIBLIOGRAPHY

Acemoglu, Daron, Simon Johnson and James A. Robinson (2000), 'The Colonial Origins of Comparative Development: An Empirical Investigation', Cambridge, MA, National Bureau of Economic Research (NBER) Working Paper No. 7771.
—— (2002), 'Reversal of Fortune: Geography and Institutions in the Making of the Modern World Income Distribution', *Quarterly Journal of Economics*, **117** (4), 1369–401.
Almond, Gabriel A. and Sidney Verba (1963), *The Civic Culture*, Boston: Little, Brown.
Archer, Ronald P. and Matthew S. Shugart (1997), 'The Unrealized Potential of Presidential Dominance in Colombia', in Scott Mainwaring and Matthew S. Shugart (eds), *Presidentialism and Democracy in Latin America*, New York: Cambridge University Press, pp. 110–59.
Buchanan, James M. and Gordon Tullock (1962), *The Calculus of Consent: Logical Foundations of Constitutional Democracy*, Ann Arbor, MI: University of Michigan Press.
Chhibber, Ajay, R. Kyle Peters and Barbara J. Hale (eds) (2006), *Reform and Growth: Evaluating the World Bank Experience*, New Brunswick, NJ: Transaction.
Corrales, Javier (2002), *Presidents without Parties: The Politics of Economic Reform in Argentina and Venezuela in the 1990s*, University Park, PA: Pennsylvania State University Press.
Cox, Gary W. and Mathew D. McCubbins (2001), 'The Institutional Determinants of Economic Policy', in Stephan Haggard and Mathew D. McCubbins (eds), *Presidents, Parliaments and Policy*, New York: Cambridge University Press, pp. 21–63.
Diamond, Jared (1997), *Guns, Germ, and Steel: The Fates of Human Societies*, New York: W.W. Norton.
Duverger, Maurice (1950), *L'Influence des Systemes Electoraux sur la Vie Politique*, Paris: Colin.
Easterly, William R. and Ross Levine (2002), 'Tropics, Germs and Crops: How

Endowments Influence Economic Development', Cambridge, MA, National Bureau of Economic Research (NBER) Working Paper No. 9106.

Evans, Peter B., Dietrich Rueschemeyer and Theda Skocpol (1985), *Bringing the State Back In*, New York: Cambridge University Press.

Fukuyama, Francis (2004), *State-Building: Governance and World Order in the Twenty-First Century*, Ithaca, NY: Cornell University Press.

Fukuyama, Francis, Björn Dressel and Boo-Seung Chang (2005), 'Facing the Perils of Presidentialism?', *Journal of Democracy*, **16** (2), 102–16.

Geddes, Barbara (1996), *Politician's Dilemma: Building State Capacity in Latin America*, Berkeley, CA: University of California Press.

Haggard, Stephan and Mathew D. McCubbins (2001), *Presidents, Parliaments and Policy*, New York: Cambridge University Press.

Horowitz, Donald (1990), 'Debate: Presidents vs. Parliaments: Comparing Democratic Systems', *Journal of Democracy*, **1** (2), 73–83.

Huntington, Samuel P. (1968), *Political Order in Changing Societies*, New Haven: Yale University Press.

—— (2004), *Who Are We? The Challenges to America's National Identity*, New York: Simon and Schuster.

Kaufmann, Daniel, Aart Kraay and Massimo Mastruzzi (2005), 'Governance Matters IV: Governance Indicators for 1996–2004', Washington, DC, World Bank Policy Research Paper No. 3630.

Knack, Stephen and Philip Keefer (1995), 'Institutions and Economic Performance: Cross-Country Tests Using Alternative Measures', *Economics and Politics*, **7** (3), 207–27.

Krastev, Ivan (2006), 'Democracy's "Doubles"', *Journal of Democracy*, **17** (2), 52–62.

Lijphart, Arend (1991), 'Constitutional Choices for New Democracies', *Journal of Democracy*, **2** (1), 72–84.

Limongi, Fernando and Argelina Figueiredo (2000), 'Presidential Power, Legislative Organization and Party Behavior in Brazil', *Comparative Politics*, **32** (2), 151–70.

Linz, Juan J. (1990), 'The Perils of Presidentialism', *Journal of Democracy*, **1** (1), 51–69.

Lipset, Seymour Martin (1995), *American Exceptionalism: A Double-Edged Sword*, New York: W.W. Norton.

Mainwaring, Scott (1997), 'Multipartism, Robust Federalism and Presidentialism in Brazil', in Scott Mainwaring and Matthew S. Shugart (eds), *Presidentialism and Democracy in Latin America*, New York: Cambridge University Press, pp. 55–109.

Mainwaring, Scott and Timothy R. Scully (1995), *Building Democratic Institutions: Party Systems in Latin America*, Stanford, CA: Stanford University Press.

Mainwaring, Scott and Matthew S. Shugart (1997), *Presidentialism and Democracy in Latin America*, New York: Cambridge University Press.

Mann, Michael (1984), 'The Autonomous Power of the State: Its Origins, Mechanisms, and Results', *European Journal of Sociology*, **25** (2), 185–213.

McClelland, David C. (1961), *The Achieving Society*, Princeton: Van Nostrand.

Nettl, J.P. (1968), 'The State as a Conceptual Variable', *World Politics*, **20** (4), 559–92.

North, Douglass C. (1990), *Institutions, Institutional Change and Economic Performance*, New York: Cambridge University Press.

Rodrik, Dani and Arvind Subramanian (2003), 'The Primacy of Institutions (And What This Does and Does Not Mean)', *Finance and Development*, **40** (2), 31–4.

Sachs, Jeffrey (1994), 'Life in the Economic Emergency Room', in John Williamson (ed.), *The Political Economy of Policy Reform*, Washington, DC: Institute for International Economics, pp. 503–23.

Sachs, Jeffrey and John W. McArthur (2001), 'Institutions and Geography: Comment on Acemoglu, Johnson and Robinson (2000)', Cambridge, MA, National Bureau of Economic Research (NBER) Working Paper No. 8114.

Sachs, Jeffrey and Andrew Warner (1995), 'Natural Resource Abundance and Economic Growth', Cambridge, MA, National Bureau of Economic Research (NBER) Working Paper No. 5398.

Shugart, Matthew S. and John M. Carey (1992), *Presidents and Assemblies: Constitutional Design and Electoral Dynamics*, New York: Cambridge University Press.

Stein, Ernesto, Mariano Tommasi, Koldo Echevarría, Eduardo Lora and Mark Payne (2005), *The Politics of Policies: Economic and Social Progress in Latin America, 2006 Report*, Washington, DC: Inter-American Development Bank.

Tommasi, Mariano (2004), 'Crisis, Political Institutions and Policy Reform: The Good, the Bad and the Ugly', in Bertil Tungodden, Nicholas Stern and Ivan Kolstad (eds), *Toward Pro-Poor Policies: Aid, Institutions and Globalization*, Washington, DC: World Bank, pp. 135–64.

Tommasi, Mariano and Sebastian Saiegh (1999), 'Why Is Argentina's Fiscal Federalism So Inefficient? Entering the Labyrinth', *Journal of Applied Economics*, **2** (1), 169–209.

Tungodden, Bertil, Nicholas Stern and Ivan Kolstad (2004), *Toward Pro-Poor Policies: Aid, Institutions and Globalization*, Washington, DC: World Bank.

Williamson, John (1994), *The Political Economy of Policy Reform*, Washington, DC: Institute for International Economics.

Zakaria, Fareed (2003), *The Future of Freedom: Illiberal Democracy at Home and Abroad*, New York: W.W. Norton.

2. Democracy and Poverty Reduction: Explorations on the Sen Conjecture

Luca Barbone, Louise Cord, Katy Hull and Justin Sandefur

Amartya Sen has famously stated that no substantial famine has ever occurred in an independent democratic country with a relatively free press (Sen 1999a). This chapter picks up on two strands of literature stimulated by Sen's conjecture, examining claims that democracy can alleviate the suffering and vulnerability of the poor by reducing income poverty and promoting human development.

We examine the impact of democracy on poverty reduction by drawing on country case studies and new cross-country empirical evidence. The case studies, drawn from the recently completed *Delivering on the Promise of Pro-Poor Growth* study, focus on four countries (Bangladesh, Ghana, Tunisia and Uganda) which experienced significant poverty reduction in the 1990s under a variety of political regimes (Besley and Cord 2006). Cross-country datasets provide a statistical check on the intuitions developed in these case studies.

Existing empirical evidence has yet to establish a resounding case that democracy reduces poverty. Reductions in income poverty can be decomposed into changes in average income and changes in the distribution of income (Bourguignon 2003). While growth would be the primary channel through which democracy might reduce income poverty, of the 47 quantitative studies reviewed by Kurzman, Werum and Burkhart (2002), less than half (19) found a robustly positive relationship between democracy and growth. Although the effects of democracy on inequality have a theoretical basis in median voter theory (Meltzer and Richard 1981), they have been hard to demonstrate empirically, in part due to difficulties in measuring inequality across countries and within countries over time.[1]

Anecdotal evidence reinforces these inconclusive findings. In the 1990s, reformist communist governments in Vietnam and China were successful in delivering significant growth with poverty reduction. Poverty was almost halved in Vietnam between 1993 and 2002[2] (Klump 2006), while in China the poverty incidence declined from 31.5 per cent to 18 per cent over the course of the 1990s (World Bank 2003).[3] Authoritarian Indonesia under President Suharto provides another example of a non-democratic government which was successful in achieving rapid, poverty-reducing growth – poverty levels fell from over 60 per cent to less than 12 per cent of the population between 1976, when the first reliable estimates were made, and 1996, the eve of the Asian financial crisis (World Bank 2001).[4]

While empirical evidence for a direct link between democracy and poverty reduction has not been conclusive, the existing theoretical literature provides two extensions of Sen's conjecture that democracy can improve the welfare of the poor. The first channel predicts that democracy will contribute to good governance by enfranchising a broader segment of society to demand effective and inclusive economic institutions. This channel incorporates the basic hypothesis of the new institutional economists: economic governance, in particular the protection of private property rights, will provide incentives for the accumulation of physical and human capital which are the proximate causes of economic growth and, in turn, poverty reduction. The second channel suggests that, by empowering economically marginalized groups to demand better standards of health and education, democratic institutions will be an effective means of holding political leaders accountable to the basic needs of the poor (McGuire 2001). Following from this notion, it predicts that democracies will be better than autocracies at providing public services which benefit the poor, resulting in improved human development outcomes.

Not all democracies, however, are created equal. While the theoretical links between democracy and poverty reduction are premised on an assumption that democracy will empower the poor, fragmentation along ethnic and economic lines, and poverty itself, could impede the extent to which the poor form a politically cohesive group or engage in politics at all. In sum, the initial conditions of a country should determine the extent to which democracy produces pro-poor outcomes.

These basic hypotheses are summarized in Figure 2.1. At the top of the diagram, democratic processes interact with country-specific cultural and economic factors to determine the quality of economic governance and the provision of public services. In democratic polities with a sizeable middle class and low social and economic fractionalization, democratic systems produce broad economic enfranchisement (access to property rights and incentives for physical and human capital investment) and political accountability for the provision of quality public services to a large segment of society. Establishing strong economic governance will contribute to growth and poverty reduction, while the accountable public services will enable improved human development outcomes, such as health and education, for any given level of per capita income.

Figure 2.1   Two Potential Channels Linking Democracy to Poverty Reduction

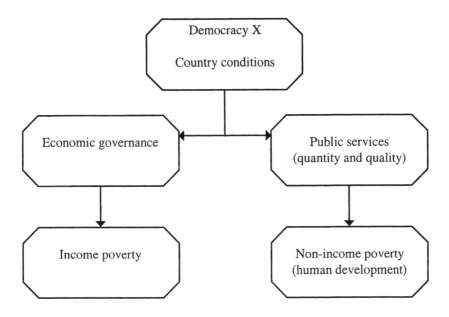

DATA AND DEFINITIONS

We attempt to quantify the channels described above using data on (1) political regimes, (2) poverty outcomes including dollar-a-day head-count ratios and child mortality, (3) country conditions, such as ethnic fractionalization and inequality, which may affect the functioning of democratic systems, and (4) intermediate mechanisms linking democracy to poverty reduction, including public spending on health and subjective measures of economic governance.

Quantifying Political Regimes

Our primary index of democracy is based on the Polity IV database developed by Marshall and Jaggers (2002) and incorporates subjective evaluations of at least three dimensions that we believe are important for understanding the impact of democracy on the poor. The first is electoral competition – the degree and breadth of popular participation in the selection of political leaders. However, while the occurrence of 'free and fair' elections is certainly a necessary feature of strong democracies, elections alone are only sufficient to guarantee majoritarianism. Thus the second dimension of democracy that we wish to capture is the constraints placed on the executive. This is the hallmark of liberal democracy, in which electoral competition takes place within the confines of the rule of law and respect for individual liberties.

The final dimension of democracy is duration – the length of democratic experience in a given country. As Keefer (2005a) argues, the efficacy of democratic participation is likely to be particularly weak in young regimes. The early decades of a new democratic regime, supposing it is not overturned, are commonly referred to as a period of 'democratic consolidation'. In order to capture this observation, we follow Besley and Kudamatsu (2006) in measuring democracy by the number of years since 1956 that a country has been rated as democratic (Polity score > 0) by Marshall and Jaggers (2002). An additional advantage of this approach is that it minimizes the sensitivity of our results to small, and sometimes debatable, changes in the numerical Polity score assigned to a country over time. Other than binary regime change, the movements over time in the index relate to an objective measure of democratic legacy.

Dimensions of Poverty

We make two key distinctions in our measurement and definition of poverty. First, we distinguish between income and non-income poverty or human development. This distinction is important not only because of the enormous international variance which exists in indicators of well-being such as literacy and life expectancy at a given level of per capita income (Anand and Sen 2000), but also because these other indicators of well-being may have alternative, direct links to democratic government which do not pass through income growth. Second, within our analysis of income poverty we distinguish poverty reduction related to movements in mean income from those produced by changes in the distribution of income at a given mean.

We measure income poverty using the head-count measure – the percentage of the population living on less than one dollar per day. The income measures are based primarily on per capita household consumption, as measured by household surveys. Chen and Ravallion (2004) provide comparable head-count poverty rates for a panel of 96 countries over the period 1977–2003. The dataset contains a total of 338 country–year observations.

Ultimately, we are concerned with quantifying the impact of these political and institutional indicators on reductions in national poverty rates. However, cross-national datasets for standard poverty indexes such as the head-count measure offer a relatively limited number of observations for statistical analysis, particularly when comparing changes over time (Kraay 2006).

To avoid this constraint we investigate institutional impacts on poverty by estimating separate equations with average incomes and the Gini coefficient as the dependent variables. The relatively close fit of a log normal approximation to most empirically observed income distributions implies that mean income and the Gini (as a measure of dispersion) are sufficient statistics to identify poverty changes (Dollar and Kraay 2002). Furthermore, decomposing poverty changes into growth and distributional components may be of independent interest. We measure mean incomes using per capita GDP in purchasing power parity (PPP) terms from the World Development Indicators dataset (World Bank 2006). The inequality data are taken from the World Income Inequality Database (WIID) which provides country-level Gini coefficients for a sample of 149 countries over the period 1950–2002 (WIDER 2005).

In addition to incomes and inequality, we are also interested in broader measures of human development. We use data on child mortality (the log of deaths under age five per 1,000 live births) taken from the World Development Indicators as a measure of human development (World Bank 2006). While child mortality is clearly a narrow measure of this broad concept, the existence of data covering a wide range of developing countries over multiple decades render it arguably the best empirical proxy available. Unlike other common indicators of human development such as life expectancy or educational attainment, child mortality rates can be expected to respond fairly quickly to improvements in public service delivery.

Additional Data Sources

With regard to the social divisions which we hypothesize may undermine democratic processes, we employ an index of ethnic fractionalization which has featured prominently in the literature (Alesina et al. 2003). The variable is constructed as one minus the Herfindahl index of ethnicity; namely, the probability that two randomly drawn individuals come from different ethnic groups.

Our measures of economic institutions are taken primarily from the International Country Risk Guide (ICRG), a dataset which provides subjective ratings of several dimensions of institutional performance on a monthly basis from 1984 to 2005 for approximately 140 countries (Political Risk Services 2005). The ICRG measure of property rights, defined as the risk of government expropriation of private property, has featured prominently in the literature on growth and institutions (Knack and Keefer 1997; Acemoglu, Johnson and Robinson 2001). In addition, the ICRG provides a measure of bureaucratic quality, designed to measure the efficiency of the public sector.

Figure 2.2   Formal and Informal Institutional Characteristics in Country Cases

	Low democracy	High democracy
Low ethnic fractionalization	Tunisia	Bangladesh
High ethnic fractionalization	Uganda	Ghana

Case Study Countries

In selecting the case studies, we focused on countries which had distinctly different levels of democracy and ethnic fractionalization, so as to create four different typologies (see Figure 2.2). The case studies enable us to explore how different regime types may be associated with improved economic governance and the provision of public services. The high fractionalization cases – Uganda and Ghana – also provide us with an opportunity to explore the impact of ethnic fragmentation on the relationship between political regimes and development outcomes.

The analysis of democracy requires numerous subtle distinctions, many of which defy the quantification at the heart of this study. Although the typologies in Figure 2.2 provide a stylized snapshot of country conditions, any investigation into specific country cases immediately highlights the shortcomings of dichotomous democracy/autocracy distinctions. As Figure 2.3 demonstrates, levels of perceived democratic accountability have changed from one decade to the next (and, in fact, one year to the next) in each country.

In the 1990s our 'high democracy' cases, Ghana and Bangladesh, made transitions to the status of electoral democracies. Both countries experienced relatively free and fair elections, although they lacked some of the essential mechanisms of accountability, transparency and the rule of law associated with liberal democracies. Our 'low democracy' cases – Tunisia and Uganda – might be best described as 'hegemonic electoral authoritarian' regimes, in which elections were primarily used as a means of reinforcing the incumbent. In short, all four countries in our selection are best understood as 'hybrid regimes' (Diamond 2002). The case study approach provides an opportunity to analyze how the nuances in political institutions will influence the depth and quality of accountability mechanisms which, as we hypothesize, are important for poverty reduction and human development.

Turning to the high fractionalization cases in Figure 2.2, the populations of

Figure 2.3   Evolution of Democracy in Case Study Countries

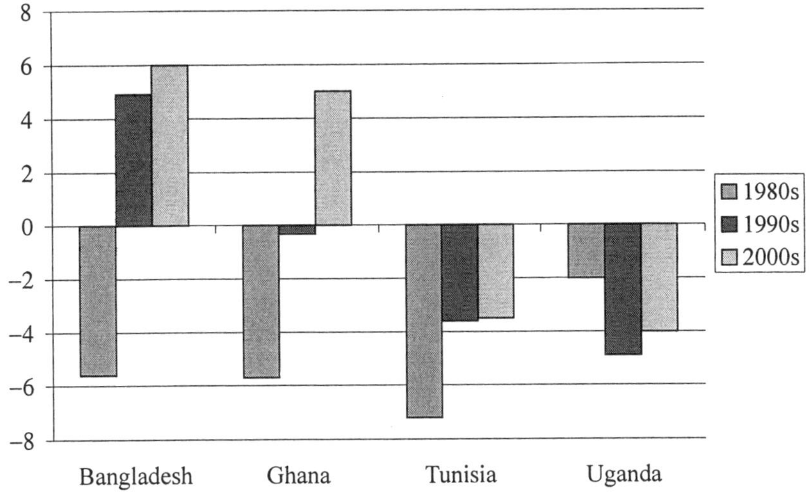

Source: Monty G. Marshall and Keith Jaggers (2002), 'Polity IV Data Set'.

Ghana and Uganda, like most countries in Sub-Saharan Africa, are made up of multiple ethnic groups. The largest single ethnic group in Uganda – the Baganda – makes up only 17 per cent of the population. Ghana has four major ethnic groups, the largest of which – the Akan – makes up 44 per cent of the population (Freedom House 2005). The extent to which this fractionalization impedes the responsiveness of institutions to the needs of the poor is discussed below.

TWO CHANNELS LINKING DEMOCRACY AND POVERTY

Democracy and Income Poverty

Our first hypothesis is that democracy might affect poverty reduction by enabling a broader segment of society to demand effective economic governance, primarily in the form of broad-based and secure property rights. Countries with more secure property rights achieve better rates of growth through higher investments in physical and human capital (North 1981). By encouraging firms to invest in new technologies, secure property rights will facilitate the absorption of innovation. And by making future returns on investment more certain, good property rights regimes will encourage individuals to invest in human and physical capital and to take economic risks.

While there is a near consensus around the notion that high-quality institutions of economic governance are good for growth, there is less agreement as to whether these institutions are more prevalent under democratic regimes. Classical theorists from Macaulay to Marx have suggested that the enfranchisement of the poor will undermine property rights by empowering the economically deprived to expropriate the wealth of the privileged classes (Przeworski and Limongi 1993). More recent research, however, has suggested that political inclusion is a precondition for stable, inclusive economic institutions and broad-based growth (World Bank 2005a; Acemoglu, Johnson and Robinson 2005).

Country Studies

Our case studies only partially support our first hypothesis – that democracy can reinforce the development of broad-based property rights regimes which are preconditions of growth and poverty reduction. Figures 2.4 and 2.5 show the evolution of democratic accountability and the investment profile (which includes measures of the security of property rights) in Ghana and Tunisia, respectively.

In Ghana, the overall trend for indexes of both democratic accountability and investment climate has been upward, from the mid-1980s to the present (see Figure 2.4). Causality, however, cannot be determined by the correlation and, indeed, the most obvious contributor to an improved investment climate has been the policies pursued under Ghana's economic recovery program, that started in 1983, some years before the transition to multiparty democracy.

But in Tunisia, declining democratic accountability ratings in the 1990s, due to growing restrictions on press freedom and civil society activism, were accompanied by an opposite trend of overall improvements in the investment profile (see Figure 2.5). Again, although these correlations do not suggest causality, they indicate that infringements of political and civil liberties may not be perceived as antithetical to an increasingly stable investment climate.

Empirical Results

Moving from specific cases to average statistical relationships, we attempt to estimate the cross-country link between democracy and income poverty. The data we use constitute a panel of 92 countries, with 316 observations from 1977 to 2002. The dependent variable is the percentage of the population living on less than one dollar per day in country i at time t. To test the hypothesis that democracy will create secure and broad-based property rights regimes which

Figure 2.4   International Country Risk Guide Profile: Ghana

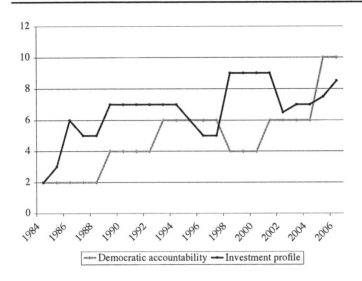

Figure 2.5   International Country Risk Guide Profile: Tunisia

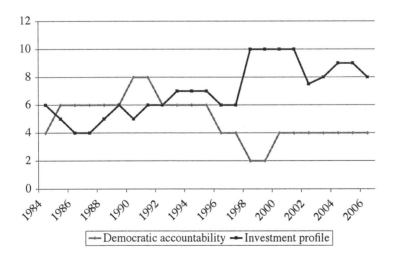

Table 2.1   Summary Statistics

	Regression Sample			Availability	
	Mean	Median	Std. dev.	Countries	Years
Head-count poverty, %	16.31	8.16	18.81	94	1977–2002
Under-five mortality	106.37	93.00	76.08	151	1960–2003
Per capita GDP (PPP$)	3879.25	3193.63	2919.07	128	1975–2003
Gini coefficient	42.44	43.30	11.46	117	1950–2003
Democracy	9.51	5.00	11.30	126	1950–2003
ICRG Inv. Profile	6.14	6.00	2.04	100	1984–2003
ICRG Gov. Eff.	1.69	2.00	0.95	100	1984–2003
Health budget/GDP	2.31	1.98	1.40	82	1990–2004

Note: The sample is restricted to low- and middle-income countries, based on categories from the World Development Indicators, 2006. In the first three columns, summary statistics are based on any observations falling in the regressions in Tables 2.2 to 2.4. The fourth and fifth columns report data availability for each variable on low- and middle-income countries, regardless of whether this full range of data enters the regression samples.

enable poverty-reducing growth, we regress these head-count poverty ratios on our index of democracy and, in later specifications, additional controls:

$$Poverty_{it} = \alpha_0 + \alpha_1 Democracy_{it} + \eta_i + \lambda_t + \varepsilon_{it} \qquad (2.1)$$

The η_i term in equation (2.1) is a country dummy controlling for unobserved, time-invariant differences between countries which may otherwise explain our results, as discussed below; λ_t is a vector of year dummies and ε_{it} is a random error. In later regressions we include indices of economic governance as additional regressors to test the importance of these as channels between democracy and poverty reduction. Additionally, we also experiment with a measure of ethnic fractionalization and its interaction with democracy to measure the impact of social polarization on the democracy–poverty link.

The basic results from this regression of income poverty on our democracy index are presented in columns 1 and 2 of Table 2.2. The univariate, cross-sectional regression of head-count poverty rates on democracy (column 1) produces a significant negative coefficient, implying that ten additional years of democracy yields a 35 per cent lower poverty rate.

However, there are compelling reasons to be skeptical of this finding. Here we focus on the problem of omitted variable bias.[5] Our failure to control for other dimensions of institutional development which are potentially (1) correlated with democracy and (2) causing cross-country differences in poverty rates will lead to a spurious finding of a democracy–poverty link. Since we have data on a panel of countries, we can largely address this problem by including country fixed effects (the η_i term in equation [2.1]) which control for all observed and unobserved cross-country differences which do not vary over time. As seen in column 2, after including country fixed effects, the negative association between democracy and poverty is completely undetectable. In sum, the Chen and Ravallion head-count poverty dataset provides no evidence of an association between democracy (as defined here) and poverty reduction within countries.

An alternative way to compute the poverty impact of democratization is by analyzing the impacts on the mean and variance of income distributions separately.[6] Toward this end, we estimate separate regressions using the (log of) mean per capita GDP and the Gini coefficient of income inequality, respectively, as the dependent variable. Numerous studies have found a significant association within countries between democracy and economic growth (Krieckhaus 2004) and cross-country evidence suggests that growth spells will have, on average, a proportional impact on the poor (Dollar and Kraay 2002; Kraay 2006).

As seen in columns 1 and 2 of Table 2.3, the positive relationship between democracy and mean income is robust to the inclusion of country effects, indicating that economic growth is linked to democracy. However, when we restrict the sample to countries for which poverty data are available (columns 8–10), this relationship disappears. Furthermore, turning to Table 2.4, we find no systematic relationship between democracy and within-country changes in income inequality, suggesting that rising (or falling) inequality does not affect a country's democracy score.[7]

What explains the reduced-form relationship between democracy and incomes in the full GDP sample? Based on the discussion above, we investigate whether improved economic governance in countries with a longer democratic legacy can explain this association. Inasmuch as the effect of democracy on incomes operates via some mechanism, in this case governance, then including governance in the regression of income on democracy should reduce the magnitude and statistical significance of the democracy coefficient. Columns 2 and 3 of Table 2.3 perform this test for per capita GDP, using ICRG indicators of the investment profile and government effectiveness as measures of governance. Both of these governance indicators enter positively and significantly at the 1 per cent level. Additionally, the inclusion of these variables reduces the magnitude of the democracy effect to approximately one-third its original size.

How can we reconcile the various results presented in this section? We found that: (1) democratization is significantly associated with higher average

Table 2.2   Democracy and Poverty

	(1)	(2)	(3)	(4)	(5)	(6)	(7)	(8)
Democracy	-.350 (.078)***	-.024 (.214)	.079 (.241)	.068 (.331)	-.026 (.216)	-.391 (.427)	-.035 (.065)	.154 (.180)
Property rights			-.074 (.374)					
Gov. effectiveness			-2.155 (.770)***					
Dem. × fract.				-.188 (.598)				
Dem. × L.I.C.					.039 (.329)			
Gini						672 (.128)***		
Dem. × Gini						.004 (.007)		
ln(mean income)							-15.989 (1.177)***	-15.299 (1.627)***
Country dummies	No	Yes	Yes	Yes	Yes	Yes	No	Yes
Countries	92	92	78	91	92	90	92	92
Obs.	316	316	258	314	316	302	316	316
R²	.602	.145	.175	.145	.145	.277	.758	.408

Notes: ***Significant at 1 per cent level.
Dependent variable: head-count poverty rate. Time span: 1977–2002.
The construction of the democracy index and other regressors are described in the text.

54

Table 2.3   *Democracy and Average Income (1977–2003)*

	Full sample								Poverty sample		
	(1)	(2)	(3)	(4)	(5)	(6)	(7)	(8)	(9)	(10)	(11)
Democracy	.029	.010	.003	.023	.038	.017	.011	.020	.019	−.005	−.005
	(.001)***	(.001)***	(.001)**	(.003)***	(.003)***	(.002)***	(.001)***	(.004)***	(.003)***	(.004)	(.004)
Property rights			.016								.008
			(.003)***								(.007)
Gov. effectiveness			.043								.011
			(.006)***								(.014)
Fractionalization				−.635							
				(.061)***							
Dem. × fract.				.014	−.016	−.015					
				(.006)**	(.005)***	(.004)***					
Dem. × L.I.C.							−.008				
							(.002)***				
Gini								−.0003			
								(.001)			
Dem. × Gini								−.0003			
								(.00007)***			
C. Dummies	No	Yes	Yes	No	No	Yes	Yes	Yes	No	Yes	Yes
Countries	115	115	92	114	114	114	115	99	78	78	78
Obs.	2633	2633	1616	2619	2619	2619	2633	1517	253	253	253
R²	.52	.102	.201	.557	.538	.107	.109	.201	.626	.438	.447

Note: ***Significant at 1 per cent level; **significant at 5 per cent level.
Dependent variable is the natural logarithm of average per capita GDP in 2000 PPP dollars. Columns 9–11 are confined to countries and time periods for which the poverty data used in Table 2.2 are available.

55

Table 2.4   Democracy and Inequality (1977–2003)

	(1)	(2)	(3)	(4)	(5)
Democracy	.077	−.018	.029	.115	−.007
	(.037)**	(.100)	(.169)	(.157)	(.100)
Property rights			−.278		
			(.222)		
Govt. effectiveness			.431		
			(.559)		
Dem. × fract.				−.347	
				(.287)	
Dem. × L.I.C					−.219
					(.188)
Country dummies	No	Yes	Yes	Yes	Yes
Countries	101	101	81	99	101
Obs.	739	739	513	729	739
R^2	.49	.127	.133	.135	.129

Note: The dependent variable is the Gini coefficient for per capita household income/expenditure.
**Significant at 5 per cent level.

incomes within countries in the full sample, (2) evidence is consistent with the hypothesis that the democracy–income link operates via improved economic governance but (3) democracy is uncorrelated with poverty or average incomes in the poverty sample. One possibility is that the sample of countries for which poverty data are available is simply too small to identify the relevant effects. Another possibility is that the instrumental benefits of democracy simply fail to materialize in the economies for which Chen and Ravallion present comparable poverty data – predominantly low- and middle-income countries.

Democracy and Human Development

Our second hypothesis is that democracy will hold political leaders accountable to the basic needs of the poor, resulting in the improved targeting of public services to human development goals.

Amartya Sen's assertion that famines are less likely to occur in democracies indicates that democratic accountability can be instrumental in raising the voices of the poor to an effective level. In dictatorships, the absence of opposition parties, elections and public criticism will mean that those in power will not suffer political consequences for a failure to respond to the most desperate needs of the poor (Sen 1999b). 'The response of a government to the acute suffering of its people often depends on the pressure that is put on it. The exercise of political rights (such as voting, criticizing, protesting, and the like) can make a real difference to the political incentives that operate on a government' (Sen 1999a). Though Sen's arguments are primarily about how democratic institutions can avert famines and alleviate acute suffering, they have been subsumed into broader discussions of the performance of democratic regimes with regard to human development (Ghobarah, Huth and Russett 2004; Bueno de Mesquita et al. 2000).

Why might democracies not only spend more on public services but be more effective at delivering these services to the poor? Citizens in democracies might demand better health and education, and elections might ensure that politicians are held accountable for their promises. Democratic accountability might also lead to greater scrutiny of public spending, lowering the risks of corruption and diversion of funds. McGuire (2001) finds that electoral competition and civil society activism in democracies have been instrumental in the creation of welfare-state institutions, resulting in improved life expectancy and infant survival rates.

Country Studies

Our case studies provide some evidence to support the finding that electoral accountability can boost the provision of public services to the poor, while also showing that the quality and depth of democratic mechanisms will determine the extent to which politicians are held accountable for their promises throughout the electoral cycle.

Political competition in Bangladesh, Ghana and Uganda has brought human development concerns, particularly education, to the forefront of public discourse around election times. After political parties were legalized in 1986, General Hossain Mohammed Ershad, the military ruler of Bangladesh, accelerated education policy formulation in a bid to win wider support (Unterhalter, Ross and Alam 2003). Legislation was passed to make primary education mandatory in 1990, and universal primary education has remained a major topic in hotly contested elections since the advent of democracy in Bangladesh.

One month prior to Ghana's most recent presidential and parliamentary elections in December 2004, the ruling New Patriotic Party announced plans to expand the years of free education offered at the preschool and secondary levels. The election-time focus on education reflected public concerns, with an official opinion poll showing that education was voters' top priority.[8]

Uganda, though lacking a system of multiparty competition until 2005, has been described by Stasavage (2005) as a clear case of a country in which elections have reoriented government spending toward primary education.

President Yoweri Kaguta Museveni's promise of free, universal primary education carried nation-wide appeal and provides one explanation for his successful electoral campaigns in 1996 and 2001.

Our case studies also demonstrate that elections alone will not provide adequate accountability to ensure improved delivery of public services. Whether or not electoral promises are fulfilled will depend in part on the extent to which institutional mechanisms enable ongoing oversight and accountability. Weaknesses in the structure of democratic institutions or a lack of political maturity can hinder the delivery of improved services. These findings support the notion that failures in the political marketplace will undermine the material benefits of democracy for the poor.

While Bangladesh is the most established democracy among our case study countries (see Figure 2.2), the structure of democratic institutions has insulated political leaders from the needs of the poor. Parliamentary politics are dictated by personalized party loyalties; backbenchers have only weak oversight capacities and a first-past-the-post electoral system has resulted in a combative relationship between the two major parties (World Bank 2002). Summing up the democratization process in Bangladesh the International Crisis Group (2006) reflects: 'Boycotts, general strikes and mass protests have become the normal tool of politics, leading to immense disillusionment among the public with the political process.' Often nongovernmental organizations – not the government – have been the major providers of informal primary education, healthcare and family planning services to the poor (World Bank 2005b). Some have argued that, by virtue of their success, NGOs may perpetuate weak accountability mechanisms between citizens and the state, placing beneficiaries in a charitable, rather than rights-based, relationship with service providers (Haque 2002).

Evidence from Ghana suggests that weak accountability mechanisms stem in part from the novelty of democracy. Decades of dictatorial rule created a particular political culture which has endured beyond the advent of democracy. A secretive approach to government fostered 'a culture in which the first instinct was to refuse requests for information', even after the advent of multiparty democracy (Foster and Zormelo 2002). With few available statistics on poverty and government performance, the political opposition and the media lack the tools to hold the ruling party accountable for its shortcomings. A 1999 Afro-barometer survey found that ordinary Ghanaians were much more likely to seek out help from a personal contact (religious leader, chief or patron) than from an elected official (Bratton, Lewis and Gyimah-Boadi 2001). Perhaps tellingly, a similar survey conducted four years later found a growing trust between citizens and their elected representatives, indicating that as a democratic culture became ingrained over time, there would be a narrowing of the 'representation gap' in Ghanaian politics (Gyimah-Boadi and Mensah 2003).

Empirical Results

Having reviewed country case studies that lend some support to Sen's assertion that democratic accountability will enable human development, we now turn to cross-country statistical evidence. We regress child mortality rates on our democracy index and additional controls, as shown below.

$$Mortality_{it} = \beta_0 + \beta_1 Democracy_{it} + \beta_2 Y_{it} + \omega_i + \delta_t + u_{it} \qquad (2.2)$$

$Mortality_{it}$ is the log of child mortality in country i at time t, and other variables are defined as in equation (2.1). In later regressions we also control for the log of per capita GDP, denoted by Y, to measure the impact of democracy on human development, conditional on average incomes. The data constitute an unbalanced panel of up to 114 countries (453 data points) observed in 1980, 1990, 1995 and 2000.

Column 1 of Table 2.5 shows a highly significant, positive relationship between democracy and child mortality. Furthermore, the magnitude of this coefficient is large in economic terms, implying that an additional ten years of democratic rule will be associated with a roughly 25 per cent lower rate of child mortality. This result is in line with Besley and Kudamatsu (2006), who find a strong link between a similar democracy measure and life expectancy.

To test the robustness of this finding, we examine the impact of controlling for income or other unobserved factors. Previous studies have found that the vast bulk of international variation in child mortality can be explained by income differences (Filmer and Pritchett 1999). However, comparing columns 1 and 2, we see that only about half of the statistical association between democracy and child mortality can be attributed to the higher average incomes of democracies in the cross-section. Furthermore, the democracy effect is surprisingly robust to the inclusion of country fixed effects, as seen in column 3. The point estimate on democracy is virtually unchanged and remains highly significant.

Having established a fairly robust reduced-form correlation between democracy and child mortality, we turn to examining one potential mechanism that could explain this link: public health spending. Column 7 of Table 2.5 regresses child mortality on democracy, controlling for per capita GDP, but restricts the sample to data points with health data. Column 8 adds health spending to the equation; health enters with a negative and significant coefficient but fails to reduce the democracy coefficient. Finally, when including country fixed effects in column 9, democracy remains surprisingly robust while health spending falls out of the equation completely. Thus, while we find that levels of health spending cannot account for the democracy–child mortality link in

Table 2.5 Democracy and Child Mortality

	Full sample						Government spending sample			
	(1)	(2)	(3)	(4)	(5)	(6)	(7)	(8)	(9)	(10)
Democracy	−.028	−.014	−.013	−.024	−.016	−.009	−.006	−.015	−.016	−.020
	(.003)***	(.003)***	(.003)***	(.005)***	(.003)***	(.009)	(.004)	(.004)***	(.004)***	(.005)***
ln(p.c. GDP)		−.548	−.220	−.212	−.206	−.259	−.276	−.569	−.507	−.051
		(.035)***	(.048)***	(.048)***	(.047)***	(.067)***	(.073)***	(.050)***	(.049)***	(.098)
Dem. × fract.				.023						
				(.010)**						
Dem. × L.I.C.					.018					
					(.005)***					
Gini						.00008				
						(.003)				
Dem. × Gini						−.00002				
						(.0002)				
Gov. effectiveness							−.041			
							(.015)***			
Health/GDP									−.129	.015
									(.025)***	(.014)
Country dummies	No	No	Yes	Yes	Yes	Yes	Yes	No	No	Yes
Countries	114	114	114	113	114	96	91	72	72	72
Obs.	453	400	400	397	400	233	250	208	208	208
R²	.632	.781	.667	.673	.684	.813	.6	.806	.829	.438

Notes: Dependent variable: natural logarithm of child deaths under five years of age per 1,000 live births. Time periods: 1980, 1990, 1995 and 2000. Columns 8–10 are confined to countries for which government health spending data are available.

cross-country data, this leaves open various alternative hypotheses, such as that democratic polities will vote for more equitable provision of public services or exercise greater oversight over their effective provision (rendering health programs more effective at reducing child mortality for each dollar spent).

DEMOCRACY AND DEVELOPMENT IN CONTEXT

Our third hypothesis is that specific country conditions will hinder the extent to which democratic systems can produce both sound economic governance and improved service delivery to the poor. The list of conditions which could potentially influence how well the poor engage in the democratic process is essentially inexhaustible: culture, historical experience, literacy levels, degree of urbanization, etc. We examine just three conditions which might be expected to matter for the poor: income levels, inequality and ethnic fractionalization. The first two conditions are chosen because of some indication, both in the broader literature and our own empirical research, that the relationship between democracy and poverty reduction may be weaker in poor countries (Przeworski et al. 2000) or among poor groups (Brusco, Nazareno and Stokes 2002; Ross 2006). Ethnic fractionalization is chosen because of evidence that ethnic diversity is harmful to growth because it encourages rent-seeking behavior and reduces the consensus for public goods (Easterly and Levine 1997).

There is some evidence to suggest that democracy can alleviate the negative effects of poverty and fractionalization by providing a consensual framework for diverse groups to negotiate mutually beneficial outcomes (Rodrik 1999; Collier 1998). There is, however, a strong counter-argument to suggest that fragmented polities will create fragmented politics. As the work of various researchers (Brusco, Nazareno and Stokes 2002; Keefer 2005; Drèze and Sen 2002) indicates, patterns of social fragmentation are likely to be reproduced in the dynamics of politics. Economically and/or socially marginalized groups, if they are engaged in politics, will tend not to vote according to their best economic interests. In highly fragmented societies, in particular, ethnic or social affiliations will trump economic concerns and the poor are unlikely to vote as a cohesive group. This research suggests that full enfranchisement, rarely achieved by elections alone, will depend on the social inclusion of historically excluded members of society. By implication, the more fragmented a polity, the lower the likelihood that democratization will automatically enfranchise the poor and the greater the challenge of creating meaningful and effective political inclusion.

Case Studies

How can democratic accountability mediate the negative effects of ethnic fractionalization on economic development? The answer to this question partly depends on the particular ethnic makeup of each country and the specific form of accountability mechanisms. The intricacy of this subject precludes simple conclusions. However, two of our case study countries – Ghana and Uganda – provide insights into the complex relationships that are found in many highly fractionalized polities. In both countries, nebulous ethnic groupings overlap with cultural, historical and economic divisions. Both countries also have hybrid political institutions which qualify them as neither fully fledged liberal democracies nor politically closed authoritarian regimes. Moreover, their political institutions have undergone significant – and relatively recent – changes. These simple facts should caution against drawing specific policy lessons from the observations below. Indeed, the main implication of the Ghana and Uganda cases is that there is no single magic bullet which can mediate the negative impact of ethnic fractionalization on development.

Ghana's gradual transition to an electoral democracy in the 1990s caused concern that political competition would exacerbate ethnic strife. Contrary to these expectations, there is evidence to suggest that the democratic process has created incentives for inter-ethnic coalition building. The complex divisions among groups in Ghana mean that no single ethnic group can win competitive elections by appealing to its cohorts alone. In order to gain a majority in the first multiparty elections in 1992, the National Defense Council (NDC) forged alliances with three minor parties. In the 2000 election both the ruling NDC and the main opposition National Patriotic Party (NPP) ensured that their presidential tickets reflected an ethno-regional balance, so that if the presidential candidate was from the southern part of Ghana, the running mate would be from the northern part (Asante and Gyimah-Boadi 2004). The NPP's ultimate success in those elections was ascribed to a campaign fought on the basis of transcendental economic issues which appealed to the socially disadvantaged and urban youth, irrespective of ethnicity (Nugent 2001). In Ghana's case the transition to democracy indicated that ethnicity, although important, was not destiny.

Uganda's 'no-party democracy' under Yoweri Museveni was premised on a claim that multiparty politics had continuously exacerbated sectarian tensions. A self-styled 'movement' form of government was not, however, entirely devoid of mechanisms of accountability: the 1995 Constitution was the result of a four-year consultative process with individuals, local organizations and trade unions; a five-tiered local council system was designed to enhance village-level participation; and Uganda's press, while not free from political harassment, was described as one of the liveliest and most critical in Africa

(Kasfir 1998). A 2000 Afro-barometer poll found that most Ugandans did not consider the ban on multiparty politics to be incompatible with the freedom to criticize government or the rights of minority groups (Bratton, Lambright and Sentamu 2000). In sum, institutions of accountability were instrumental in bringing various groups into the political and civil processes, even in the absence of multiparty democracy.

Despite various forms of inclusion, participation and voice, ethnic divisions and historical patterns of neglect persist in both Ghana and Uganda, and they are reflected in geographically uneven patterns of development. Although democracy has been a conduit for intergroup cohesion in Ghana, there is some evidence to suggest that democracy will also delineate the limits of political inclusion: dominant parties may not forge political coalitions beyond those necessary for electoral success, perpetuating a disregard for the northern regions (Fayemi, Jaye and Yeebo 2003) which suffer from lower public resource allocations despite their dire needs. These regions had the lowest levels of subsidies per school-age child, the highest pupil-to-teacher ratios and some of the lowest rates of public healthcare provision in Ghana, according to a 1992–98 public expenditure review (Canagarajah and Ye 2001). In Uganda, accusations have been made that Westerners are benefiting more than other Ugandans from political appointments and promotions in parastatals. Northerners' virtual boycott of a 2000 referendum on multipartyism was a challenge to the movement system's claim to embody national aspirations: a silent protest against official disregard for a region beset by continued unrest and the highest poverty rates in the country (Leggett 2001). Both the Ghana and Uganda cases indicate that ethnic divisions, especially when they overlap with economic disparities, pose massive developmental challenges to any state, whatever the political system.

Empirical Results

Our empirical results so far have established a strong statistical relationship, robust to controls for unobserved heterogeneity, between democracy and both per capita GDP and child mortality. However, the preceding discussion suggests that this relationship may fail to hold in fractionalized, unequal or extremely poor societies. To test this suggestion, we include two interaction terms in our GDP and child mortality equations: the interaction of democracy and ethnic fractionalization, democracy and a dummy variable for 'low-income country' (L.I.C.) status and, finally, democracy and Gini coefficient for income inequality. Our basic hypothesis is that the coefficient on these interaction terms should be negative. However, interpreting interaction coefficients is open to some debate, so we attempt to place our findings in the context of the literature.

Consider the following regression of the log average per capita income on democracy and an interaction term:

$$Y_{it} = \gamma_0 + \gamma_1 Dem_{it} + \gamma_2 Frac_i + \gamma_3 (Dem_{it} \times Frac_i) \, \eta_i + \lambda_t + \varepsilon_{it} \qquad (2.3)$$

The partial effect of democracy on average income is expressed as $\partial \ln Y / \partial Dem = \gamma_1 + \gamma_3 Frac$. At least two other studies we know of examine this same interaction effect. Collier (1998) and Alesina and La Ferrara (2005) use average annual GDP growth rates as their dependent variable and interact a measure of ethnic or ethno-linguistic fractionalization with the Gastil index of political liberties on the right-hand side. Their results are consistent with the estimates reported in column 4 of Table 2.3 where we include democracy, fractionalization and their interaction on the right-hand side but exclude country fixed effects. Both Collier and Alesina and La Ferrara interpret this pattern of coefficient signs ($\gamma_1 > 0$, $\gamma_2 < 0$, $\gamma_3 > 0$) as indicating that democracy can have a particularly strong, positive effect on growth in fractionalized societies.

However, when we extend the cross-section approach pursued by Collier and Alesina and La Ferrara to a panel of countries and include country fixed effects, this story seems to fall apart. Column 6 shows a positive coefficient of .017 on democracy and a coefficient on the democracy–fractionalization interaction term of –.015. Thus, after ten additional years of democratic history, a hypothetical country with zero fractionalization would see an 18 per cent increase in per capita income over its non-democratic income path; meanwhile, a country with perfect fractionalization would see effectively zero income gain (.017–.015) from democratization. To summarize, previous studies have stressed that democracy will mediate ethnic conflicts in fractionalized societies. In contrast, our empirical evidence is consistent with the interpretation that ethnic fractionalization undermines the material benefits of democracy.

How do our empirical findings hold up against insights from our case studies? Our empirical findings affirm that, for a given level of ethnic fractionalization, democracies tend to grow more quickly than non-democracies. Our case study of Ghana bolsters this conclusion: there is no evidence that electoral democracy in this fractionalized society has led to ethnic strife or undermined economic performance. However, our results contrast with earlier studies in finding that the marginal impact of democracy on income tends to be lower in fractionalized societies.[9] Consistent with this finding, evidence from both Ghana and Uganda suggests that fractionalization challenges the effectiveness of democratic institutions at reducing poverty and improving human development outcomes among economically marginalized groups.

CONCLUSION

Extending Sen's conjecture that democracy can enhance the welfare of the vulnerable and the poor, we have distinguished between two instrumental roles for democracy: one relating to income poverty and the other to broader human development outcomes. Three basic conclusions emerge from both our case studies and empirical estimations. First, the relationship between democracy and reductions in income poverty is weak and contingent on specific country conditions. Second, democratic political systems are better than non-democratic regimes at delivering public services to the poor and, in turn, raising human development outcomes. Third, initial country conditions, including levels of poverty, inequality and ethnic fractionalization, will inhibit the extent to which democracy benefits the poor.

Addressing the relationship between democracy and poverty reduction via economic governance, our case studies provide anecdotal evidence to suggest that non-democratic regimes can achieve poverty-reducing growth by promoting relatively stable property rights and attractive investment climates. Estimating a simple, cross-country reduced-form relationship between our democracy index and dollar-a-day head-count poverty rates, we find virtually no evidence of a link between democratization and reductions in income poverty.

The lack of a relationship between democratic legacy and income poverty requires some explanation. Numerous estimates, including our own, show a positive and significant association between democracy and average income based on national accounts data. Yet, we find no relationship between democracy and inequality once controlling for time-invariant country effects. Moreover, the democracy–income relationship disappears when we limit our sample to countries reporting head-count poverty rates. This leaves open at least two interpretations.

First, poverty data may be too scarce or too noisy to detect the genuine impact of democratic institutions. Alternatively, the material benefits of democracy may not be homogeneous across countries. Specifically, 'political market failures' may undermine democratic accountability in the low-income countries which dominate the poverty dataset. Since the positive association between democracy and average income is weaker in highly fractionalized countries, this suggests that electoral processes and constraints on the executive are less correlated with growth in fragmented polities.

Turning to the relationship between democracy and human development, our case studies suggest that democratic processes can bring the provision of public services to the forefront of public debate. The hybrid regimes represented by our case studies provide numerous indications (both positive and negative) of valuable sources of accountability: parliamentary oversight, availability of information and freedom of the media, to name just a few. Shortcomings in accountability mechanisms – whether a relatively weak parliament in Bangladesh or a 'culture of silence' in Ghana (Bratton, Lewis and Gyimah-Boadi 2001) – can impair the ability of democracy to deliver improved policies and institutions to the poor. The main point here is that while democracy is relevant to human development outcomes, elections alone will not provide sufficient levels of accountability to empower the poor.

Our empirical estimations support the notion that democratic political systems do better at delivering public services to the poor and, in turn, raising human development outcomes. Unlike our inconclusive results for the relationship between democracy and income poverty, the (negative) democracy–child mortality link appears statistically robust and rather large.[10] We further investigate the channel from democracy to human development by controlling for health spending. Total health spending as a share of GDP is higher among democracies and is negatively associated with child mortality in the cross-section. However, its effect is not robust and its inclusion in our regressions does nothing to diminish the 'direct effect' of democracy.

To what extent does the positive relationship between democracy and human development hold in poor and fractionalized societies? Our case studies indicate that institutions of accountability – whether in the context of Ghana's gradual transition to multiparty democracy or Uganda's movement system of government – can play an important role in mediating ethnic tensions. Although our case studies are far too narrow in scope to enable broad conclusions about the suitability of democracy in highly fragmented societies, they show that, at least in the case of Ghana and Uganda, institutions of accountability have helped, rather than hindered, political inclusion. The developmental impact of increased accountability is, however, far from resounding. Regional inequalities, overlapping with ethnic divisions, persist and are a testimony to the depth of the challenge of poverty reduction in highly fractionalized states.

Our empirical estimations confirm that initial conditions – namely poverty, income inequality and ethnic fractionalization – will hinder the positive effects of democracy on the poor. The robustly negative relationship between democracy and child mortality appears to be restricted to less-fractionalized and/or middle-income countries. Moreover, since low-income countries dominate the poverty dataset, this finding may explain the absence of a link between democracy and income in countries which report head-count poverty rates. In short, democracy appears to be good for the poor – except in poor countries.

If our modest goal has been to contribute to the understanding of the relationship between political regimes and development, our conclusions are perhaps more modest still. Our research indicates the inherent difficulty in measuring complex notions such as democratic accountability and ethnic fractionalization with the goal of arriving at generalizable conclusions. Of all our findings, we can be perhaps most confident of the importance of country specificity, since historical patterns of inclusion and exclusion and traditions of accountability, among many other factors, will influence the extent to which democracy helps the poor. An improved understanding of the relationship between democracy and poverty reduction rests, first, on a definition of democracy which includes the aspects of accountability which matter most for the poor and, second, on further investigation of the impediments to the effective enfranchisement of the poor.

In moving this agenda forward, indicators which go beyond the more traditional national measures of democracy are needed to measure accountability at the national and local levels. Institutional indicators, as they are currently designed, tend to be country-wide measures of political regime, government effectiveness and public accountability and do not measure the differentiated impact of the quality of public institutions facing poor households and regions. In addition, indicators of government effectiveness naturally do not take into account the role of non-governmental institutions in delivering services to the poor. A measure of service delivery assessing the range of governmental and non-governmental services available to the poor would provide a more accurate portrayal of the reality on the ground than current indicators which focus wholly on the state provision of these services. Subnational and sectoral institutional indicators – including the share of land that is titled in rural and urban areas, the quality of local service delivery and corruption and governance indicators which reflect regional variations – would help us to better understand the differentiated institutional fabric of developing countries, yielding important insights into how local and national conditions affect the impact of democracy on the poor.

NOTES

1. Inequality data vary between countries and even within countries from year to year. Inequality can be measured by pre-tax or post-tax income or expenditure and can be per capita or per household (Li, Squire and Zou 1998). Also, changes in relative prices can stimulate short-term changes in inequality.
2. Using calculations based on the national poverty rate head-count index, the poverty rate fell from 58.1 per cent to 28.9 per cent of the population (Klump 2006).
3. Figures from 1990 and 1999, calculated using the World Bank's $1/day consumption measure.
4. Based on head-count index and national poverty line data from SUSENAS, the Indonesian national socioeconomic survey.
5. Simultaneity bias is an equally important concern. An enormous literature in economics

and political science has investigated the inverse of the relationship investigated here: from economic development (for which head-count poverty measures are a reasonable proxy) to democracy (Lipset 1959; Acemoglu, Johnson and Robinson 2005). However, lacking convincing instruments for democracy, we are not in a position to address this concern rigorously. Interestingly, however, attempts by Acemoglu, Johnson and Robinson (2001) to rigorously test this reverse causation using various instruments for per capita income found no effect.

6. For a detailed exposition of the relationship between poverty lines and a mean-variance decomposition, see Kraay (2006) or Bourguignon (2003).

7. The lack of a significant relationship between democracy and inequality may also arise from problems in measuring inequality and the fact that short-term changes in the Gini coefficient often reflect spurious changes in relative prices and are not the result of concerted policy reforms.

8. Some 42 per cent of the 6,000 people interviewed in a nation-wide survey of voter attitudes published by Ghana's National Commission for Civic Education in August 2004 described education as their number one concern (United Nations Office for the Coordination of Humanitarian Affairs 2004).

9. The immediate explanation for this difference is the choice of econometric specification. Unlike Collier (1998) and Alesina and La Ferrara (2005), we use income levels as opposed to growth rates as our dependent variable and control for time-invariant unobservables using country fixed effects. The question of which specification is more informative is open to debate. However, rather than attempting to squeeze more information out of existing cross-country data, we believe future research could more fruitfully focus on detailed micro-level studies of the interaction between ethnic tensions and political institutions. Our case studies attempt to take a first step in this direction.

10. It should be noted that these divergent results are based on different datasets covering a slightly different set of countries and time periods. Nevertheless, they appear to point the way toward further research refining our understanding on how democracy may contribute to development.

BIBLIOGRAPHY

Acemoglu, Daron, Simon Johnson and James A. Robinson (2001), 'The Colonial Origins of Comparative Development: An Empirical Investigation', *American Economic Review*, **91** (5), 1369–401.

Acemoglu, Daron, Simon Johnson and James A. Robinson (2005), 'Institutions as the Fundamental Cause of Long-Run Growth', in Philippe Aghion and Steven Durlauf (eds), *The Handbook of Economic Growth*, Amsterdam: Elsevier, pp. 385–472.

Acemoglu, Daron, Simon Johnson, James A. Robinson and Pierre Yared (2005), 'Income and Democracy', London, Centre for Economic Policy Research (CEPR) Discussion Paper No. 5273.

Alesina, Alberto and Eliana La Ferrara (2005), 'Ethnic Diversity and Economic Performance', *Journal of Economic Literature*, **43** (3), 762–800.

Alesina, Alberto, Arnaud Devleeschauwer, William Easterly, Sergio Kurlat and Romain Wacziarg (2003), 'Fractionalization', *Journal of Economic Growth*, **8** (2), 155–94.

Anand, Sudhir and Amartya Sen (2000), 'The Income Component of the Human Development Index', *Journal of Human Development*, **1** (1), 83–106.

Asante, Richard and E. Gyimah-Boadi (2004), 'Ethnic Structure, Inequality and Governance of the Public Sector in Ghana', Geneva, United Nations Research

Institute for Social Development, unpublished paper.

Besley, Timothy and Louise J. Cord (eds) (2006), *Delivering on the Promise of Pro-Poor Growth*, New York: Palgrave.

Besley, Timothy and Masayuki Kudamatsu (2006), 'Health and Democracy', *American Economic Review, Papers and Proceedings*, **96** (2), 313–18.

Bourguignon, François (2003), 'The Growth Elasticity of Poverty Reduction: Explaining Heterogeneity across Countries and Time Periods', in Theo S. Eicher and Stephen J. Turnovski (eds), *Inequality and Growth: Theory and Policy Implications*, Cambridge, MA: MIT Press, pp. 3–26.

Bratton, Michael, Gina Lambright and Robert Sentamu (2000), 'Democracy and Economy in Uganda: A Public Opinion Perspective', Cape Town, South Africa, Afro-barometer Working Paper No. 4.

Bratton, Michael, Peter Lewis and E. Gyimah-Boadi (2001), 'Constituencies for Reform in Ghana', *Journal of Modern African Studies*, **39** (2), 231–59.

Brusco, Valeria, Marcelo Nazareno and Susan C. Stokes (2002), 'Does Poverty Erode Democracy? Evidence from Argentina', University of Chicago, unpublished paper.

Bueno de Mesquita, Bruce, James Morrow, Randolph M. Siverson and Alastair Smith (2000), 'Political Institutions, Political Survival, and Policy Success', in Bruce Bueno de Mesquita and Hilton Root (eds), *Governing for Prosperity*, New Haven: Yale University Press, pp. 59–84.

Canagarajah, Sudharshan and Xiao Ye (2001), 'Public Health and Education Spending in Ghana in 1992–98', Washington, DC, World Bank Policy Research Working Paper No. 2579.

Chen, Shaohua and Martin Ravallion (2004), 'How Have the World's Poorest Fared since the Early 1980s?', *World Bank Research Observer*, **19** (2), 141–69.

Collier, Paul (1998), 'The Political Economy of Ethnicity', Oxford, University of Oxford, Centre for the Study of African Economies Working Paper Series No. 98-8.

Diamond, Larry (2002), 'Thinking about Hybrid Regimes', *Journal of Democracy*, **13** (2), 21–35.

Dollar, David and Aart Kraay (2002), 'Growth Is Good for the Poor', *Journal of Economic Growth*, **7** (3), 195–255.

Drèze, Jean and Amartya Sen (2002), *India: Development and Participation*, New York: Oxford University Press.

Easterly, William and Ross Levine (1997), 'Africa's Growth Tragedy: Policies and Ethnic Divisions', *Quarterly Journal of Economics*, **112** (4),1203–50.

Fayemi, Kayode, Thomas Jaye and Zaya Yeebo (2003), 'Democracy, Security and Poverty in Ghana: A Mid-Term Review of the Kufuor Administration', *Democracy and Development: Journal of West African Affairs*, **3** (2), 51–84.

Filmer, Deon and Lant Pritchett (1999), 'The Effect of Household Wealth on Educational Attainment: Evidence from 35 Countries', *Population and Development Review*, **25** (1), 85–120.

Foster, Mick and Douglas Zormelo (2002), 'How, When and Why Does Poverty Get Budget Priority? Poverty Reduction Strategy and Public Expenditure in Ghana', London, Overseas Development Institute Working Paper No. 164.

Freedom House (2005), *Freedom in the World*, New York: Freedom House.

Ghobarah, Hazem Adam, Paul Huth and Bruce Russett (2004), 'Comparative Public Health: The Political Economy of Human Misery and Well-Being', *International*

Studies Quarterly, **48** (1), 73–94.

Gyimah-Boadi, E. and Kwabena Amoah Awuah Mensah (2003), 'The Growth of Democracy in Ghana Despite Economic Dissatisfaction: A Power Alternation Bonus?', Cape Town, South Africa, Afro-barometer Paper No. 28.

Haque, M. Shamsul (2002), 'The Changing Balance of Power between the Government and NGO's in Bangladesh', *International Political Science Review*, **23** (4), 411–35.

International Crisis Group (2006), 'Bangladesh Today', Islamabad and Brussels, Asia Report No. 121.

Kasfir, Nelson (1998), 'No-Party Democracy in Uganda', *Journal of Democracy*, **9** (2), 49–63.

Keefer, Philip (2005a), 'Democratization and Clientelism: Why Are Young Democracies Badly Governed?', Washington, DC, World Bank Policy Research Working Paper No. 3594.

—— (2005b), 'Democracy, Public Expenditures, and the Poor: Understanding Political Incentives for Providing Public Services', *World Bank Research Observer*, **20** (1),1–27.

Klump, Rainer (2006), 'Pro-Poor Growth in Vietnam: Miracle or Model?', in Timothy Besley and Louise C. Cord (eds), *Delivering on the Promise of Pro-Poor Growth*, New York: Palgrave, pp. 119–46.

Knack, Stephen and Philip Keefer (1997), 'Does Social Capital Have an Economic Payoff? A Cross-Country Investigation', *Quarterly Journal of Economics*, **112** (4), 1251–88.

Kraay, Aart (2006), 'When Is Growth Pro-Poor? Evidence from a Panel of Countries', *Journal of Development Economics*, **80** (1), 198–227.

Krieckhaus, Jonathan (2004), 'The Regime Debate Revisited: A Sensitivity Analysis of Democracy's Economic Effect', *British Journal of Political Science*, **34** (4), 635–55.

Kurzman, Charles, Regina Werum and Ross E. Burkhart (2002), 'Democracy's Effect on Economic Growth: A Pooled Time-Series Analysis, 1951–1980', *Studies in Comparative International Development*, **37** (1), 3–33.

Leggett, Ian (2001), *Uganda*, Oxford, UK: Oxfam.

Li, Hongyi, Lyn Squire and Heng-fu Zou (1998), 'Explaining International and Intertemporal Variations in Income Inequality', *Economics Journal*, **108** (446), 26–43.

Lipset, Seymour Martin (1959), 'Some Social Requisites of Democracy: Economic Development and Political Legitimacy', *American Political Science Review*, **53** (1), 69–105.

Marshall, Monty G. and Keith Jaggers (2002), 'Polity IV Data Set', [Computer file; version p4v2002] College Park, MD: University of Maryland Center for International Development and Conflict Management.

McGuire, James (2001), 'Social Policy and Mortality Decline in East Asia and Latin America', *World Development*, **29** (10), 1673–97.

Meltzer, Allan H. and Scott F. Richard (1981), 'A Rational Theory of the Size of Government', *Journal of Political Economy*, **89** (5), 914–27.

North, Douglass (1981), *Structure and Change in Economic History*, New York, NY: W.W. Norton.

Nugent, Paul (2001), 'Ethnicity as an Explanatory Factor in the Ghana 2000 Elections', *African Issues*, **29** (1/2), 2–7.

Political Risk Services (2005), *International Country Risk Guide*, East Syracuse, NY: PRS Group.

Przeworski, Adam and Fernando Limongi (1993), 'Political Regimes and Economic Growth', *Journal of Economic Perspectives*, **7** (3), 51–69.

Przeworski, Adam, Michael E. Alvarez, José Antonio Cheibub and Fernando Limongi (2000), *Democracy and Development: Political Institutions and Well-Being in the World, 1950–1990*, New York: Cambridge University Press.

Rodrik, Dani (1999), 'The Asian Financial Crisis and the Virtues of Democracy', *Challenge*, **44** (4), 44–59.

Ross, Michael (2006), 'Is Democracy Good for the Poor?', *American Journal of Political Science*, **50** (4), 860–74.

Sen, Amartya (1999a), 'Democracy as a Universal Value', *Journal of Democracy*, **10** (30), 3–7.

—— (1999b), *Development as Freedom*, New York: Alfred A. Knopf.

Stasavage, David (2005), 'Democracy and Education Spending in Africa', *American Journal of Political Science*, **49** (2), 343–58.

United Nations Office for the Coordination of Humanitarian Affairs (2004), 'Ghana: Kufuor Faces Old Opponent in his Bid for a Second Term', IRINnews.org. Available at http://www.irinnews.org/report.asp?ReportID=43183&SelectRegion= West_Africa. Accessed on 20 October 2006.

Unterhalter, Elaine, Jake Ross and Mahmudul Alam (2003), 'A Fragile Dialogue? Research and Primary Education Formation in Bangladesh, 1971–2001', *Compare*, **33** (1), 85–99.

World Bank (2001), *Indonesia: Country Assistance Strategy*, Washington, DC: World Bank, East Asia and Pacific Region.

—— (2002), *Taming Leviathan: Reforming Governance in Bangladesh, an Institutional Review*, Washington, DC: World Bank, South Asia Region.

—— (2003), *China. Promoting Growth and Equity – Country Economic Memorandum*, East Asia and Pacific Region, Washington DC: World Bank.

—— (2005a), *World Development Report, 2006: Equity and Development*, Washington, DC: World Bank.

—— (2005b), *Bangladesh: Attaining the Millennium Development Goals in Bangladesh*, Washington, DC: World Bank.

—— (2006), *World Development Indicators*, Washington, DC: World Bank.

World Institute for Development Economics Research (WIDER) (2005), World Income Inequality Database, version 2.0a.

3. Democratization, Institutional Quality and Economic Growth

Victor Polterovich and Vladimir Popov

Democracy is widely regarded as one of the goals of development and reform. There are disagreements, however, on how important this goal is in relation to others, such as higher income, more equitable income distribution, longer life expectancy and rising educational levels. John Rawls put a very high, if not an absolute, weight on democratic values. Civil liberties, he said, including political rights 'are not subject to political bargaining or to the calculus of social interests' (1971, 3). Yet proponents of Asian values, often citing Confucian tradition, argue that the interests of society as a whole are superior to the interests of an individual. Thus civil or political rights can, in principle, be sacrificed to benefit the community, such as for more rapid and equitable economic growth. As Amartya Sen puts it, 'Lee Kuan Yew, the former prime minister of Singapore and a great champion of the "Asian values", has defended authoritarian arrangements on the ground of their alleged effectiveness in promoting economic success' (Sen 1997, 33).

Few scholars, not even the defenders of Asian values, seriously dispute the intrinsic values of democracy. The debate is rather about the *price* of these values, the relative cost of democratic values compared with other developmental goals. The value placed on democratic (political) rights has changed dramatically throughout human history, but there is still no theory to explain the change. This chapter focuses instead on the more modest and more easily tested issue of the *cost* of democratization; that is, the existence of tradeoffs between democratization and growth. The conventional wisdom today appears to be either that these tradeoffs do not exist or that democracy complements economic growth and other development goals. The price of democratization then becomes largely irrelevant, because democracy becomes both means and end. However, if such a tradeoff exists – if democratization under particular conditions is really associated with costs – the price of democratization becomes tangible and highly important.

Many scholars have recently expressed their disappointment with the

72

performance of the 'third wave' democracies – countries which have democratized since 1974[1] – both in terms of their ability to ensure political and other civil rights and in terms of their economic and social progress. Thomas Carothers believes that of nearly 100 countries which are considered newcomers to the democratic world from authoritarianism, only 18 (10 countries of Eastern Europe plus Brazil, Chile, Mexico, Uruguay, Taiwan, the Philippines, South Korea and Ghana) 'are clearly en route to becoming successful, well-functioning democracies or at least have made some democratic progress and still enjoy a positive dynamic of democratization' (2002, 9).

Fareed Zakaria (2003) looks at the rise of 'illiberal democracies': countries where competitive elections are introduced before law and order is established. While European countries in the nineteenth century and, more recently, East Asian countries moved from establishing law and order to gradually introducing democratic elections,[2] democratic political systems were introduced in Latin America, Africa and now in many former Soviet republics in societies without firm law and order. Authoritarian regimes (including communist ones) gradually built property rights and institutions while filling the law and order vacuum via authoritarian means (lawless order). After democratization occurred and illiberal democracies emerged, leaders found themselves deprived of old authoritarian instruments to ensure order but without the newly developed democratic mechanisms needed to guarantee property rights, contracts and order in general.

There is an extensive literature on the interrelationship between economic growth and democracy (for surveys see, e.g., Przeworski and Limongi 1993; Przeworski et al. 2000; UNDP 2002). Democracy is said to undermine investment (because of populist pressure for increased consumption) and to block 'good' economic policies and reforms because governments in democratic societies are exposed to pressures from particularistic interests. Autocratic regimes are believed to be better suited than democratic ones to oppose popular pressure to redistribute income and resources (Alesina and Rodrik 1994). There have been relatively few cases of successful simultaneous economic and political reforms (Intriligator 1998), and some studies suggest that introducing voting in post-communist countries may even harm the economy (Cheung 1998).

Taiwan, South Korea, Chile before the late 1980s and China until now are usually cited as examples of autocracies which successfully implemented liberalization and reform. Yet Olson (1991) argues that autocracies can be predatory, since there is no one to control the autocrat. He also believes that the populist problem of democracies can be dealt with by introducing constitutions which require supermajorities for certain government actions (Olson 2000). For Sen (1999), the comparative studies now available suggest that there is no relation between economic growth and democracy in either direction and that all major famines occurred under authoritarian, not under democratic, regimes.[3]

Przeworski and Limongi (1993) analyzed 18 earlier studies and found mixed results. The only pattern they discovered is that most studies published after 1987 find a positive link between democracy and growth, whereas earlier studies, although using the same samples and timeframes, generally found that authoritarian regimes grew faster. There are also conflicting studies of the impact of democracy on growth in transition economies. Fidrmuc (2003) reports a moderate negative initial and direct effect that is countered by a positive indirect effect (democratization facilitates economic liberalization which is good for growth). But Popov (2000, 2007) finds a positive effect from economic performance on the rule-of-law-to-democracy index and negative effects on growth from democratization and liberalization, at least in the first ten years of transition.

A number of other studies differentiate between young and mature democratic regimes. Clague et al. (1996, 1) found that 'The age of a democratic system is strongly correlated with property and contract rights.' Akhmedov and Zhuravskaya (2004) demonstrate that political cycles are deeper and therefore more costly under immature democratic regimes. Ross (2006) shows that while democracies spend more money on education and healthcare than non-democracies, the benefits seem to accrue to middle- and upper-income groups, meaning democracy has little or no effect on infant and child mortality rates.

Kaplan (2000) argues that democratic transitions are highly risky in low-income settings with poor institutions and ethnic divisions. They can cause an upsurge in violence, crime, official corruption and anarchy. Chua (2002) blames the West for promoting a version of capitalism and democracy which Westerners have never fully adopted themselves and which leads to an accumulation of wealth by 'market dominant minorities' and increased political power for a disenfranchised majority. Using panel data regressions based on POLITY IV measures of regime change, Rodrik and Wacziarg (2005) argue with Chua, Kaplan and Zakaria; their results show that growth of GDP per capita actually accelerates immediately after a democratic transition. But Rodrik and Wacziarg control for the 'state failure' dummy (which actually turns out to be most significant), so it is very probable that this dummy is in fact endogenous to democratization and captures the negative effects of democratization on institutions. Without this dummy the impact of democratization on growth turns out to be insignificant.

According to the 2002 UN *Human Development Report*, 'Political freedom and participation are part of human development, both as development goals in their own right and as means for advancing human development' (UNDP 2002, 52). It argues that there is no tradeoff between democracy and growth and that democracies actually contribute to stability and equitable economic and social development. Rodrik (1997) does not find significant correlation between democracy and economic growth for 1970–89, after controlling for initial income, education and the quality of governmental institutions, but he provides evidence that democracies have more predictable long-run growth rates, produce greater stability in economic performance, handle adverse shocks much better than autocracies and pay higher wages. These findings are very much in line with Przeworski et al. (2000). According to them, while there is no substantial difference in long-term growth rates, democracies appear to have smaller variance in the rates of growth than autocracies (fewer growth miracle stories, but also fewer spectacular failures), a higher share of labor in value added and a lower share of investment in GDP.[4]

Writing in 1996, Barro concluded that the overall effect of democracy on growth is weakly negative. He also considered a nonlinear regression and found that the middle level of democracy is most favorable to growth, the lowest level comes second and the highest level comes third. In a subsequent study, Barro writes:

> The idea that democracy – in terms of electoral rights – is necessary for growth is just as false as the proposition that dictatorship is essential for poor countries to escape poverty .... For a country that starts with weak institutions – weak democracy and little rule of law – an increase in democracy is less important than an expansion of the rule of law as a stimulus for economic growth and investment. In addition, democracy does not seem to have a strong direct role in fostering the rule of law. Thus one can not argue that democracy is critical for growth, because democracy is a prerequisite for the rule of law. (2000, 47).

Barro also states that for given measures of the standard of living, the democracy level is not connected with the rule of law in either direction (1999, 174). Similarly, Liew (2001) attributes China's economic success of the 1980s and 1990s to more effective governance, not to democracy.

This chapter offers two innovations not seen in previous literature on democracy and growth. First, we study not the influence of the democracy level itself, but changes in this level in the 1970s–90s as measured by increments of a Political Rights Index. Second, we elaborate on Zakaria's distinction between democracy and law and order; order based on legal rules is measured by the rule of law, investors' risk and corruption indices. We try to test two interconnected threshold hypotheses. First, in countries where law and order are strong enough, democratization stimulates economic growth, whereas democratization undermines growth in countries with poor law and order. Second, if democratization occurs under the conditions of poor law and order (i.e., an illiberal democracy arises) then the shadow economy expands, the quality of governance worsens and macroeconomic policy is less prudent. Our findings are very similar to Wang's chapter in this volume, that argues that efficient government is needed to reap the benefits of democratization.

HOW DEMOCRATIZATION AFFECTS LAW AND ORDER AND GROWTH

The process of democratization is associated with few costs and many benefits, if carried out in liberal autocracies; that is, in countries which have already created a system of protection of civil rights (but not political rights) or established mechanisms and traditions for maintaining law and order (Zakaria 2003). But when democratization occurs in illiberal autocracies – countries which maintain order but not based on law – the result is the emergence of illiberal democracies. These regimes have the worst record for ensuring institutional capacities, that predictably has a devastating impact on economic growth.

In this chapter we use a narrow definition of democracy which includes the right to vote, to be elected and to form political parties, as well as free political competition.[5] Democracy is usually contrasted with authoritarianism, a system which grants basic decision-making power and control to a single official or to a very narrow group. Authoritarian governments are often described as 'grabbing hands'; they are often corrupted and select officials based on loyalty, not merit (Frye and Shleifer 1997). Therefore, even if such leaders want to promote growth, they are not able to choose correct policies. But there are many well-known cases of relatively clean authoritarian regimes (Hong Kong, Taiwan, South Korea, Singapore at different periods) which carry out good economic policies resulting in quite successful economic performance.

In contrast, some analysts argue that democracy facilitates the formation and selection of growth-oriented laws and policies, professional policymakers, effective control and timely turnovers of high-ranking officials. These beliefs, however, are primarily based on observations of mature democracies. A certain level of wealth, education and civil society development are prerequisites for effective democratization, because democracy is costly for both citizens and the state. It may be considered a 'luxury good' which is demanded when a buyer becomes wealthy enough. There are other prerequisites as well, such as strong law and order. Quick democratization creates many rent-seeking opportunities. Destructive redistribution activities can lead to chaos, that may be prevented only if strong order, based on law, is established in the society.[6]

If these prerequisites are absent, democracy may degenerate as follows:

Due to quick democratization a citizen receives a resource – the right to vote – which has no intrinsic value for the citizen, but may have a price because it is in demand by organized political groups. The temptation to sell votes is strong, and if law and order is weak many votes could be bought and used for redistribution in favor of a particular group.

Under these circumstances, democracy becomes 'marketized', and parliamentarians turn out to be representatives of vested interests, not citizens, because all positions and decisions are bought and sold as commodities. Corruption flourishes not only within the thin stratum of officials, but across the entire country, as citizens become involved in selling and buying votes, laws, orders, permissions and positions. An increase in corruption slows economic growth by decreasing the level of the rule of law and the quality of governance.

In the rest of the chapter we concentrate on law and order as the most important prerequisite for successful democratization, and we try to identify the channels through which democratization influences economic growth. Figure 3.1 shows potential channels of impact. Weak democracies produce weak governments which are prone to the pressure of industrial lobbies and populist groups; civil service in weak democracies is being corroded by corruption and crony relationships. Their governments cannot ensure high tax compliance and cannot contain the expansion of the shadow economy. They cannot collect enough revenue to finance their expenditure and thus resort to inflationary financing. Very often the problem is exacerbated by the resource abundance which gives rise to resource rent (and the fight for its redistribution) and income inequalities.[7] As a result, growth rates in weak democracies are low; the collapse of preventive healthcare for low-income groups holds back any potential increases in life expectancy (Ross 2006), as do growing income and social inequalities and rising crime and murder rates (Przeworski et al. 2000). The most important mechanisms which undermine growth in illiberal democracies are indicated with thick arrows.

DEMOCRATIZATION IN DEVELOPED COUNTRIES

Democratization occurred very gradually in the countries currently labeled 'developed'. Initially voting rights were granted based on property, education, residency, age and gender requirements, so that only a very small minority of male property-owners had access to the ballot box. For example, in France the proportion of voters amounted to only 0.25–0.3 per cent of the population in 1815–30, and about 0.6 per cent in 1830–48. Universal male suffrage was introduced in 1848, but women were disenfranchised until 1946. In England

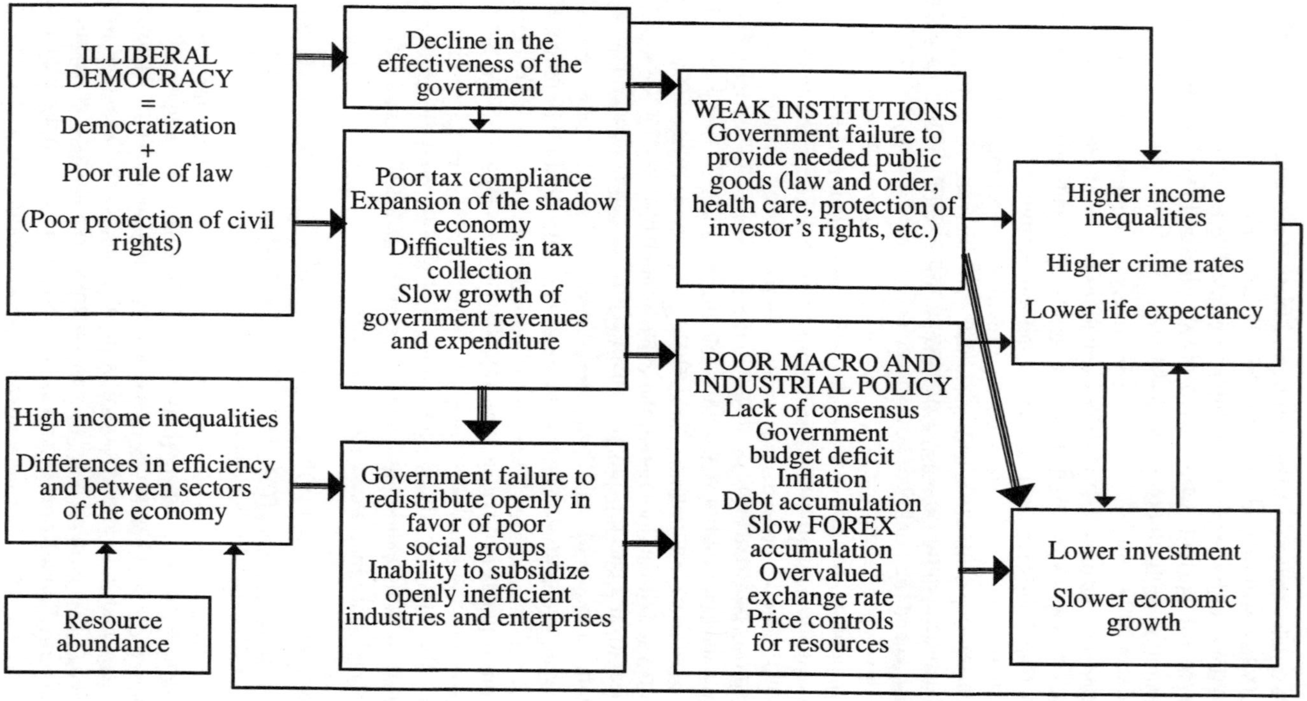

Figure 3.1 Economic and Social Costs of Illiberal Democracies

suffrage was extended by the Reform Act of 1832. Nevertheless, voting rights were confined to 14–18 per cent of the male population. Universal male suffrage was introduced in 1928. In Germany, Italy and Belgium women were not given voting rights until after World War II. Rich countries were generally late in introducing universal suffrage: 1965 for the United States; 1970 for Canada and 1971 for Switzerland (Chang 2002, 71–6).

There is a simple explanation for the slow pace of democratization: the ruling classes did not want to dilute their power. Another reason, however, could have been the fear that quick democratization is associated with a number of costs. The U.S. experience of the nineteenth century is a clear demonstration of this possibility. Between 1815 and 1840 there was a period of rapid democratization and political party formation; simultaneously corruption flourished and the quality of governance deteriorated. Party political machines were developed to appoint people to bureaucratic positions and to control the government, police and courts. Elections were falsified. Party leaders hired individuals to vote multiple times and to intimidate potential opponents and prevent them from voting.

Aspiring police officers often had to pay a party machine to get a job. In the 1890s patrolmen had to pay $300 for their jobs in New York City, sergeants paid $1,600 and captains $12,000. According to one study, 'the police were primarily a political tool rather than a professional law enforcement agency… political loyalty was the only real qualification for appointment' (Walker 1977; cited in Knott and Miller 1987, 27).

One of the prime bureaucratic postings in the federal government was at the customs offices in New York. According to trial testimony in 1907, for years customs officials had registered lower shipment weights for sugar, defrauding the government of millions of dollars of duties on raw sugar (Knott and Miller 1987, 30). It took nearly 70 years for the United States to initiate a serious fight against corruption and to get out of the corruption trap.

DEMOCRATIZATION IN DEVELOPING COUNTRIES

Almost all of the countries which successfully caught up to the developed world economically either delayed democratization or kept the same ruling party throughout the growth period. Taiwan, South Korea, Singapore, Chile before the late 1980s and China until today followed the first strategy, whereas Japan, Germany and Italy after World War II are examples of the second approach. As Sen (1997) pointed out, 'We cannot really take the high economic growth of China or South Korea in Asia as "proof positive" that authoritarianism does better in promoting economic growth – any more than we can draw the opposite conclusion on the basis of the fact that Botswana, the fastest-growing African country (and one of the fastest-growing countries in the world), has been an oasis of democracy in that unhappy continent'. Indeed Freedom House gives Botswana very high scores in terms of political rights. But researchers question whether Botswana should be classified as a democracy (Przeworsky et al. 2000, 23–26). The same party has ruled Botswana since it gained independence in 1966, and we do not know whether it would yield power if faced with a defeat at the polls.

Among the former communist countries with weak law and order, the less democratic regimes (Belarus, China, Kazakhstan, Turkmenistan, Uzbekistan, Vietnam) enjoyed better economic performance, whereas poor rule-of-law but more democratic regimes (other post-Soviet countries, the Balkan states, Mongolia) generally performed less successfully in terms of GDP change, life expectancy and income inequalities (Popov 2000, 2007).

AN ECONOMETRIC STUDY OF GROWTH AND DEMOCRATIZATION

The Data

In the next section we use econometric techniques to analyze the relationship between growth and democratization. All economic indicators are taken from the World Development Indicators database for 1970–99 unless otherwise specified. The dataset covers over 200 countries, but not all data are available for each country.

Research on the economic consequences of democracy usually looks at levels of democracy rather than at changes in these levels. The data collected by Freedom House since 1972 for over 180 countries make it possible to evaluate the impact of changes in democracy, i.e. democratization per se, on economic and social development, while controlling for the level of democracy.

The proxy for law and order (civil rights/liberalism) is the Investment Climate Index from the International Country Risk Guide (www.icrgonline. com), that is available for 1984–90, the middle of the period of economic growth (1975–99). Investors care more about guarantees and the predictability of property and contract rights than about democratic or political rights, so liberal authoritarian regimes like Hong Kong (before and after the handover to China) get very high scores.

Another measure is the Rule of Law Index from the World Bank database, based on polls of experts and surveys of residents. It ranges from –2.5 to +2.5; the higher the value, the stronger the rule of law (Kaufmann, Kraay and Zoido-

Lobatón 1999). This database contains separate indices for transparency and accountability, political stability, rule of law, control of corruption, government effectiveness and quality of regulations, but these indices are available only for recent years. We also use Corruption Perception Indices based on Transparency International estimates for over 50 countries from 1980 to 1985.

Table 3.1 presents descriptive statistics for 'new democracies' compared with all other countries. We do not control for factors such as the level of development, but the results are quite similar for new democracies in post-communist and in developing countries. The growth of GDP per capita in 1975–99 is slower than in other countries, the increase in government revenues is less pronounced, the Index of Government Effectiveness is lower and the shadow economy is larger. In addition, new democracies in developing countries seem to run higher budget deficits, have higher inflation, lower levels of foreign exchange reserves, slower accumulation of foreign exchange reserves and lower energy prices. Only increases in life expectancy in the new democracies among developing countries in 1970–2000 are larger (7.6 years) than elsewhere (7.0 years), but in multiple regressions (controlling for rule of law and for initial level of life expectancy in the early 1970s) both the level of democracy and the increase in democratization in the last three decades negatively affect life expectancy.

Rate of Growth and Democratization

The impact of democratization is different for developed and developing countries, especially when the strength of the rule of law is taken into account: for developing countries with poor rule of law, greater democratization in 1975–99 was associated with lower growth rates.

More accurate estimates – cross-country regression results – are presented in our background paper (Polterovich and Popov 2005): average growth rates of GDP per capita in 1975–99 are explained by conventional factors (investment, population growth, initial level of GDP per capita), democratization and the Rule of Law Indices. The regression results with the interaction term of the rule of law and democratization reveal that there is a threshold level[8] of the rule of law:

$$y = CONST + CONTR\_VAR + 0.18\Delta(RL - 0.72) \qquad (3.1)$$

($N = 84$, adjusted $R^2 = 63$ per cent, Significance: –7 per cent and less) where:

y = growth rates of GDP per capita in 1975–99,

Δ = democratization (based on the Change in Democracy Index for 1970–2000),[9]

RL = Rule of Law Index for 2000–2001.

The control variables include annual average population growth rates in 1975–99 (n), average share of investment in GDP in 1975–99 (I) and initial level of GDP per capita in 1975 (Y).

The critical level of the Rule of Law Index is 0.72 (more than in the Czech Republic, Jordan, Malta and Uruguay; but less than in Cyprus, Estonia, Hungary, Slovenia and Tunisia). If the index is higher, democratization has a positive effect on growth; if it is lower, the impact is negative.[10] To put it differently, equation (3.1) shows that only countries which managed to reach a certain level of rule of law benefited from democratization.

The shortcoming of Rule of Law indices is that they are available only for recent years, whereas we are interested in the quality of institutions at the beginning (or at least in the middle) of the period of economic growth. Using the Rule of Law indices for the end of the growth period poses an endogeneity problem; we tried to find appropriate instrumental variables but did not succeed. We later used other measures of law and order (investment climate and corruption indices) which are available for the earlier period.

The Corruption Perception Index (CPI) for 1980–85 is available from Transparency International for over 50 countries and is appropriate for our analysis. For example, in 1980–85 corruption levels in the Soviet Union registered between that of developed and developing countries, whereas today Russia is at the bottom of the list of developing countries. The CPI is measured on a scale of zero to ten, with higher index numbers indicating lower levels of corruption, so more accurately this is an index of cleanness, not of corruption.

The detailed results are presented in Polterovich and Popov (2005); here we report only the basic equations:

$$y = CONST + CONTR\_VAR + 0.053\ \Delta\ (CPI - 7.8) \qquad (3.2)$$
$$(3.50) \quad (-4.91)$$

($N = 45$, $R^2 = 73$ per cent, Significance: -1 per cent, t-values in parentheses).

where *CPI* is the average Corruption Perception Index in 1980–85.

The same control variables are used: annual average population growth rates in 1975–99 (n), average share of investment in GDP in 1975–99 (I) and initial level of GDP per capita in 1975 (Y).

If the Corruption Index was higher than 7.8 (the approximate level of Japan), democratization had had a positive impact on growth. If it was lower, democratization had had significant negative impact on growth. The level of democracy in 1972–75, when added to the control variables, turns out to be

Table 3.1   Descriptive Statistics for New Democracies (Countries Where Freedom House Index of Political Rights Improved by at Least 1.5 points between 1972–75 and 1999–2002)

Country	A	B	C	D	E
Improvement of the Index of Political Rights (points)	3.31	3.98	3.00	–0.20	0.98
Investment Climate Index, 2000 (%)	65.10	66.02	64.59	68.92	67.42
Ratio of Investment Climate Index to Increase of Democracy Index (%)	9.01	8.28	9.43	20.18	15.79
PPP GDP per capita in 1999 (US$)	5510	6900	4885	9588	8059
Increase in life expectancy (years)	5.75	1.96	7.55	7.02	6.57
Annual average growth of GDP per capita in 1975–99 (%)	0.82	0.30	0.88	1.41	1.23
Index of Government Effectiveness in 2001 (ranges from –2.5 to +2.5)	–0.19	–0.16	–0.21	0.09	–0.01
Unofficial economy, 1st estimate (%)*	35.10	28.20	40.50	21.80	28.20
Unofficial economy, 2nd estimate (%)*	33.60	24.80	40.40	23.30	28.30
Share of central government revenues in GDP in 1995–99 as a % of 1971–75	132.00	56.00	136.00	164.97	154.00
Average annual budget balance, 1975–99, % of GDP ('–' indicates deficit)	–4.49	–3.26	–5.01	–3.94	–4.13
Average annual inflation, 1975–99 (%)	30.30	16.60	31.10	13.24	18.80
Average foreign exchange reserves in 1970–99 (months of imports)	3.12	2.62	3.35	3.36	3.27
Increase in foreign exchange reserves, 1980–1999 (months of imports)	1.53	3.14	0.81	0.45	0.84
Ratio of prices of energy to prices of clothing in 1993 (%) (price level for all goods in the US = 100%)	101.00	48.90	145.10	117.62	110.90

Note: A. All new democracies (62); B. New democracies in transition countries (20); C. New democracies in developing countries (42); D. All except new democracies (148); E. All countries (210). *Two estimates of the size of the shadow economy are compiled by Friedman et al. (1999). For some countries they are the same, for the others they are different.

Sources: World Bank, World Development Institute, Freedom House, UNDP data; Friedman et al. (1999).

insignificant, although all other indicators retain their significance.

Inclusion of the corruption index, *CPI*, as a linear variable makes both the *CPI* and interaction term (*CPI*Δ) insignificant:

$$y = CONST + CONTR\_VAR. + 0.11CPI + 0.036\Delta\ CPI - 0.34\Delta \quad (3.3)$$
$$\qquad\qquad\qquad (0.48) \qquad (1.00) \qquad (-1.95)$$

(N = 45, R^2 = 73 per cent, same control variables, t-values in parentheses).

If 'corruption index' is included as a linear variable only, i.e. excluding the interaction term (*CPI*Δ), we get inferior results – all coefficients become less statistically significant, whereas the adjusted R^2 falls slightly:

$$y = CONST + CONTR\_VAR + 0.31CPI - 0.194\Delta \quad\quad (3.4)$$
$$\qquad\qquad\qquad (3.18) \qquad (-2.41)$$

(N = 45, R^2 = 72 per cent, same control variables, t-values in parentheses).[11]

Because we use CPIs for the initial part of the period in consideration, but not for the very beginning of the period, there is a chance that both CPI values and democratization depend on the rate of economic growth. Therefore we tried to instrument democratization and interaction terms using three instrumental variables: initial democracy (*D*); Islamic (*Is*); which is equal to one if a country is a member of the Organization of Islamic Conference and equal to zero otherwise; and average share of fuel imports for 1960–75 (*FI*). They are weakly correlated with rate of growth (correlation coefficients are equal to –0.3, –0.16 and 0.2, respectively) but they explain a substantial part of the variation in democratization:

$$\Delta = 3.16 + 0.487D - 1.23Is + 0.014FI \quad\quad (3.5)$$
$$\quad (11.06) \quad (7.61) \quad (-4.02) \quad (2.75)$$

(N = 137, adjusted R^2 = 0.34, t-values in parentheses).

Again, the detailed results are presented in Polterovich and Popov 2005; here we report only the best equation:

$$y = 5.03 - 0.001Y + 0.160I - 1.55n - 0.859\Delta + 0.156\Delta CPI =$$
$$\quad 5.03 - 0.001Y + 0.160I - 1.55n + 0.156\Delta\ (CPI - 5.51) \quad (3.6)$$

Thus the threshold level of CPI is equal to 5.51, close enough to the level found earlier, whereas the significance of democratization variables is still reasonable.

Other indicators of law and order are the Investment Climate Index (*IC*), average Investment Climate Index 1984–90 (*IC*$_{2000}$) and average *IC* for 2000 from the International Country Risk Guide; this value ranges from 0 to 100 per cent, higher values mean better climate (World Bank 2001).

Below we present one of the regressions where Investment Climate Index is used instead of the CPI:

$$y = 0.883 - 0.0004Y + 0.122I - 0.559n - 0.981\Delta + 0.016\Delta IC =$$
$$(-4.07) \qquad (3.29) \ (-2.35) \ (-5.16) \quad (4.66)$$

$$0.883 - 0.0004 \ Y + 0.122I - 0.559n + 0.016\Delta \ (IC -61.31) \qquad (3.7)$$

($N = 90$, $R^2 = 51.62$ per cent, *t*-values in parentheses).

Equation (3.7) reveals that the Investment Climate Index threshold is equal to 61.3 per cent. Democratization affected growth positively if and only if the *IC* of a country exceeded this threshold level, corresponding to the Investment Climate Index of Albania, Colombia and India. Including the *IC* indicator as a linear variable together with democratization and the interaction term makes all three coefficients insignificant. Inclusion of the *IC* as a linear variable instead of the interaction term, *IC*Δ, yields worse results: the statistical significance of the investment climate and democratization variables declines (and Δ even becomes insignificant) and R^2 decreases slightly:

$$y = 0.883 - 0.0004Y + 0.122I - 0.559n + 0.08IC - 0.10\Delta \qquad (3.8)$$
$$(-4.08) \quad (3.26) \ (-2.78) \quad (4.54) \ (-1.31)$$

($N = 90$, $R^2 = 51.58$ per cent, *t*-values in parentheses).

Again, the regression may suffer from the endogeneity problem. Unfortunately we were not able to find proper instrumental variables to get a stable result. By using initial democracy (*D*), Islam (*Is*) and average share of fuel imports for 1960–75 (*FI*) as instrumental variables and controlling for *Y*, we can support the threshold hypothesis with a threshold level of 57.7, which is close enough to the previous result. However, the hypothesis is not supported if we control for population growth or investment.

DO INSTITUTIONS DECAY IN WEAK DEMOCRACIES?

The importance of institutional factors for economic growth has been pointed out more than once for various countries and regions (see Aaron 2000 and Acemoglu, Johnson and Robinson 2004 for surveys). Using instrumental variables for institutions and foreign trade, Rodrik, Subramanian and Trebbi (2002) conclude that institutions are more important than either openness or geography for explaining the growth record of particular countries. Rodrik (1996) found that nearly all variations in the rates of growth in labor productivity in Southeast Asian countries in 1960–94 can be explained by per capita income in 1960, average length of education and an index of the quality of institutions derived from surveys conducted in the 1980s. Other studies found that 70 per cent of the variations in investment in 69 countries can be explained by only two factors – GDP per capita and institutional capacity (World Bank 1997). Stiglitz (1999) wrote about an emerging post-Washington Consensus view which places greater emphasis on the role of institutions, while Polterovich (1998) discusses mechanisms for the institutional traps that stall growth.

Institutions are usually viewed as exogenous, at least in the short and medium term. There are few studies offering clues to the patterns of institutional rise or decay. In this chapter we try to prove that there is a price to pay for early democratization; specifically, when competitive elections are introduced before major liberal rights (personal freedom and safety, property, contracts, fair trial in court, etc.) are well established. Below we try to check this proposition by testing a number of hypotheses arguing that democratization under poor traditions of law and order leads to the deterioration of institutional quality: weakening law and order, increasing corruption,[12] worsening investment climate, expanding shadow economy and decreasing government effectiveness. These are potential channels through which early democratization may hamper economic growth. To be sure, these consequences of democratization under weak institutions are correlated between themselves. Figure 3.2 shows that the expansion of the shadow economy normally goes hand in hand with a decline in the Government Effectiveness Index.

The Shadow Economy and Democratization

Using the Corruption Perception Index as a proxy for rule of law in 1980–85, we get the following equation for the unofficial economy: S_1 = average share of the shadow economy in GDP in the 1990s, first estimate; S_2 = second estimate (Hellman, Jones and Kaufmann, 2000):

$$S_1 = 37.50 - 0.002Y - 22.70Tr + 3.74\Delta - 0.86CPI\Delta$$

Figure 3.2 Index of Government Effectiveness in 2001 and the Share of Shadow Economy in GDP in the 1990s

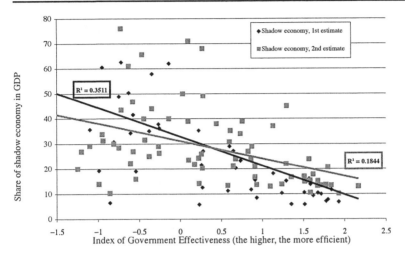

$$S_1 = 37.50 - 0.002Y - 22.70\text{Tr} - 0.86\Delta(4.35 - CPI) \qquad (3.9)$$
$$\quad (4.25) \quad (-2.44) \quad (-4.16) \qquad (-6.59)$$

($N = 33$, adjusted $R^2 = 0.78$, significance: -2 per cent).

where, as above, Δ = democratization in 1970–2000, CPI = Corruption Perception Index in 1980–85, Y = PPP GDP per capita in 1975 and Tr denotes a dummy variable for transition countries. Thus in relatively 'clean' countries democratization reduces the share of the shadow economy, but in corrupt countries democratization actually increases the unofficial economy. The threshold level of the Corruption Perception Index in 1980–85 was 4.35, in between Portugal and Greece.

The second measure of the shadow economy produces a similar result (3.10). However, the threshold level is higher at 5.64.

$$S_2 = 35.31 - 0.022Y - 21.45Tr + 3.78\Delta - 0.67CPI\Delta \qquad (3.10)$$
$$\quad (3.23) \quad (-2.09) \quad (-3.39) \quad (4.83) \quad (-4.22)$$
($N = 33$, adjusted $R^2 = 0.78$, significance: -2 per cent).

If we include *CPI* as a linear term in equation (3.9) or (3.10), it turns out to be most insignificant and does not increase the R². Thus our threshold hypothesis is supported.[13]

Rule of Law and Democratization

We regress the Rule of Law Index for 2000 on democratization during the previous 30 years and the interaction term between democratization and corruption for 1980–85. The result (3.11) seems to show that democratization increases the rule of law level only if the 'initial' law and order (measured by average CPI for 1980–85) is strong enough. The threshold level is equal to 3.04.

$$RL = -0.28 - 0.17\Delta + 0.056CPI\Delta = -0.28 + 0.056\Delta(CPI - 3.04) \quad (3.11)$$
$$(-0.09) \ (-2.81) \qquad (7.69)$$

($N = 52$, adjusted $R^2 = 0.55$, significance: -1 per cent).

However, if we control for population density (*PopDens*), net fuel imports (*FI*), the corruption index in 1980–85 (*CPI*) and the initial level of democracy (*D*), the sign of the democratization variable changes:

$$RL = 0.003 + 0.0002PopDens - 0.009FI - 0.24D + 0.20CPI + 0.22\Delta \quad (3.12)$$
$$(5.51) \qquad (3.46) \quad (-5.25) \ (6.54) \quad (5.66)$$

($N = 51$, adjusted $R^2 = 0.87$, significance: -0.1 per cent).

This regression explains 87 per cent of the variation, and the coefficients are extremely significant. Moreover, if the democratization variable is instrumented with the Islam dummy variable, as we did earlier, the parameters of regression virtually do not change. So it turns out that this second hypothesis (no threshold, strictly positive linear impact of democratization on the rule of law) is preferable: high population density, high initial level of democracy and cleanness and fast democratization all contribute to higher rule of law at the end of the period.

Corruption and Democratization

Corruption could be another proxy for law and order. Using this proxy yielded mixed results as well. The threshold is calculated with a regression of average Corruption Perception Index for 2002–2003 on democratization during the previous 30 years and the interaction term between democratization and corruption for 1980–85 and controlling for initial GDP per capita (Y), and the average ratio of the sum of exports and imports to GDP for 1980–99 (T), an indicator of economic openness (equation [3.13]). Recall that the Corruption Perception Index is higher for cleaner countries.

$$CPI_{2002} = 2.0 + 0.00044Y + 0.02T + 0.08\Delta(CPI - 2.3) \qquad (3.13)$$
$$\phantom{CPI_{2002} = 2.0 + }(4.72) \quad (5.77) \quad (3.45) \quad (-1.83)$$

($N = 45$, adjusted $R^2 = 0.83$, significance: -7 per cent).

The threshold here is very low (but still 10 countries out of 53 were below the threshold: Bangladesh, Brazil, Egypt, Hungary, Indonesia, Mexico, Nigeria, Pakistan, the Philippines and Uganda).

Nevertheless, if we control for initial corruption level (CPI), equation (3.13) falls apart. The best regression we got to explain corruption in 2002–2003 does not contain democratization at all:

$$CPI_{2002} = 1.0 + 0.01T + 0.0003Y + 0.48CPI \qquad (3.14)$$
$$\phantom{CPI_{2002} = 1.0 +}(3.84) \quad (2.99) \quad (3.92)$$

($N = 45$, adjusted $R^2 = 0.84$, significance: -2 per cent).

Investment Climate and Democratization

Measuring law and order using the 2000 Investment Climate Index produces a seemingly convincing result in equation (3.16):

$$IC_{2000} = 37.7 + 9.7\log Y - 1.0D + 0.003PopDens + 0.06\Delta\,(IC - 45) \qquad (3.15)$$
$$\phantom{IC_{2000} = }(4.84) \quad (-1.78) \quad (7.99) \qquad (3.92) \qquad\qquad (-2.23)$$

($N = 85$, adjusted $R^2 = 0.66$, significance: -8 per cent).

Democratization had a positive influence only if the average 1984–90 Investment Climate Index (IC) was larger than a threshold level of 45 per cent. This was the level of Argentina, Egypt, Namibia and the Philippines.

However, democratization turns out to be insignificant if we include a linear IC term. Here is the best linear regression, that does not contain democratization at all:

$$IC_{2000} = 14.8 + 0.35IC + 10.3\log Y + 0.002PopDens \qquad (3.16)$$
$$(5.95) \quad (5.53) \qquad (6.12)$$

($N = 85$, adjusted $R^2 = 0.66$, significance: -0.1 per cent).

Thus we have two different explanations for the *IC* dynamics: (1) democratization improves investment climate only if it was already above a certain threshold (*IC* > 45 per cent) and (2) democratization always improves investment climate.

Government Effectiveness and Democratization

Detailed regression results for the Government Effectiveness Index are in Polterovich and Popov (2005). Controlling for GDP per capita and the Rule of Law Indices, and even for all other measures of institutional capacity, any democratization which occurred between 1970 and 2000 had a clear negative impact on the efficiency of the government (*GE*), measured as the Index of Government Effectiveness in 2001, and ranges from −2.5 to +2.5 (World Bank 2001; Kaufmann, Kraay and Zoido-Lobatón 1999).

If the Corruption Perception Index is used as a proxy for institutional capacity in the beginning of the growth period, we get the following equation:

$$GE = -2.6 + 0.91\log Y + 0.007FI + 0.025\Delta(CPI - 3.7) \qquad (3.17)$$
$$(-2.64) \quad (4.49) \qquad (1.76) \qquad (2.95) \qquad (-2.44)$$

($N = 45$, adjusted $R^2 = 0.73$, *t*-values in parentheses).

where Δ = democratization in 1970–2000, *CPI* = the Corruption Perception Index in 1980–85 and *FI* = net fuel imports as a per cent of total imports in 1960–99.

This means that democratization in relatively 'clean' countries (with CPI over 3.7 – higher than Colombia but lower than India) raises the effectiveness of the government, whereas in corrupt countries it undermines the effectiveness of the government.

As happened when explaining corruption and the Investment Climate Index, it is possible to find a better equation without the democratization variable at all:

$$GE = -2.5 + 0.65\log Y + 0.007FI + 0.17CPI \qquad (3.18)$$
$$(-4.74) \quad (3.40) \qquad (2.08) \qquad (4.93)$$

($N = 45$, adjusted $R^2 = 0.77$, significance: -4 per cent).

Similar results are obtained if the quality of institutions is proxied by the Investment Climate Index for 1984–90 (*IC*). Two equations with virtually the same goodness of fit (R^2 = 77 per cent) – one with the threshold and the other without it – can be obtained for a larger sample of countries (about 100) by using the Investment Climate Index instead of the Corruption Perception Index.

Dealing with Endogeneity

The results of the econometric study presented here may seem dubious. For all indices which describe the quality of the institutions (rule of law, corruption perception, government effectiveness and investment climate) equations with the threshold work well, but it is possible to find a better equation (with higher R^2 and sometimes better *t*-values) where democratization affects the quality of institutions positively or where democratization does not play any role at all. There may be several explanations. First, given the previously established threshold relationship between a shadow economy and democratization, one may conclude that subjective indices estimated by experts are inferior measures of the quality of institutions compared with such objective measures as share of the shadow economy. None of the four subjective indices that we used helps explain the share of the shadow economy in GDP after controlling for the level of GDP per capita. This is very much against intuition and raises serious concerns about the quality of these subjective indices.

A second interpretation is that the impact of democratization on the Rule of Law Index is actually uncertain and that the threshold impact of democratization on economic growth is due mostly to its impact on the size of the government and on macroeconomic policies, as discussed below.

A third interpretation may be the most plausible; it is based on accounting for the endogeneity between institutions and democratization. Indeed, in another paper (Polterovich, Popov and Tonis 2006) we show that the stability of the newly born democracies depends on the initial level of democracy in 1972–75 and the quality of the institutions at the beginning of the period (Investment Climate Index for 1984–90 or Corruption Perception Index).

But the quality of institutions at the end of the period is affected by the magnitude of democratization itself. It means that in countries with weak institutions at the beginning of the period, democratization attempts were very likely unsuccessful, so at the end of the period they returned to authoritarianism, whereas the institutional quality was damaged by the democratization attempts anyway. Thus, what we observe by the end of the period is poor institutions with no change in the level of democracy. To put it differently, our previous indicator of the increase in the level of democracy (Δ) may not be appropriate to capture correctly the impact of democratization on institutions because it excludes by definition cases of democratization under poor institutions which ended up in a return to authoritarianism.

The evidence is provided by the following regression, that uses a new variable to characterize the instability of democratization (*AUTlast_MIN*), that is the ratio of the Index of Political Rights in 2002 to its minimum value in the period 1972–2002. It is a crude but reasonable measure of the success of democratization: the closer it is to one, the less pronounced was the retreat from the highest point of democracy registered for the whole period. This indicator captures not only the direction of change in the political regime, but also the persistence of this change:

$$CPI_{2002} = 2.14 + 0.55CPI + 0.00034Y + 0.00037PopDens -$$
$$\quad\quad (3.53) \quad\ (4.74) \quad\quad\ (2.63) \quad\quad\quad\quad (3.71)$$

$$1.05*10^{-12}(POP*Y) - 0.73AUTlast\_MIN \quad\quad\quad\quad (3.19)$$
$$(-2.62) \quad\quad\quad\quad\quad (-2.08)$$

(N = 44, adjusted R^2=0.85, significance: –5 per cent).

where *(POP*Y)* is the total PPP GDP of a country in 1975, a measure of the country's size.

Equation (3.19) suggests that high cleanness in 2002 (lower corruption, higher CPI_{2002}), controlling for the initial level of corruption in 1980–85 (*CPI*), was observed in countries which became democratic and were still democratic at the end of the period or which returned to the achieved earlier level of democracy by the end of the period.

Thus, the conclusion is that democratization under weak institutions does indeed ruin them even further, but we could not capture this effect earlier because low Δ countries include some cases of successful democratization (from democracy to authoritarianism and back to democracy), as well as some cases of unsuccessful democratization (from authoritarianism to democracy and then back to authoritarianism). *AUTlast_MIN* allows us to better account for what may be called successful democratization (if a country was democratic at one point in the middle of the period but ended up in authoritarianism, *AUTlast_MIN* > 1 and this case is not considered a success).

Similar results not reported here are obtained for other indices which characterize the quality of institutions. Besides, these results hold when using a different measure of 'successful democratization' instead of *AUTlast_MIN*, an indicator of the stability of democracy which is computed as the R^2 in the equation describing the time trend of the Index of Political Rights. One of the equations is reported here as an example:

$$GE = -2.1 + 0.6\log Y - 0.16D + 0.0003PopDens + 5.3*10^{-10}POP*Y -$$
$$(4.76)\quad (-4.19)\quad (8.17)\qquad\quad (1.68)\quad (-2.36)$$

$$0.34Is + 0.2\Delta(IC-33) + 0.005IC(\Delta R^2)\qquad\qquad (3.20)$$
$$(5.87)\qquad (-2.82)\qquad\quad (1.94)$$

($N = 87$, adjusted $R^2 = 0.78$, t-values in parentheses).

where ΔR^2 is the indicator of the stability of democracy. According to equation (3.20), government effectiveness, after controlling for initial GDP per capita, population density, total initial GDP, Islam and the initial level of democracy, is influenced positively by democratization, if initial investment climate was good, but negatively if it was bad; on top of that the stability of the change in the Index of Political Rights (in either direction) had a positive effect on government effectiveness.

Obviously more research is needed to properly account for the endogeneity between democratization and institutional quality.

Democratization and the Size of Government

The institutional capacity of a state is determined by the efficiency of the government (measured as the provision of public goods per $1 of government spending), as well as by the financial strength of the government (share of state revenues/expenditure in GDP). It appears that democratization in countries with poor law and order may have had an adverse effect on the size of the government. Perhaps nowhere else in the world was the process more pronounced than in the transition economies in the 1990s. Most of them experienced a dramatic reduction in the share of government spending in GDP and in the efficiency of state institutions (Popov 2000, 2007). The post-communist transition story, however, is by no means unique and has broader implications. The following regression demonstrates that democratization leads to the slowdown of growth of government revenues:

$$Rev_{1999} = 73.02 + 0.075Y - 10.80Rev + 67.71D - 34.08\Delta\qquad (3.21)$$
$$(2.77)\quad (-2.57)\quad\quad (2.41)\quad\quad (-2.15)$$

($N = 66$, adjusted $R^2 = 0.67$, significance: -5 per cent).

Recall that Rev_{1999} is the average share of central government revenues in

GDP in 1995–99 as a percentage of the 1971–75 level, and *D* is the level of democracy in 1972–75 (lower values mean more democracy). Thus the increase in the ratio of government revenues to GDP in 1975–99 depends positively on initial levels of GDP per capita, *Y*, and negatively on both initial levels of the average share of central government revenues in GDP in 1971–75 (*Rev*) and democracy. Most importantly, democratization, Δ, slows down the growth of central government revenues (positive values denote increases in democracy).

Democratization and other variables (except *Rev*) lose their significance if *CPI* is added into the set of control variables, but the goodness of fit falls dramatically, to 25 per cent or lower.

Democratization and Macroeconomic Policy

Research on Latin America and other countries has proven that the 'transitional democracies' are less efficient than either authoritarian regimes or well-established democratic regimes in resisting macroeconomic populism (Kaufman and Stallings 1991; Dornbush and Edwards 1989; Sachs 1989). Weak governments which cannot collect taxes cannot balance the budget and have to resort to inflationary financing of budget deficits.

Cross-country regressions (see Polterovich and Popov 2005 for details) reveal that democratization contributes to inflation, when controlling for the law and order and other variables. If two countries had the same levels of Investment Climate Index in 1984–90, average inflation was higher in the country which had lower authoritarianism (higher initial democracy level) in 1972–75 and experienced deeper democratization in the subsequent three decades (see equation [3.22]).

$$Lg\ Inflation_{75-99} = 5.2 - 0.048IC - 0.20D + 0.18\Delta \qquad (3.22)$$
$$(9.36)\ (-7.29)\quad (-4.02)\quad (3.55)$$

($N = 91$, adjusted $R^2 = 0.44$, significance: -0.1 per cent).

Results do not change even when we control for the previous inflationary experience (annual average inflation in 1960–99). We were not able to find any statistically significant threshold, however.

CONCLUSION

There may be several reasons why extensive research on the link between democracy and growth produces conflicting results. First, previous studies looked mostly at the level of democracy, but not at changes in this level. Our regressions show that the influence of initial democracy level on growth is either positive or insignificant, but the influence of democratization (increase in the level of democracy) is often negative.

Second, and probably most important, very often the distinction between law and order (civil rights) and democracy (political rights) is not rigorous. This study controls for law and order, defined as the state's ability to enforce rules and regulations based not on arbitrary practices but on well-established legal rules (measured by the share of shadow economy, corruption, government effectiveness, rule of law and investor climate indices), and examines the impact of democratization on economic growth. We presented considerable evidence to support our first threshold hypothesis: democratization in countries with strong law and order stimulates economic growth, whereas in countries with poor law and order democratization undermines growth. Thus, a certain threshold level of law and order is required to reap the benefits of democratization. Our findings make plausible the second threshold hypothesis: in countries with poor traditions of law and order, rapid democratization undermines institutional capacity and the quality of macroeconomic policy with predictable adverse effect on economic growth.

The practical implication of this analysis is that introducing democracy overnight may not be the best way to transform authoritarian regimes.[14] Democracy building, like market-type reforms, should be gradual, rather than shock therapy, and should go hand in hand with the strengthening of law and order. Democracy, participation in decision making and civil society are precious developmental goals by themselves, and they should not be compromised by poor implementation.

NOTES

1. According to Samuel Huntington (1991), the 'third wave' of democratization started in Southern Europe in 1974; the 'second wave' occurred after World War II and the first wave began after 1800. The emergence of new democracies in the post-communist world in the 1990s is sometimes referred to as the 'fourth wave'. Later we use the term 'new democracies' to refer to countries where the Freedom House index of political rights improved by at least 1.5 points between 1972–75 and 1999–2002 (see Table 3.1).

2. The most obvious example of law and order without democracy is Hong Kong before and after handover to China in 1997.

3. Ellman (2000) challenges this point by referring to the lack of famines in the authoritarian USSR after 1947 and to the Sudanese famine which occurred under the democratic regime in 1985–89. Sen himself (1997) points out another example, the Irish famine of the 1840s, but he claims, 'English rule over Ireland at that time was, for all practical purposes, a colonial rule'.

4. One of the most startling findings is about population dynamics and life expectancy. In a democracy birth rates and death rates are lower and life expectancy higher than in an autocracy

with the same income per capita (Przeworski et al. 2000).

5. Even liberal authoritarian regimes (i.e., Hong Kong, nineteenth century Europe) can guarantee freedom of speech, as well as freedom from ethnic, religious, gender and other forms of discrimination.

6. A different question concerns the determinants of democracy independently on its efficiency. Barro (1999) finds that the propensity for democracy rises with per capita GDP, primary schooling, middle-class share of income and smaller reliance on natural resources. Przeworski et al. (2000) show that any country, even a poor one, can *become* democratic, but in order to *stay* democratic a certain level of income and other conditions need to be in place. Ross (2001) provides very strong evidence that oil exports and mineral exports hinder democracy and analyzes the mechanisms of such a relationship.

7. Fuel-exporting countries are more likely to fall into the trap of unstable democratic regimes; that is, to experience a periodic return to authoritarianism after democratization (Ross 2001; Polterovich, Popov and Tonis 2006).

8. The idea of the threshold regressions is used extensively in our joint paper, 'Stages of Development and Economic Growth', where we show that different policies (trade protectionism, accumulation of foreign exchange reserves, increase in government spending, liberalization of migration and of capital flows, etc.) are good for economic growth in countries with low levels of GDP per capita and good quality of institutions, but bad for wealthier countries, especially if their institutions are weak. We try to determine the threshold level of GDP (and other indicators, such as the rule of law) in every case. The paper is available from the authors. See also Victor Polterovich and Vladimir Popov (2004).

9. D = average level of democracy in 1972–75, equal to the Freedom House Index of Political Rights, ranging from one to seven for every year; the absolute level shows the degree of authoritarianism, so, lower values mean more democracy. See http://www.freedomhouse.org. Δ = Democratization 1973–75 to 1999–2002 equals the change in democratization levels for the whole period and calibrated to make the indicator always positive and showing the increase in democratization, not in the authoritarianism: $\Delta = 4 - (D_{99-02} - D_{73-75})$.

10. Other policy variables, such as inflation, import taxes, increase in foreign exchange reserves and changes in the size of the government, were included into the regression to see if the results still hold. They do; these regressions are not reported here to save space but are available from the authors.

11. Results for developing countries only are even stronger.

12. We do not assert that institutions are better in autocracies than in weak democracies. We only show that in autocracies with weak institutions democratization worsens them even more. This may explain Treisman's (1999) finding that the current degree of democracy has no significant impact on the level of corruption; it is only the long exposure to democracy that limits corruption.

13. To test the robustness, we ran similar regressions with the Investment Climate Index in 1984–90, using IC as a proxy for institutional capacity:

$$S_1 = 100.7 - 21.3\log Y + 0.12\Delta(63 - IC) \qquad (1a)$$
$$(3.07) \quad (-2.19) \quad (3.45) \quad (-3.13)$$

($N = 47$, adjusted $R^2 = 0.71$, significance – 3 per cent).

$$S_2 = 35.31 - 22.8\log Y + 0.09\Delta(60 - IC) \qquad (2a)$$
$$(3.29) \quad (-2.35) \quad (2.39) \quad (-2.25)$$

($N = 47$, adjusted $R^2 = 0.64$, significance – 2 per cent).

The results are very similar (threshold Investment Climate Index is 60–63 per cent), the regression is quite robust, and the parameters of the regressions deteriorate once IC is included as a linear term.

14. In his study of Arab political reform, Daniel Brumberg wrote, 'It is far from clear how to reform liberalized autocracies.... Encouraging rapid change, such as completely free elections, might invite radical forces and even retreat to full autocracy' (Brumberg 2003).

BIBLIOGRAPHY

Aaron, Janine (2000), 'Growth and Institutions: A Review of the Evidence', *World Bank Research Observer*, **15** (1), 99–135.

Acemoglu, Daron, Simon Johnson and James A. Robinson (2004), 'Institutions as the Fundamental Cause of Long-Run Growth', Cambridge, MA, National Bureau of Economic Research (NBER) Working Paper No. 10481.

Acemoglu, Daron, Simon Johnson, James A. Robinson and Pierre Yared (2005), 'Income and Democracy', Cambridge, MA, National Bureau of Economic Research (NBER) Working Paper No. 11205.

Akhmedov, Akhmed and Ekaterina Zhuravskaya (2004), 'Opportunistic Political Cycles: Test in a Young Democracy Setting', *Quarterly Journal of Economics*, **119** (4), 1301–38.

Alesina, Alberto and Dani Rodrik (1994), 'Distributive Politics and Economic Growth', *Quarterly Journal of Economics*, **109** (2), 465–90.

Barro, Robert J. (1996), 'Democracy and Growth', *Journal of Economic Growth*, **1** (1), 3–27.

—— (1999), 'Determinants of Democracy', *Journal of Political Economy*, **107** (6), 158–83.

—— (2000), 'Rule of Law, Democracy and Economic Performance', Heritage Foundation, available at http://www.heritage.org/research/features/index/chapters/pdfs/Index2000_Chap2.pdf.

Brumberg, Daniel (2003), 'Liberalization Versus Democracy. Understanding Arab Political Reform', Washington, DC, Carnegie Endowment for International Peace Working Paper No. 37.

Carothers, Thomas (2002), 'The End of the Transition Paradigm', *Journal of Democracy*, **31** (1), 5–21.

Chang, Ha-Joon (2002), *Kicking Away the Ladder: Development Strategies in Historical Perspective*, New York: Cambridge University Press.

Cheung, Steven N.S. (1998), 'The Curse of Democracy as an Instrument of Reform in Collapsed Communist Societies', *Contemporary Economic Policy*, **16** (2), 247–9.

Chua, Amy (2002), *World on Fire: How Exporting Free Market Democracy Breeds Ethnic Hatred and Global Instability*, New York: Doubleday.

Clague, Christopher, Philip Keefer, Steven Knack and Mancur Olson (1996), 'Property and Contract Rights in Autocracies and Democracies', *Journal of Economic Growth*, **1** (2), 243–76.

Dethier, Jean-Jacques, Hafez Ghanem and Edda Zoli (1999), 'Does Democracy Facilitate the Economic Transition?', Washington, DC, World Bank Policy Research Working Paper No. 2194.

Diamond, Larry (1997), 'Is the Third Wave of Democratization Over? An Empirical Assessment', South Bend, Indiana, University of Notre Dame, Helen Kellogg Institute for International Studies Working Paper No. 236.

Dornbush, Rudiger and Sebastian Edwards (1989), 'The Economic Populism Paradigm', Cambridge, MA, National Bureau of Economic Research (NBER) Working Paper No. 2986.

Ellman, Michael (2000), 'The 1947 Soviet Famine and the Entitlement Approach to Famines', *Cambridge Journal of Economics*, **24** (5), 603–30.

European Bank for Reconstruction and Development (1997), *Transition Report 1997*, London: EBRD.

Fernandez, Raquel and Dani Rodrik (1991), 'Resistance to Reform: Status Quo Bias in the Presence of Individual Specific Uncertainty', *American Economic Review*, **81** (5), 1146–55.

Fidrmuc, Jan (1998), 'Political Support for Reforms: Economics of Voting in Transition Countries', *European Economic Review*, **44** (8), 1491–513.

—— (2003), 'Economic Reform, Democracy and Growth during Post-Communist Transition', *European Journal of Political Economy*, **19** (3), 583–604.

Freedom House, Datasets at http://www.fredomhouse.org/index.htm.

Friedman, Eric J., Simon Johnson, Daniel Kaufmann and Pablo Zoido-Lobatón (1999), 'Dodging the Grabbing Hand: The Determinants of Unofficial Activity in 69 Countries', New Brunswick, NJ, Rutgers University, Department of Economics Working Paper No. 199921.

Frye, Timothy and Andrei Shleifer (1997), 'The Invisible Hand and the Grabbing Hand', *American Economic Review*, **87** (2), 354–8.

Hellman, Joel, Geraint Jones and Daniel Kaufmann (April 2000), 'How Profitable Is Buying the State Officials in Transition Economies?' *Transition: The Newsletter About Reforming Economies*, 8–11.

Huntington, Samuel P. (1991), *The Third Wave: Democratization in the Late Twentieth Century*, Norman, OK: University of Oklahoma Press.

Intriligator, Michael D. (1998), 'Democracy in Reforming Collapsed Communist Economies: Blessing or Curse?', *Contemporary Economic Policy*, **16** (2), 241–6.

Kaplan, Robert D. (2000), *The Coming Anarchy: Shattering the Dreams of the Post Cold War*, New York: Random House.

Kaufman, Robert R. and Barbara Stallings (1991), 'The Political Economy of Latin American Populism', in Rudiger Dornbush and Sebastian Edwards (eds), *Macroeconomics of Populism in Latin America*, Chicago: University of Chicago Press, pp. 15–44.

Knott, Jack H. and Gary J. Miller (1987), *Reforming Bureaucracy: The Politics of Institutional Choice*, Englewood Cliffs, NJ: Prentice Hall.

Liew, Leong (2001), 'Marketization, Democracy and Economic Growth in China', in Anis Chowdhury and Iyanatul Islam (eds), *Beyond the Asian Crisis: Pathways To Sustainable Growth*, Northampton, MA: Edward Elgar, pp. 300–23.

Olson, Mancur (1991), 'Autocracy, Democracy and Prosperity', in Richard J. Zeckhauser (ed.), *Strategy and Choice*, Cambridge, MA: MIT Press, pp. 131–57.

—— (2000), *Power and Prosperity: Outgrowing Communist and Capitalist Dictatorships*, New York: Basic Books.

Polterovich, Victor (1998), 'Institutional Traps and Economic Reforms', Moscow, New Economic School Working Paper No. 98/004.

—— (2002), 'Political Culture and Transformational Recession: A Comment on the article by A. Hillman "En Route to the Promised Land"', *Economics and Mathematical Methods* (in Russian) **38** (4), 95–103.

Polterovich, Victor and Vladimir Popov (2002), 'Accumulation of Foreign Exchange

Reserves and Long Term Economic Growth', paper presented at the New Economic School Tenth Anniversary conference, Moscow, December.

—— (2004), 'Appropriate Economic Policies at Different Stages of Development', Moscow, New Economic School Working Paper.

——(2005), 'Democracy and Growth Reconsidered: Why Economic Performance of New Democracies Is Not Encouraging', paper presented at the GDN Sixth Annual Conference, Dakar, Senegal, 24–26 January.

Polterovich, Victor, Vladimir Popov and Alexander Tonis (2006), 'Resource Abundance, Political Corruption and the Instability of Democracy', Moscow, New Economic School Working Paper No. WP2007/73.

Popov, Vladimir (2000), 'Shock Therapy versus Gradualism: The End of the Debate (Explaining the Magnitude of the Transformational Recession)', *Comparative Economic Studies*, **42** (1), 1–57.

—— (2007), 'Shock Therapy versus Gradualism Reconsidered: Lessons from Transition Economies after 15 Years of Reforms', *Comparative Economic Studies*, forthcoming.

Przeworski, Adam and Fernando Limongi (1993), 'Political Regimes and Economic Growth', *Journal of Economic Perspectives*, **7** (3), 51–69.

Przeworski, Adam, Michael E. Alvarez, José Antonio Cheibub and Fernando Limongi (2000), *Democracy and Development: Political Institutions and Well-Being in the World, 1950–1990*, New York: Cambridge University Press.

Rawls, John (1971), *A Theory of Justice*, Cambridge, MA: Belknap Press, Harvard University.

Rodrik, Dani (1995), 'Understanding Economic Policy Reform', *Journal of Economic Literature*, **34** (1), 9–41.

—— (1996), 'Institutions and Economic Performance in East and South East Asia', paper presented at the International Economics Association conference 'Institutional Foundations of Economic Development in East Asia', Tokyo, 16–19 December.

—— (1997), 'Democracy and Economic Performance', paper presented at a conference on democratization and economic reform, Cape Town, South Africa, 16–19 January.

Rodrik, Dani and Romain Wacziarg (2005), 'Do Democratic Transitions Produce Bad Economic Outcomes?', *American Economic Review*, **95** (2), 50–55.

Rodrik, Dani, Arvind Subramanian and Francesco Trebbi (2002), 'Institutions Rule: The Primacy of Institutions over Geography and Integration in Economic Development', Harvard University, Department of Economics, unpublished paper.

Ross, Michael (2001), 'Does Oil Hinder Democracy?', *World Politics*, **53** (3), 325–61.

—— (2006), 'Is Democracy Good for the Poor?', *American Journal of Political Science*, **50** (4), 860–74.

Sachs, Jeffrey D. (1989), 'Social Conflict and Populist Policies in Latin America', Cambridge, MA, National Bureau of Economic Research (NBER) Working Paper No. 2897.

Sen, Amartya (1997), 'Human Rights and Asian Values: What Lee Kuan Yew and Lee Peng Don't Understand About Asia', *New Republic*, 14 July, 33–41.

——(1999), 'The Value of Democracy', *Development Outreach*, (Summer), 5–9.

Stiglitz, Joseph (1999), 'Whither Reform? Ten Years of Transition', paper presented at the World Bank's Annual Bank Conference on Development Economics, Washington, DC, 28–30 April.

Treisman, Daniel (2000), 'The Causes of Corruption: A Cross-National Study', *Journal of Public Economics*, **76** (3), 399–457.

United Nations Development Programme (2002), *Human Development Report 2002: Deepening Democracy in a Fragmented World*, New York: Oxford University Press.

Wang, Shaoguang (2007), 'Democracy and State Effectiveness', in Natalia Dinello and Vladimir Popov (eds), *Political Institutions and Development: Failed Expectations and Renewed Hopes*, Cheltenham, UK: Edward Elgar, pp. 140–67.

World Bank (1997), *World Development Report 1997: The State in a Changing World*, New York: Oxford University Press.

—— (2001), *World Development Indicators, 2001*, New York: Oxford University Press.

——(2007), 'Governance Indicators dataset', at http://info.worldbank.org/governance/kkz2005/tables.asp.

World Development Institute (2001), Worldwide Governance Research Indicators Datasets, 2000–2001 and 1997–98, available at http://info.worldbank.org/governance/beeps/.

Zakaria, Fareed (2003), *The Future of Freedom: Illiberal Democracy at Home and Abroad*, New York: W.W. Norton.

4. Federalism and Political Centralization

Ruben Enikolopov and Ekaterina Zhuravskaya

Fiscal decentralization can encourage the provision of public goods if public officials have the proper political incentives. We define fiscal decentralization as the devolution of authority over public revenue and expenditure to lower levels of government, and we use this term interchangeably with federalism. Previous studies identify three channels which make fiscal decentralization beneficial – interjurisdictional competition (Tiebout 1956), informational advantages (Hayek 1948) and higher preference homogeneity (Oates 1972). All three rely on the premise that local politicians have political incentives to respond to the needs of the local population. A classic cost of federalism – regionalist policies in the presence of interjurisdictional spillovers (Musgrave 1969; Oates 1972) – relies on the premise that political incentives drive local politicians to cater to their own constituency but ignore the preferences of populations in other jurisdictions of the country. This logic gives rise to a tradeoff between national and local preferences in the political incentives of local officials in a federation: local politicians should have sufficiently high weight placed on the preferences of the population of their own jurisdiction in order to realize the benefits of federalism. However, to minimize interjurisdictional externalities, local politicians should place some weight on voter preferences in other jurisdictions of the country. The latter side of this tradeoff – having local political incentives aligned with national interests – represents political centralization. Since political incentives are shaped by political institutions, a fiscally decentralized country needs political institutions which strike a balance between the interests of local and national constituencies.

Riker, in his seminal book *Federalism: Origins, Operation, Significance* (1964), identified two political institutions which facilitate political centralization: strong national political parties and administrative subordination (i.e., having central authorities appoint local governments rather than having them directly elected). According to Riker, only strong national political parties achieve the necessary balance between national and local interests. Even with very strong national political parties, he argues, the presence of local elections ensures that local politicians are held accountable to their constituencies. However, strong national parties align the political incentives of local politicians with national objectives by affecting the career prospects of local politicians. First, strong parties are better able to promote local politicians to national-level politics than weak parties. Second, political support from a strong national party during local elections is more valuable to local politicians than support from a weak party. Thus, local politicians internalize the interjurisdictional externalities of their policies in the search for promotion and political support by their national governing party, because the party cares about national-level performance.

Riker's second institution, administrative subordination, weakens local accountability. It solves the problem of interjurisdictional externalities by having central-level politicians reappoint only those local officials who are 'well behaved' from central officials' point of view. This power, however, undermines the benefits of federalism in the first place: as they focus on pleasing their bosses, appointed officials may stop caring for the preferences of the local population, even though they know them better than central politicians.

Several recent studies point to an additional potential cost of federalism – local capture. In this situation, special interests have more influence on public policy at the local level than the central level (Bardhan 2002; Sonin 2003). Blanchard and Shleifer (2001) indicated that if local governments are more vulnerable to capture than central governments, then appointing local officials in a federation is beneficial. This condition is very restrictive, however; it could be the case that neither central nor local authorities serve broad public interests (Bardhan and Mookherjee 2000). If this condition holds, strong national parties also will help alleviate local capture by dangling career advancement opportunities as incentives to resist regional special interests.

Scholars have not reached a consensus on the overall effect of decentralization in developing and transition countries. One camp argues that the benefits of decentralization outweigh the costs (e.g., Qian and Weingast 1996; Qian and Roland 1998; Maskin, Qian and Xu 2000); whereas the second view argues for the opposite (e.g., Tanzi 1996; Cai and Treisman 2004; Bardhan 2002). Previous empirical studies of the effects of decentralization have produced inconclusive results which vary across samples and time periods.[1] This can be partly explained by the fact that these studies overlooked the importance of political institutions.

We shed light on this debate by testing Riker's two predictions about political centralization and finding solid empirical support for both. Using cross-section and panel data on 75 developing and transition countries over 25 years, we evaluate the effect of national political party strength and appointments of local officials on the outcomes of fiscal decentralization. We have two principal results. First, strong political parties (measured by the age of main parties and fractionalization of government parties) substantially improve the effect of decentralization on growth, public goods provision and government quality. Second, administrative subordination of local authorities to higher-level governments (measured by dummies indicating whether provincial and municipal politicians are appointed or elected) does not significantly affect the outcomes of fiscal decentralization. We also provide case-study evidence on the channel of influence. Comparisons of party systems and decentralizations in two pairs of countries – Argentina versus Chile and Russia versus China – yield the conclusion that career concerns provided by strong national political parties play an important role in disciplining local politicians.[2]

To the best of our knowledge, there are only two studies which consider Riker's argument. Blanchard and Shleifer (2001) build a very simple model to illustrate the logic behind the need for political centralization. They argue that the stark contrast between outcomes of fiscal decentralization in China and Russia during the transition can be explained by differences in the level of political centralization in these countries. Gennaioli and Rainer (2004) confirm that decentralization works better in the absence of local capture by showing that precolonial centralization of tribes in Sub-Saharan Africa is associated with better modern public goods provision and significantly more so for countries and public goods with higher special interest influence. Gennaioli and Rainer, however, do not distinguish between political and fiscal decentralization. Our study shows that fiscal decentralization produces better outcomes in countries with political centralization taking the form of strong national political parties.

MEASURING POLITICAL INSTITUTIONS

National Political Party Strength

Our first hypothesis is based on Riker's theory that the strength of national parties is an important determinant of political incentives at the local level. Strong national political parties indirectly influence the policies of local politicians by affecting their career prospects. Specifically, politicians in local governments depend on their parties' political and financial support at the time of their reelection and on the possibility of their promotion to the national government. Since stronger parties can provide better career opportunities to their members, local politicians place greater weight on the policy preferences of their party when their national party is strong.[3] In turn, national governing parties have an incentive to punish – not support or promote – local politicians who pursue regional interests, because voters evaluate national governing parties according to overall national performance.

The best available proxies for the strength of national parties are the age of the main parties (the average age of the two main governmental parties and the main opposition party) and the fractionalization of governing parties (the probability that two members of parliament picked at random from governing parties belong to different parties). We chose the first measure because in developing and transition countries a higher age of the main parties indicates a more stable party system and stronger political parties (Huntington 1968). The stability of a political system is an important determinant of career concerns, because local politicians take the expected horizon of their party into account when deciding how much effort to allocate to career advancement within the party. The second measure reflects the average relative political weight of each governing political party in national policymaking, providing another important factor in decisions about career advancement for local politicians. Low fractionalization of government parties indicates that a government consists of a small number of strong parties, each having substantial impact on policy decisions; while high fractionalization is an indicator of a larger number of weak governing parties, each of which has little influence over policies. Since the ability to influence policy is what makes national political offices attractive, higher government fractionalization results in lower career concerns.[4]

Using these measures of party strength, we can formulate a testable prediction: holding everything else constant, a younger age of main parties and a higher fractionalization of government parties, according to Riker's theory, are associated with less efficient decentralization.

However, both of our measures of political centralization are highly imperfect: they correlate with several other variables which may affect decentralization outcomes. To make sure that our measures adequately reflect career concerns provided by strong national parties, we use a number of covariates. First, government fractionalization depends on the electoral and governmental systems, both of which can have an independent effect on the efficiency of decentralization (Persson and Tabellini 2003). In order to avoid spurious correlation, we control for countries' government system and electoral rules in regressions for government fractionalization as a measure of national party strength. Second, cross-country differences in party fractionalization and decentralization efficiency may depend on the degree of diversity among voters and on the presence of special ethnically or religiously distinct autonomous regions within federal states. To account for these effects, we control for ethno-linguistic fractionalization and the presence of contiguous autonomous regions in the country. Finally, the age of the main parties may reflect the age of countries or age of democracy and, therefore, may be correlated with institution-building processes present in young democracies which, in turn, could affect decentralization. Thus, it is also necessary to control directly for the age of countries and the age of democracy, as discussed below.

To the best of our knowledge, there is little quantitative comparative analysis of the strength of party systems. Data do not allow for a systematic check of how well the cross-country and time-series variations in the average age of main parties and fractionalization of government parties reflect the relative weight of national interests in the utility calculations of local politicians. We can check the validity of our measures only for a few special cases. Garman, Haggard and Willis (2001) provide cross-sectional ranking of countries according to the centralization of political parties for five Latin American countries. Among those countries, Brazil and Colombia have the most decentralized parties; Argentina is an intermediate case; and Mexico and Venezuela have the most centralized political parties. Both of our measures of party strength yield the same ranking, with the exception of the age of the main parties in Colombia – an obvious and well-known outlier because of the peculiarity of its party system (Roland and Zapata 2005).[5] Camp (1998) and Carrion (1998) study the changes over time in party strength in Mexico and Peru. They show that Mexico and Peru experienced a substantial decline in the strength of their national parties in the 1990s. A large number of independent candidates and candidates from recently formed parties were elected as mayors, governors and legislators. Accordingly, we observe a sharp decrease in the average age of main parties and a sharp increase in the fractionalization of government parties in both countries at that time. Thus, in these cases our measures adequately capture the cross-sectional and time variation in party strength. As usual for country-level comparisons, there are few (but notable) exceptions, such as Colombia for which the two measures perform very poorly.

The literature provides alternative views on whether direct election of local officials helps or hinders the efficiency of fiscal decentralization. Seabright (1996) builds a model to illustrate that (under certain fairly restrictive assumptions) elected local officials are more accountable than elected central officials. Thus, Seabright's conclusion is that if the problem of interjurisdictional spillovers is excluded, then local elections should help the efficiency of fiscal decentralization. In contrast, Riker's focus is on interjurisdictional spillovers. Nonetheless, he argues that appointing local governments is not an effective mechanism for aligning local incentives with national objectives, precisely because appointed local officials lack the local accountability which is essential to realizing the benefits of decentralization. Riker concludes that appointing local public officials does not improve decentralization outcomes despite the need for some degree of political centralization. The opposite view is that in immature democracies the election mechanism often fails and does not provide accountability (Bardhan 2002); and strong parties are hard to build. Blanchard and Shleifer (2001) argue that appointing local politicians is a feasible and effective second-best solution to problems of regionalist policies and local capture in decentralized states. However, their conclusion relies on the assumption that state capture is lower at the central level than at the local level.

To test Riker's conjecture about the effectiveness of administrative subordination in disciplining local public officials against the predictions of Blanchard and Shleifer's model, we use dummy variables indicating whether municipal and provincial executives are elected or appointed. Following Riker, we formulate our second hypothesis as follows: appointment (rather than election) of local public officials does not improve the outcomes of fiscal decentralization.

CASE-STUDY EVIDENCE ABOUT THE CHANNELS OF INFLUENCE

The formal empirical tests in this chapter document the link between outcomes of fiscal decentralization and our measures of two aspects of political centralization – party strength and administrative subordination. The data, however, do not allow us to test for the channels through which these political institutions affect the efficiency of decentralization. In this section, we consider two case studies to illustrate how local politicians' concerns about promotion to national politics form an important channel.

Argentina versus Chile

Both Argentina and Chile experienced fiscal decentralization in the 1980s and 1990s, but with a substantial difference in outcomes. About 10 per cent of total government revenues and expenditures were shifted from central to subnational budgets in Chile and 15 per cent in Argentina.[6] In Chile the transfer of expenditure responsibilities and financial resources from central to municipal governments helped to improve the provision of public health services (Bossert et al. 2003) and education (Winkler and Rounds 1996; Parry 1997). In contrast, decentralization is viewed as one of the main reasons for Argentina's macroeconomic destabilization and economic crisis (Tommasi, Saiegh and Sanguinetti 2001). The differing results can be explained by the differing levels of political centralization and national party strength in the two countries.

Argentine national political parties are weak, and the main political arena in Argentina lies at the provincial level (Corrales 2002; De Luca, Jones and

Tula 2002; Spiller and Tommasi 2003). Patronage, pork-barrel politics and clientelism are much more important in local and province-level elections than the support of a national party (Jones and Samuels 2005). Importantly, Argentine politicians generally have province-focused career paths. National politicians tend to return home to political posts in their own provinces after holding a national office (Jones et al. 2002). Thus, not only do province-level politicians have no political incentives to care about national-level performance, but also most national-level politicians pursue the interests of their home province.

In stark contrast, Chile has a strong political party system with parties which are highly centralized and national in scope (Londregan 2000). National party affiliation in Chile is important both for local elections and for the career concerns of government officials at all levels (Scully 1995; Eaton 2004). Municipal political offices offer lucrative career opportunities through advancement within the national political parties. Many local politicians, particularly from large municipalities, became prominent central-level politicians as a result of being promoted by their respective parties following successful terms in local offices.[7] At the same time, there are no known examples of Chilean politicians who returned to the local political arena after serving in a national office.

Overall, local politicians in Chile have strong career concerns about advancement to the central level via national political parties, whereas in Argentina the most attractive careers for politicians are at the provincial level. Thus, in Chile national political parties serve as a mechanism for disciplining local authorities and aligning the incentives of local politicians with national objectives, whereas in Argentina they do not. These differences may account for at least some of the differences in the outcomes of decentralization in these two countries.

Russia versus China

While decentralization promoted growth in China, it proved an obstacle to growth in Russia (Jin, Qian and Weingast 2005; Zhuravskaya 2000). Blanchard and Shleifer (2001) explain this divergence by the difference in the political centralization levels of the two countries. In China decentralization has taken place under the tight administrative control of the Communist Party; whereas in Yeltsin's Russia, economic decentralization was accompanied by large-scale political decentralization. Career concerns play an important role in disciplining provincial governors in China. The Communist Party leadership evaluates the performance of provincial leaders and makes promotion – and dismissal – decisions based on whether each province followed growth-promoting policies (Huang 2002; *Economist* 2005). But in Russia the central government was too weak throughout the 1990s to extend any influence on regional governors, and national parties are at an embryonic stage of development. As a result, regional governments often adopted policies such as inter-regional trade barriers and money surrogates which imposed significant negative externalities on the rest of the country (Shleifer and Treisman 2000; Yakovlev and Zhuravskaya 2006). The comparison between the transitions in China and Russia highlights the importance of career concerns for local politicians to align their incentives with national objectives.

DATA

We use data on political institutions, fiscal decentralization, government performance, economic growth, public goods provision and various control variables for up to 75 developing and transition countries for the years 1975– 2000. The list of countries in our sample is given in Table 4A.1. Definitions and sources of all variables are given in Table 4A.2. Summary statistics and correlations between the variables are also presented in Tables 4A.3 and 4A.4, respectively.

We use the share of subnational revenues in total government revenues as the main measure of fiscal decentralization. The results are robust to using the share of subnational expenditures in total government expenditures as an alternative measure of fiscal decentralization. The data come from the IMF's Government Finance Statistics. These measures are the most commonly used in the empirical literature on the effects of fiscal decentralization. Although they are highly imperfect and do not reflect information on the distribution of decision-making authority between the levels of government, they provide a useful proxy for the relative level of countries' fiscal decentralization.[8]

All measures of political centralization were taken from the Database on Political Institutions (Beck et al. 2001) and updated using various additional sources (see Table 4A.2). To measure the quality of government we use the Transparency International corruption index and the World Bank indexes of control over corruption, quality of governance, regulation quality and rule of law (Kaufmann, Kraay and Zoido-Lobatón 2002). To measure the quality of public goods provision we use data on DPT immunization, infant mortality, illiteracy and pupil-to-teacher ratio from the World Bank World Development Indicators.[9] Changes in GDP per capita purchasing power parity (PPP) are used to measure economic growth.

METHODOLOGY

We use standard methodology for growth regressions and regressions of the quality of government (Barro 1997; La Porta et al. 1999; Treisman 2000) and add explanatory variables which describe the level of fiscal decentralization, political institutions and our focus, their interaction term.

We analyze the effect of political institutions on the efficiency of decentralization using two distinct approaches. First, we study the determinants of cross-sectional variation in the quality of government, public goods and economic growth across countries. Second, we explore the determinants of short-run over-time variation in public goods provision within countries using panel country fixed-effects regressions.[10]

For the purposes of cross-sectional analysis, we use the following regression model:

$$Y_i = \alpha_1 + \alpha_2 Polit_i + \alpha_3 Decentr_i + \alpha_4 Polit_i * Decentr_i + \alpha_5 X_i + \varepsilon_i \quad (4.1)$$

where i indexes countries. Y_i is one of the following outcomes: an index of corruption or government quality in year 2001 (the year for which data are available), the logarithm of change in GDP per capita at PPP between 2000 and 1975, or the average measure of public goods for years 1975–2000. $Polit_i$ denotes a measure of political institutions described earlier. $Decentr_i$ denotes a measure of fiscal decentralization. For $Polit_i$ and $Decentr_i$ we take average values for the period 1975–2000 or the largest subperiod for which data are available in each country. X is the following set of control variables: initial values of the logarithm of GDP per capita at PPP and of the logarithm of population, share of Protestants, ethno-linguistic fractionalization, latitude, legal origin, initial democratic traditions (measured by the average value of the democracy index for 50 years prior to the initial year) and the current level of democracy. In regressions which use fractionalization of governing parties as a measure of party strength, the set of control variables also includes dummy variables for electoral rule and government system. The initial values are taken from 1975 or the year closest to 1975 for which data are available; all other control variables are averages over 1975–2000. In the regression for economic growth, we add the following control variables measured in 1975: the level of fixed investments, openness of economy (measured as the residual share of exports and imports in GDP after regressing on area of country and population size) and logarithm of fertility.[11] We estimate equation (4.1) by two-stage least squares, with the geographical area of countries used as an instrument for fiscal decentralization.

We also use panel regressions with fixed effects to estimate short-run changes in public goods provision:[12]

$$Y_{it} = \alpha_i + \rho_t + \beta_1 Polit_{it} + \beta_2 Decentr_{it} + \beta_3 Polit_{it} Decentr_{it} + \beta_4 X_{it} + \varepsilon_{it} \qquad (4.2)$$

where i indexes countries and t years. Y_{it} is a measure of an outcome of public goods provision. As above, $Polit_{it}$ and $Decentr_{it}$ denote variables which describe political institutions and fiscal decentralization. We control for country and year fixed effects (α_i and ρ_t). X_{it} is a set of control variables which includes logarithm of GDP per capita at PPP lagged one year and logarithm of fertility. To eliminate possible endogeneity in panel regressions, we instrument political institutions, fiscal decentralization and their interaction term with lagged values. Finally, we report standard errors, adjusted to heteroscedasticity, both allowing and not allowing clusters by country.

RESULTS

Figure 4.1 illustrates our results. The figure presents plots of the residual values from regressions of dependent variables on control variables as a function of the interaction term of decentralization and measures of party strength. The top row presents the relationship between countries, whereas the bottom row presents the relationship within countries.

Strength of National Parties

Table 4.1 presents cross-section results for the age of main parties. Having older parties significantly improves the effect of decentralization on all indices of government quality except for the Transparency International Index of Corruption. Party age also improves the effect of decentralization on immunization, infant mortality and economic growth. The pupil-to-teacher ratio also has the right sign and is almost statistically significant. About 20 per cent of the developing countries in our sample have parties old enough for decentralization to have a positive effect on indices of government quality, and 70–90 per cent of them have parties old enough for decentralization to be beneficial for public goods provision and economic growth.

Table 4.2 presents cross-sectional results for the fractionalization of government parties. Fractionalization significantly hampers the effect of decentralization on all outcomes without exception. More than half of the developing countries in our sample have fractionalization low enough for decentralization to have a positive effect on indices of control of corruption, regulation quality, rule of law, immunization and illiteracy, whereas for the indices of corruption, government effectiveness, pupil-to-teacher ratio, infant mortality and economic growth, the share is almost 90 per cent.

The results of panel regressions with fixed effects for party and government fractionalization are presented in Table 4.3. In interpreting these results it is important to note that immunization and pupil-to-teacher ratio are much more likely to be immediately affected by changes in the efficiency of education and healthcare spending compared to illiteracy and infant mortality, that probably respond to changes in fiscal policies only with a lag.[13] Thus, we expect the results in the short run to come from the former two outcomes of public goods provision. Indeed, we find that party age positively and significantly affects the immediate effect of fiscal decentralization on immunization and the ratio of teachers to pupils. Fractionalization of government parties also significantly (but negatively) affects the ratio of teachers to pupils. The coefficient of the cross-term of the revenue decentralization and government fractionalization in regression for immunization also has an expected sign, but is insignificant (with *t*-statistics above unity). Note that there are a few influential observations in each of the panel regressions with immunization and pupil-to-teacher ratio as dependent variables (one or two observations from India, Colombia and Guatemala). None of them increase the significance of our results and most actually bias the results towards zero. If influential observations are excluded from the sample, all of the coefficients of the cross-terms of decentralization and our measures of party strength are highly statistically significant and have the expected sign in regressions for immunization and pupil-to-teacher ratio (including the regression with government fractionalization effect on immunization, that is insignificant in the whole sample). As a baseline, we report results on the whole sample which are the most conservative estimates of the within relationship. In contrast, there is no short-run relationship between illiteracy and infant mortality and our main variable of interest.

Overall, the results are consistent for the two measures of party strength and for cross-section and panel regressions. Therefore, the data provide strong evidence in favor of Riker's hypothesis that strong national political parties improve the results of fiscal decentralization.

Administrative Subordination

Tables 4.4 and 4.5 present the results for the effect of elections of state and municipal executives in cross-section regressions. The results are practically absent. There are no significant results for the regressions with appointed municipal executives as explanatory variation; and in only three out of ten cases, do we observe significantly worse outcomes of fiscal decentralization

Figure 4.1   Illustration of Estimated Relationships: Partial Residual Scatter Plots

4.1a Fractionalization of government parties and effect of decentralization on the rule of law index in cross-section.

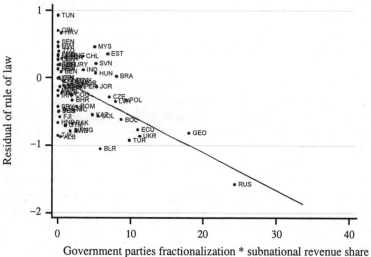

4.1b Party age and effect of decentralization on the rule of law index in cross-section.

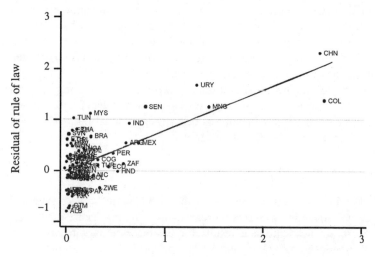

Age of main parties * subnational revenue share

Figure 4.1   (continued)

4.1c Fractionalization of government parties and effect of decentralization on pupil-to-teacher ratio, within relationship.

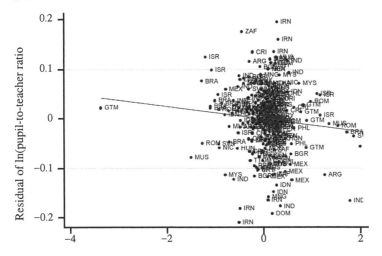

Government parties fractionalization * subnational revenue share

4.1d Party age and effect of decentralization on pupil-to-teacher ratio, within relationship.

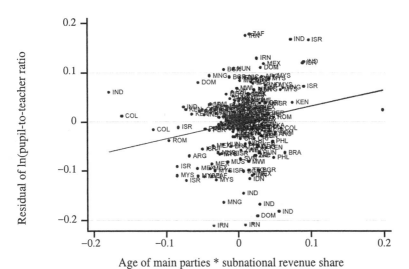

Age of main parties * subnational revenue share

Political Institutions and Development

Table 4.1   Party Age (Cross-Section Regressions)

	TI index	Effective-ness	Regulation quality	Corruption control	Rule of law
			Quality of government		
CROSS-TERM:					
Subnational revenue share	1.068	1.135	1.179	0.964	1.127
and age of main parties	(0.77)	(4.28)***	(2.56)**	(2.10)**	(2.60)**
Subnational rev. share	0.053	−0.020	−0.039	−0.027	−0.033
	(0.60)	(1.24)	(1.44)	(0.94)	(1.26)
Age of the main parties	−11.586	−15.233	−15.195	−11.786	−16.482
	(0.52)	(3.30)***	(1.91)*	(1.78)*	(2.32)**
Log. (GDP per capita)	0.694	0.136	0.040	0.114	0.043
	(2.14)**	(1.76)*	(0.47)	(1.10)	(0.45)
Democratic traditions	0.129	0.027	−0.076	0.053	0.014
	(1.26)	(0.66)	(1.73)*	(1.37)	(0.34)
Current level of democ.	0.077	0.032	0.101	0.036	0.075
	(0.67)	(0.86)	(2.51)**	(1.16)	(2.43)**
Logarithm (population)	−0.405	−0.082	−0.060	−0.086	−0.070
	(1.54)	(1.51)	(0.92)	(1.49)	(1.15)
Share of Protestants	0.031	−0.001	0.004	0.002	−0.004
	(1.99)*	(0.07)	(0.45)	(0.21)	(0.60)
Ethnoling. fraction.	−2.580	−0.123	−0.267	−0.400	0.183
	(1.83)*	(0.32)	(0.52)	(0.91)	(0.40)
Latitude	−0.829	2.618	1.545	2.274	3.177
	(0.17)	(2.56)**	(1.01)	(1.57)	(2.44)**
English legal origin	0.710	−0.070	0.273	−0.175	−0.328
	(0.76)	(0.24)	(1.08)	(0.65)	(1.18)
Socialist legal origin	−1.237	−1.152	−0.755	−0.831	−1.127
	(1.41)	(4.54)***	(2.66)**	(3.15)***	(4.60)***
French legal origin	−0.311	−0.076	0.262	−0.162	−0.407
	(0.25)	(0.22)	(0.82)	(0.58)	(1.41)
Logarithm (fertility)	na	na	na	na	na
Fixed investments	na	na	na	na	na
Openness	na	na	na	na	na
Observations	53	70	70	69	70
R^2	0.43	0.48	0.43	0.51	0.51

Note: Absolute values of robust t-statistics are in parentheses. ***Significant at 1 per cent level; **significant at 5 per cent level; *significant at 10 per cent level.

Table 4.1 (continued)

	Public goods and growth				
CROSS-TERM:	Immu-nization	Negative of infant mortality	Negative of illiteracy	Negative of log (pupil/teacher)	GDP growth
Subnational rev. share	28.256	31.737	13.564	0.370	1.356
and age of main parties	(1.87)*	(2.78)***	(1.21)	(1.67)	(3.61)***
Subnational rev. share	−1.429	−0.919	−0.716	−0.001	−0.049
	(1.26)	(1.10)	(0.89)	(0.55)	(1.06)
Age of the main parties	−339.950	−314.043	−90.900	−4.688	−16.735
	(1.34)	(1.73)*	(0.51)	(1.34)	(2.69)***
Log. (GDP per capita)	1.934	22.726	14.114	0.169	−0.530
	(0.55)	(7.63)***	(4.85)***	(3.77)***	(3.67)***
Democratic traditions	1.504	3.737	0.958	0.014	0.050
	(1.12)	(2.17)**	(0.70)	(0.57)	(0.99)
Current level of democ.	−0.138	−0.203	0.742	0.018	0.035
	(0.14)	(0.16)	(0.65)	(0.88)	(0.98)
Logarithm (population)	0.078	−0.050	2.680	−0.011	0.142
	(0.02)	(0.01)	(0.83)	(0.21)	(0.80)
Share of Protestants	−0.257	−0.254	0.080	−0.006	−0.006
	(1.30)	(1.36)	(0.28)	(1.94)*	(0.88)
Ethnoling. fraction.	2.842	−12.362	6.553	0.223	0.013
	(0.16)	(0.81)	(0.48)	(0.70)	(0.02)
Latitude	68.007	4.866	7.913	0.774	3.364
	(1.02)	(0.12)	(0.16)	(0.83)	(1.24)
English legal origin	−4.626	−48.053	−29.177	0.174	−0.746
	(0.42)	(5.44)***	(3.02)***	(1.37)	(2.93)***
Socialist legal origin	8.694	−19.111	−9.207	0.375	−2.119
	(1.02)	(2.40)**	(1.13)	(3.18)***	(6.47)***
French legal origin	−0.003	−34.646	−22.062	0.134	−0.337
	(0.00)	(3.13)***	(1.51)	(0.72)	(0.66)
Logarithm (fertility)	na	na	na	na	−0.653
	na	na	na	na	(1.63)
Fixed investments	na	na	na	na	−0.001
	na	na	na	na	(0.09)
Openness	na	na	na	na	0.005
	na	na	na	na	(1.19)
Observations	70	70	64	70	70
R^2	0.46	0.73	0.57	0.67	0.68

Table 4.2   Fractionalization of Government Parties (Cross-Section Regressions)

CROSS-TERM:	Quality of government				
	TI index	Effectiveness	Regulation quality	Corruption control	Rule of law
Subnational rev. share & fract. of govt. parties	−0.184	−0.062	−0.096	−0.074	−0.084
	(2.34)**	(3.29)***	(4.68)***	(3.45)***	(4.75)***
Subnational rev. share	0.070	0.023	0.020	0.014	0.015
	(1.58)	(1.74)*	(1.42)	(0.94)	(1.33)
Fract. of govt parties	4.429	1.157	1.702	1.256	1.663
	(2.95)***	(2.54)**	(3.44)***	(2.41)**	(3.91)***
Log. (GDP per capita)	−0.826	−0.170	0.285	−0.156	−0.133
	(1.36)	(0.88)	(1.23)	(0.84)	(0.77)
Proport. electoral rule	−0.299	0.285	0.008	0.004	0.167
	(0.48)	(1.33)	(0.04)	(0.02)	(0.96)
Parliamentary system	0.669	0.130	−0.021	0.105	0.011
	(2.05)**	(1.45)	(0.20)	(0.93)	(0.13)
Democratic traditions	0.221	0.037	−0.049	0.077	0.031
	(2.25)**	(0.79)	(0.94)	(1.58)	(0.75)
Current level of democ.	0.008	0.020	0.068	0.034	0.057
	(0.08)	(0.53)	(1.73)*	(0.96)	(1.92)*
Logarithm (population)	−0.107	−0.061	−0.072	−0.047	−0.049
	(0.51)	(0.86)	(0.88)	(0.72)	(0.84)
Share of Protestants	0.039	0.001	0.009	0.006	−0.001
	(3.82)***	(0.11)	(1.03)	(0.62)	(0.10)
Ethnoling. fract.	−2.163	−0.361	−0.629	−0.676	−0.125
	(2.51)**	(1.01)	(1.69)*	(2.30)**	(0.45)
Latitude	1.034	1.538	0.108	1.428	2.150
	(0.44)	(1.54)	(0.12)	(1.42)	(2.56)**
English legal origin	0.231	−0.464	0.229	−0.358	−0.681
	(0.26)	(1.54)	(0.74)	(1.09)	(2.55)**
Socialist legal origin	−1.114	−1.136	−0.407	−0.604	−1.036
	(1.43)	(4.01)***	(1.28)	(2.11)**	(4.34)***
French legal origin	0.22	−0.26	0.23	−0.14	−0.54
	(0.27)	(0.71)	(0.72)	(0.46)	(1.93)*
Logarithm (fertility)	na	na	na	na	na
Fixed investments	na	na	na	na	na
Openness	na	na	na	na	na
Observations	55	73	73	72	73
R²	0.50	0.36	0.36	0.44	0.55

Table 4.2   (continued)

CROSS-TERM:	Public goods and growth				
	Immu-nization	Negative of infant mortality	Negative of illiteracy	Negative of log(pupil/teacher)	GDP growth
Subnational rev. share & fract. of govt parties	−1.533	−2.136	−0.943	−0.023	−0.067
	(5.33)***	(3.34)***	(1.80)*	(2.57)**	(2.82)***
Subnational rev. share	0.256	0.608	0.027	0.011	0.051
	(0.72)	(1.10)	(0.06)	(1.54)	(1.48)
Fract. of govt parties	14.996	51.619	16.804	0.560	1.170
	(1.85)*	(3.20)***	(1.35)	(3.10)***	(2.04)**
Log. (GDP per capita)	−4.817	0.502	−1.543	0.012	−0.152
	(1.32)	(0.08)	(0.24)	(0.12)	(0.79)
Proport. electoral rule	3.014	−0.690	−1.875	0.059	0.339
	(0.76)	(0.08)	(0.30)	(0.56)	(1.29)
Parliamentary system	3.338	18.768	13.218	0.144	−0.361
	(1.64)	(4.82)***	(3.77)***	(3.16)***	(1.77)*
Democratic traditions	0.778	4.821	1.588	0.016	0.017
	(0.78)	(2.88)***	(1.06)	(0.77)	(0.40)
Current level of democ.	0.523	−0.893	0.407	0.013	−0.027
	(0.77)	(0.72)	(0.34)	(0.72)	(0.59)
Logarithm (population)	−1.938	−0.377	2.153	−0.026	−0.086
	(1.13)	(0.13)	(0.87)	(0.62)	(0.54)
Share of Protestants	−0.160	−0.081	0.127	−0.004	−0.002
	(1.20)	(0.33)	(0.41)	(1.21)	(0.31)
Ethnoling. fract.	−13.662	−35.393	−4.266	−0.082	−1.127
	(2.07)**	(2.71)***	(0.38)	(0.37)	(1.68)*
Latitude	17.512	−37.180	−11.212	−0.026	−1.181
	(0.93)	(1.00)	(0.52)	(0.05)	(0.58)
English legal origin	−5.663	−49.403	−28.554	0.119	−0.778
	(0.69)	(4.99)***	(2.98)***	(0.95)	(2.83)***
Socialist legal origin	9.688	−7.514	−3.110	0.442	−2.427
	(1.77)*	(0.70)	(0.33)	(2.98)***	(7.16)***
French legal origin	−5.603	−31.274	−18.843	0.064	−0.870
	(1.01)	(2.99)***	(2.16)**	(0.46)	(1.82)*
Logarithm (fertility)	na	na	na	na	0.011
	na	na	na	na	(1.03)
Fixed investments	na	na	na	na	−0.003
	na	na	na	na	(0.54)
Openness	na	na	na	na	−1.369
	na	na	na	na	(3.75)***
Observations	73	73	67	73	73
R^2	0.72	0.76	0.63	0.69	0.61

Note: Absolute values of robust t-statistics are in parentheses. ***Significant at 1 per cent level; **significant at 5 per cent level; *significant at 10 per cent level.

Political Institutions and Development

Table 4.3   Party Age and Fractionalization of Government Parties (Panel Regressions)

	Immu-nization	Negative of infant mortality	Negative of illiteracy	Negative of log(pupil/teacher)
CROSS-TERM:				
Subnational revenue share	51.262	−4.757	−0.834	0.459
and age of the main parties	(3.09)***	(0.91)	(0.67)	(2.66)***
	(1.72)*	(0.98)	(0.44)	(1.23)
CROSS-TERM:				
Subnational revenue share				
and fractionalization of				
government parties				
Subnational revenue share	−1.247	0.031	−0.210	−0.012
	(2.05)**	(0.12)	(3.20)***	(1.75)*
	(1.09)	(0.08)	(1.47)	(0.93)
Age of the main parties	−631.026	−130.170	15.926	−7.951
	(1.84)*	(1.45)	(0.76)	(2.62)***
	(0.78)	(0.98)	(0.37)	(1.09)
Fractionalization of				
government parties				
Logarithm (GDP per capita)	33.550	9.846	4.173	0.278
	(4.38)***	(2.73)***	(5.11)***	(3.83)***
	(1.75)*	(0.82)	(1.53)	(1.64)
Logarithm (fertility)	−81.650	−27.162	−3.860	−0.217
	(5.16)***	(3.53)***	(2.34)**	−1.420
	(2.11)**	(1.65)	(0.79)	(0.74)
Observations	334	222	416	245
Number of countries	48	51	51	45
R^2	0.36	0.65	0.62	0.5

Table 4.3   *(continued)*

	Immu-nization	Negative of infant mortality	Negative of illiteracy	Negative of log(pupil/teacher)
CROSS-TERM: Subnational revenue share and age of the main parties				
CROSS-TERM: Subnational revenue share and fractionalization of government parties	−1.342 (1.17) (0.92)	0.150 (0.28) (0.27)	−0.109 (0.90) (0.76)	−0.014 (1.80)* (1.52)
Subnational revenue share	0.364 (0.76) (0.54)	−0.015 (0.06) (0.04)	−0.157 (2.74)*** (1.28)	−0.000 (0.01) (0.01)
Age of the main parties				
Fractionalization of government parties	11.810 (0.53) (0.43)	−5.229 (0.60) (0.49)	2.654 (1.26) (0.95)	0.425 (2.63)*** (2.13)**
Logarithm (GDP per capita)	24.452 (3.54)*** (1.23)	9.275 (2.58)*** (0.88)	3.717 (4.85)*** (1.22)	0.160 (2.87)*** (1.20)
Logarithm (fertility)	−93.286 (5.85)*** (2.75)***	−35.770 (4.34)*** (2.48)**	−5.972 (3.72)*** (1.33)	−0.553 (4.39)*** (2.23)**
Observations	374	248	469	272
Number of countries	50	55	54	47
R^2	0.38	0.65	0.60	0.53

Note: Absolute values of robust t-statistics are in parentheses. The second set of t-statistics produced by clustering errors by country. ***Significant at 1 per cent level; **significant at 5 per cent level; *significant at 10 per cent level.

Political Institutions and Development

Table 4.4   State Executives Appointed or Elected (Cross-Section Regressions)

CROSS-TERM:	TI index	Effective-ness	Regulation quality	Corruption control	Rule of law
		Quality of government			
Subnat. rev. share and elected	0.025	−0.078	−0.087	−0.023	−0.057
state exec. (diff. in effects)	(0.21)	(1.61)	(1.71)*	(0.36)	(1.02)
Subnational revenue share	0.022	0.033	0.028	−0.000	0.014
(effect for appoint. state exec)	(0.27)	(1.01)	(0.79)	(0.00)	(0.41)
Elected state executives	−0.523	0.945	1.184	0.054	0.577
	(0.29)	(1.22)	(1.41)	(0.06)	(0.72)
Logarithm (GDP per capita)	0.347	0.272	0.146	0.093	0.114
	(0.62)	(1.49)	(0.78)	(0.54)	(0.63)
Democratic traditions	0.293	0.002	−0.118	0.072	−0.001
	(1.99)*	(0.03)	(1.46)	(1.28)	(0.14)
Current level of democracy	−0.076	0.009	0.098	0.022	0.059
	(0.88)	(0.17)	(1.91)*	(0.59)	(1.48)
Logarithm (population)	−0.251	−0.060	−0.098	−0.043	−0.056
	(0.86)	(0.58)	(0.91)	(0.49)	(0.59)
Share of Protestants	0.018	0.005	0.008	0.006	0.001
	(1.82)*	(0.61)	(0.87)	(0.83)	(0.25)
Ethnolinguistic fract.	−2.233	−0.669	−0.852	−0.641	−0.295
	(1.82)*	(1.13)	(1.54)	(1.16)	(0.56)
Latitude	1.862	1.396	0.249	1.846	2.267
	(0.51)	(0.81)	(0.14)	(1.34)	(1.48)
English legal origin	0.567	0.200	0.590	−0.168	−0.112
	(0.58)	(0.46)	(1.53)	(0.45)	(0.29)
Socialist legal origin	−0.128	−1.205	−0.938	−0.696	−1.179
	(0.13)	(3.31)***	(2.24)**	(1.99)*	(3.35)***
French legal origin	0.673	0.062	0.369	−0.027	−0.284
	(0.73)	(0.14)	(0.95)	(0.09)	(0.84)
Logarithm (fertility)	na	na	na	na	na
	na	na	na	na	na
Fixed investments	na	na	na	na	na
	na	na	na	na	na
Openness	na	na	na	na	na
	na	na	na	na	na
Observations	50	69	70	68	70
R^2	0.34	0.11	0.15	0.42	0.28
Subnat. rev. share in adj. regress.	0.047	−0.044	−0.059	−0.024	−0.043
(effect for elected state exec)	(0.49)	(1.56)	(1.81)*	(0.51)	(1.11)

Table 4.4 (continued)

CROS-STERM:	Immu-nization	Negative of infant mortality	Negative of illiteracy	Negative of log(pupil/teacher)	GDP growth
			Public goods and growth		
Subnat. rev. share and elected state exec. (diff. in effects)	−1.578 (1.36)	−3.074 (2.00)**	−1.798 (1.52)	−0.024 (1.16)	−0.134 (1.93)*
Subnational revenue share (effect for appoint. state exec)	0.418 (0.54)	1.858 (1.46)	0.875 (1.03)	0.016 (1.14)	0.058 (0.94)
Elected state executives	17.565 (1.02)	47.246 (1.70)*	25.304 (1.20)	0.526 (1.54)	1.965 (1.62)
Logarithm (GDP per capita)	6.123 (1.49)	31.938 (3.56)***	21.317 (3.01)***	0.230 (2.52)**	−0.231 (0.63)
Democratic traditions	0.553 (0.37)	2.215 (0.74)	0.335 (0.17)	−0.011 (0.36)	−0.064 (0.67)
Current level of democracy	−0.488 (0.66)	−1.637 (0.89)	−0.756 (0.58)	0.009 (0.48)	−0.034 (0.52)
Logarithm (population)	−3.034 (1.11)	−5.818 (1.02)	−1.330 (0.36)	−0.062 (1.14)	−0.038 (0.17)
Share of Protestants	−0.119 (0.99)	−0.171 (0.64)	0.173 (0.58)	−0.005 (1.58)	−0.003 (0.42)
Ethnolinguistic fract.	−21.879 (1.88)*	−55.302 (2.29)**	−19.204 (1.11)	−0.177 (0.58)	−1.199 (1.36)
Latitude	1.686 (0.05)	−87.267 (0.95)	−43.174 (0.93)	−0.179 (0.22)	−1.002 (0.34)
English legal origin	1.653 (0.19)	−30.597 (1.80)*	−17.307 (1.33)	0.382 (2.02)**	0.343 (0.44)
Socialist legal origin	5.703 (0.66)	−27.358 (1.76)*	−14.963 (1.27)	0.321 (1.92)*	−2.904 (3.88)***
French legal origin	−6.805 (0.97)	−35.564 (1.66)	−21.510 (2.06)**	0.096 (0.59)	−0.335 (0.72)
Logarithm (fertility)	na na	na na	na na	na na	0.035 (2.12)**
Fixed investments	na na	na na	na na	na na	0.001 (0.08)
Openness	na na	na na	na na	na na	−1.743 (2.59)**
Observations	70	70	64	70	70
R²	0.55	0.52	0.43	0.52	0.47
Subnat rev. share in adj. regress. (effect for elected state exec)	−1.159 (1.38)	−1.216 (1.19)	−0.922 (1.31)	−0.008 (0.52)	−0.076 (2.09)**

Note: Absolute values of robust t-statistics are in parentheses. ***Significant at 1 per cent level; **significant at 5 per cent level; *significant at 10 per cent level.

Table 4.5   Municipal Executives: Appointed or Elected (Cross-Section Regressions)

	Quality of government				
	TI index	Effective govt	Regulation	Corruption control	Rule of law
CROSS-TERM:					
Subnational revenue share and elected	−0.127	−0.011	−0.035	−0.026	−0.023
municipal executives (difference in effects)	(1.00)	(0.34)	(0.87)	(0.68)	(0.68)
Subnational revenue share (effect for appointed	0.168	−0.018	−0.008	−0.012	−0.013
municipal executives)	(0.94)	(0.38)	(0.15)	(0.20)	(0.25)
Elected municipal executives	2.745	0.231	0.507	0.257	0.284
	(1.10)	(0.36)	(0.66)	(0.34)	(0.41)
Logarithm (GDP per capita)	0.531	0.180	0.107	0.206	0.104
	(1.29)	(1.60)	(0.80)	(1.48)	(0.80)
Level of democracy	0.224	0.048	−0.051	0.072	0.020
	(1.86)*	(1.29)	(1.29)	(2.02)**	(0.54)
Democratic traditions	−0.013	0.016	0.081	0.037	0.072
	(0.14)	(0.46)	(2.61)**	(1.21)	(2.31)**
Logarithm (population)	−0.496	−0.013	−0.007	−0.003	−0.020
	(1.01)	(0.12)	(0.05)	(0.03)	(0.16)
Share of Protestants	0.038	−0.001	0.007	0.003	−0.003
	(1.47)	(0.15)	(0.65)	(0.29)	(0.33)
Ethnoling. fract.	−3.439	0.246	−0.287	−0.268	0.307
	(1.10)	(0.33)	(0.40)	(0.33)	(0.38)
Latitude	−0.191	3.117	1.641	2.954	3.702
	(0.03)	(2.50)**	(0.95)	(1.64)	(2.26)**
English legal origin	1.293	−0.193	0.399	0.007	−0.235
	(0.94)	(0.49)	(1.06)	(0.02)	(0.60)
Socialist legal origin	−1.313	−1.262	−0.764	−0.904	−1.255
	(1.13)	(4.36)***	(2.38)**	(3.30)***	(4.40)***
French legal origin	0.492	−0.132	0.412	0.048	−0.319
	(0.27)	(0.37)	(1.02)	(0.13)	(0.91)
Logarithm (fertility)	na	na	na	na	na
	na	na	na	na	na
Fixed investments	na	na	na	na	na
	na	na	na	na	na
Openness	na	na	na	na	na
	na	na	na	na	na
Observations	52	68	69	67	69
R^2	0.15	0.39	0.32	0.5	0.44
Subnational revenue share in adjacent regressions	0.045	−0.008	−0.025	−0.019	−0.017
(effect for elected municipal executives)	(0.63)	(0.42)	(1.16)	(0.94)	(0.83)

Table 4.5 (continued)

CROSS-TERM:	Immu-nization	Negative of infant mortality	Negative of illiteracy	Negative of log(pupil/teacher)	GDP growth
Subnational rev. share/ elected municipal executives (difference in effects)	−0.024 (0.02)	0.648 (0.47)	58.341 (0.03)	−0.012 (0.59)	−0.025 (1.29)
Subnational rev. share (effect for appointed municipal executives)	−1.619 (0.67)	−1.639 (0.89)	−62.720 (0.03)	0.009 (0.29)	−0.013 (0.39)
Elected municipal executives	−17.028 (0.49)	−9.208 (0.32)	−902.440 (0.03)	0.267 (0.61)	0.322 (0.76)
Log. (GDP per capita)	0.934 (0.13)	20.342 (3.73)***	−145.924 (0.03)	0.191 (2.74)***	−0.363 (3.46)***
Level of democracy	0.573 (0.44)	4.511 (2.78)***	−11.919 (0.03)	0.011 (0.56)	0.029 (0.90)
Democratic traditions	1.568 (0.80)	−0.234 (0.16)	39.973 (0.03)	0.006 (0.24)	0.053 (1.22)
Log. (population)	3.655 (0.55)	−0.988 (0.24)	11.358 (0.03)	−0.041 (0.62)	0.127 (1.09)
Share of Protestants	−0.218 (0.66)	−0.709 (2.13)**	−12.173 (0.03)	−0.003 (0.73)	−0.007 (1.01)
Ethnoling. fract.	21.532 (0.52)	17.076 (0.51)	950.178 (0.03)	0.041 (0.07)	0.075 (0.14)
Latitude	98.215 (0.96)	44.544 (0.74)	885.125 (0.03)	0.300 (0.30)	3.079 (1.70)*
English legal origin	−6.258 (0.32)	−63.554 (3.48)***	−647.905 (0.03)	0.200 (0.83)	−0.627 (1.90)*
Socialist legal origin	10.452 (0.78)	−31.929 (2.95)***	−176.364 (0.04)	0.304 (2.60)**	−2.310 (9.56)***
French legal origin	7.173 (0.34)	−43.333 (3.03)***	−464.032 (0.03)	0.118 (0.80)	−0.472 (1.51)
Logarithm (fertility)	na na	na na	na na	na na	0.010 (1.01)
Fixed investments	na na	na na	na na	na na	0.002 (0.97)
Openness	na na	na na	na na	na na	−0.460 (1.10)
Observations	69	69	62	69	69
R²	0.36	0.7	0.02	0.66	0.76
Subnat. revenue share in adjacent regressions (effect for elected municipal execs)	−1.643 (1.26)	−0.991 (1.18)	−4.379 (0.04)	−0.003 (0.18)	−0.038 (1.70)*

Note: Absolute values of robust t-statistics in parentheses. ***Significant at 1 per cent level;**significant at 5 per cent level;*significant at 10 per cent level. Observations for China are excluded.

Table 4.6 State and Municipal Executives Appointed or Elected (Panel Regressions)

	Immu-nization	Negative of infant mortality	Negative of illiteracy	Negative of log(pupil/teacher ratio)
CROSS-TERM: Subnational rev. share & elected state execs (difference in effects)	0.105 (0.12) (0.06)	0.382 (1.83)* (2.07)**	0.083 (1.35) (0.65)	0.048 (3.65)*** (2.95)***
CROSS-TERM: Subnational revenue share & elected municipal executives (difference in effects)				
Subnational revenue share (effect for appointed execs)	−21.320 (1.43) (0.18)	−8.876 (1.73)* (1.13)	−0.833 (0.62) (1.55)	−1.091 (3.64)*** (2.10)**
Elected state executives	3.423 (0.430) (0.73)	17.478 (4.03)*** (1.82)*	7.207 (7.61)*** (0.36)	0.099 (0.930) (3.35)***
Elected municipal executives				
Logarithm (GDP per capita)	−48.491 (3.38)*** (0.19)	−43.047 (6.24)*** (1.68)	−5.673 (4.12)*** (3.40)***	0.320 (1.37) (0.45)
Logarithm (fertility)	−0.353 (0.390) (1.48)	−0.337 (1.490) (2.46)**	−0.241 (3.36)*** (1.25)	−0.041 (2.89)*** (0.55)
Observations	237	181	276	148
Number of countries	35	36	33	25
R^2	0.56	0.73	0.66	0.36
Subnational revenue share in adjacent regressions (effect (or elected state execs)	−0.247 (0.64) (0.35)	0.045 (0.23) (0.25)	−0.158 (3.57)*** (3.06)***	0.007 (0.99) (0.86)

Table 4.6 (continued)

	Immu-nization	Negative of infant mortality	Negative of illiteracy	Negative of log(pupil/ teacher ratio)
CROSS-TERM: Subnational rev. share & elected state execs (difference in effects)				
CROSS-TERM: Subnational revenue share & elected municipal executives (difference in effects)	−13.866 (0.45) (0.26)	−0.355 (0.74) (0.83)	−0.526 (0.14) (0.14)	0.145 (4.68)*** (3.37)***
Subnational revenue share (effect for appointed execs)	13.754 (0.45) (0.26)	0.277 (0.64) (1.00)	0.396 (0.11) (0.10)	−0.135 (4.57)*** (3.48)***
Elected state executives				
Elected municipal executives	360.18 (0.45) (0.26)	16.133 (1.03) (1.42)	13.337 (0.14) (0.14)	. (.) (.)
Logarithm (GDP per capita)	25.145 (2.53)** (1.20)	15.298 (5.04)*** (1.48)	2.036 (2.17)** (0.61)	0.057 (0.87) (0.40)
Logarithm (fertility)	−33.864 (1.65)* (0.85)	−19.812 (3.17)*** (1.19)	−5.082 (2.54)** (1.03)	−0.724 (5.06)*** (3.18)***
Observations	330	271	407	217
Number of countries	49	49	46	41
R^2	0.15	0.72	0.61	0.06
Subnational revenue share in adjacent regressions (effect for elected state execs)	−0.113 (0.18) (0.12)	−0.078 (0.38) (0.25)	−0.129 (1.80)* (1.12)	0.010 (1.55) (1.10)

Note: Absolute values of robust t-statistics in parentheses. ***Significant at 1 per cent level;**significant at 5 per cent level;*significant at 10 per cent level. Observations for China are excluded.

in the case when state executives are appointed compared with when they are elected. These few significant results, however, are likely to be driven by the omitted variable bias because they are inconsistent with the panel data results. Table 4.6 presents the results of the fixed-effects panel regressions for administrative subordination. In contrast to the cross-sectional correlations, the coefficient of the cross-term between subnational revenue share and the dummy for elected state executives is always positive and, in the case of the teacher-to-pupil ratio and infant mortality, significant. The teacher-to-pupil ratio is also positively and significantly affected by the cross-term of decentralization and municipal elections dummy.

Panel regressions improve on cross-section regressions in two important ways. First and foremost, including fixed effects takes care of much of the criticism that the results are driven by the unobserved differences between countries. Second, in the panel regressions we are able to instrument measures of political institutions with their lag values. This is not a perfect instrument because our outcome variables may also be persistent, but this is better than not having instruments, because lags as instruments at least reduce the measurement error bias. Thus, we consider cross-section results to be valid only when they are confirmed by panel regression results.

Overall, we find no robust evidence that administrative subordination helps the outcomes of fiscal decentralization. Again, our results are consistent with Riker's hypothesis that administrative subordination is an ineffective mechanism of aligning local political incentives with national interests (unlike strong national political parties).

CONCLUSION

Our key finding is that political institutions play an important role in determining the results of fiscal decentralization. In line with Riker's predictions, we find that a strong national party system is a very effective way of aligning the political incentives of local politicians with national objectives, while preserving their accountability to local constituencies, a linkage which is necessary for efficient decentralization. In developing and transition countries, older and more stable party systems, as well as lower fractionalization of government parties, are associated with the better effect of fiscal decentralization on economic growth, government quality and public goods. Our findings also confirm Riker's skepticism about administrative subordination as a mechanism of ensuring efficient political incentives for the local governments in decentralized states. We find that appointing state and municipal officials does not help the results of fiscal decentralization.

Therefore, a remedy for poor governance in large, inherently decentralized countries is building strong national political parties whenever possible. Strong parties help to provide elected local officials with efficient political incentives, because their chances of reelection depend both on national party support and the satisfaction of the local constituency. This allows leaders to strike a balance between national objectives and local accountability.

NOTES

We thank Alberto Alesina, Scott Gelhbach, Sergei Guriev, James Hines, Rory MacFarquhar, Pierre Pestieau, Gérard Roland, Andrei Shleifer, Konstantin Sonin, Barry Weingast, Luigi Zingales, anonymous referees and seminar participants at the University of Michigan, CEFIR, NES, London Business School, University of California, Berkeley, Institute for Advanced Study in Princeton, Harvard University, Princeton University, participants of CEPR-WDI 2003 Transition Conference and Fiscal Federalism workshop in Barcelona in 2005 for useful comments. We also thank Alexander Rumyantsev for excellent research assistance. The work of Ruben Enikolopov was in part supported by a program of the Bureau of Educational and Cultural Affairs, U.S. Department of State, administered by the American Council for International Education. The views expressed herein are those of the authors and are not necessarily shared by ECA or ACIE. Part of the work on this study took place when Ekaterina Zhuravskaya was on leave at the Institute for Advanced Study in Princeton. The hospitality and congenial environment of the Institute are gratefully acknowledged.

1. Fisman and Gatti (2002) and de Mello and Barenstein (2001) found negative effect of decentralization on corruption across countries; Treisman (2000) reported no relationship. Zhang and Zou (1998) reported negative effect of decentralization on provincial growth in China; whereas Jin, Qian and Weingast (2005) and Lin and Liu (2000) showed that this relationship is positive once one filters out cyclical effects. Akai and Sakata (2002) reported a positive effect of decentralization on growth of U.S. states in the early 1990s, while Xie, Zou and Davoodi (1999) showed no relationship over 50 years. Woller and Phillips (1998) found no link between decentralization and growth in developing countries; in contrast, Davoodi and Zou (1998) reported a negative marginally significant relationship in developing countries and no effect in developed countries. Robalino, Picazo and Voetberg (2001) found a negative cross-country relationship between decentralization and infant mortality.
2. In this study, we restrict our attention to developing and transition countries for two reasons. First, the local capture and interjurisdictional externalities are more relevant for developing than for developed countries, since well-functioning democratic institutions and systems of checks and balances substantially limit the scope for opportunistic behavior by public officials in developed countries (Bardhan 2002). Second, two conditions necessary for our analysis hold only in developing countries: our measures of national party strength adequately reflect career concerns of local politicians only in developing countries; and measures of administrative subordination exhibit sufficient variation only in developing countries.
3. Riker (1964) noted that a necessary condition for strong national parties to have beneficial influence on career concerns of local politicians is a direct connection between national and regional political parties. One counter example to this is Canada, where the link between national and regional parties is rather weak (Uslaner 2000). The data availability does not allow us to take into account the relationship between national and regional parties.
4. We consider fractionalization of governing parties rather than fractionalization of parliament as a whole, because fractionalization in small opposition parties and the presence of independent MPs have little effect on local politicians' career concerns.

5. The fractionalizations of government parties in Mexico, Venezuela and Argentina (0; 0.11; and 0, respectively) are noticeably lower in Brazil and Colombia (0.31, in both countries). The average age of the main parties is 37 and 39 years old in Mexico and Venezuela, respectively; in Argentina it is 19, and in Brazil, 10. Colombia is an obvious outlier with the average age of the main parties equal to 147 years. According to Roland and Zapata (2005), Colombia has a very peculiar system in which parties do not have control over their own party label, allowing different party lists with the same party label. In essence, each party in Colombia is a collection of different parties which use the same party label rather than a single unified party. Thus, our measures of party strength significantly overstate party strength in Colombia. A similar system exists in Ecuador.

6. The level of decentralization, of course, has been substantially higher in federal Argentina than in unitary Chile; but, for the purposes of this case study, we are interested in the changes rather than levels.

7. For example, Joaquin Lavin and Jaime Ravinet, the two former mayors of Santiago, advanced to the very top. Lavin (a member of the Independent Democratic Union party) became one of the main opposition leaders. He lost the 1999 presidential election to Ricardo Lagos in a runoff by 200,000 votes and was a close third in the 2005 presidential race. Ravinet (a member of the Coalition of Parties for Democracy) was the minister of defense in Lagos' cabinet in 2004–2006.

8. An important shortcoming of these data is that they do not distinguish between state and municipal expenditures and revenues; this breakdown is available only for a very limited number of countries.

9. Unlike the other measures of public goods, the pupil-to-teacher ratio is not an outcome, but a characteristic of the process which might reflect inefficiencies of resource use rather than quality. For many developing countries, however, the number of teachers reflects a binding constraint. We considered and rejected enrollment in schools as another possible measure of the quality of education. It is nonlinear in the level of education: for countries with high quality of education, it takes values around 100 per cent, while for countries with poor quality of education it takes values either lower or higher than 100 per cent. The values are above 100 per cent when adults go to school.

10. The data on corruption and the quality of government are only a cross-section. In addition, we cannot use panel regressions for the analysis of economic growth, due to the insufficient number of observations in five-year averaged regressions.

11. The number of observations per country varies from country to country and, therefore, the over-time averages for 25 years at a maximum are measured with varied precision. To account for this, in regressions for public goods and growth, we weight observations by the square root of the number of years with non-missing data for political institutions and decentralization. To account for differences in the measurement accuracy of corruption and governance quality indices, we weight observations by the inverse of the standard errors of the indexes that are provided along with the measures.

12. As a robustness check, we also run panel regressions with random effects. The results prove to be similar to the results of cross-sectional analysis.

13. In addition, such measures as infant mortality and illiteracy rates are functions of not just government action, but also of characteristics of the citizens for which we do not have a proper measure.

BIBLIOGRAPHY

Acemoglu, Daron (2005), 'Constitutions, Politics and Economics; A Review Essay on Persson and Tabellini's "The Economic Effects of Constitutions",' *Journal of Economic Literature*, **43** (4), 1025–48.

Akai, Nobu and Masayo Sakata (2002), 'Fiscal Decentralization Contributes to Economic Growth: Evidence from State-level Cross-section Data for the United States', *Journal of Urban Economics*, **52** (1), 93–108.

Alesina, Alberto and Enrico Spolaore (2003), *The Size of Nations*, Cambridge, MA: MIT Press.

Arzaghi, Mohamad and J. Vernon Henderson (2005), 'Why Countries are Fiscally Decentralizing', *Journal of Public Economics*, **89** (7), 1157–89.

Bardhan, Pranab (2002), 'Decentralization of Governance and Development', *Journal of Economic Perspectives*, **16** (4), 185–205.

Bardhan, Pranab and Dilip Mookherjee (2000), 'Capture and Governance at Local and National Levels', *American Economic Review*, **90** (2), 135–9.

Barro, Robert J. (1997), *Determinants of Economic Growth: A Cross-Country Empirical Study*, Cambridge, MA: MIT Press.

Beck, Thorsten, George Clarke, Alberto Groff, Philip Keefer and Patrick Walsh (2001), 'New Tools in Comparative Political Economy: The Database of Political Institutions', *World Bank Economic Review*, **15** (1), 165–76.

Blanchard, Olivier and Andrei Shleifer (2001), 'Federalism With and Without Political Centralization: China Versus Russia', *IMF Staff Papers*, **48** (4), 171–9.

Bossert, Thomas J., Osvaldo Larrañaga, Ursula Giedion, José Arbelaez and Diana M. Bowser (2003), 'Decentralization and Equity of Resource Allocation: Evidence from Colombia and Chile', *Bulletin of the World Health Organization*, **81** (2), 95–100.

Cai, Hongbin and Daniel Treisman (2004), 'State Corroding Federalism', *Journal of Public Economics*, **88** (3–4), 819–43.

Camp, Roderic (1998), 'Battling for the Voters: Elections, Parties and Democracy in Mexico', in Kurt Von Mettenheim and James Malloy (eds), *Deepening Democracy in Latin America*, Pittsburgh, PA: University of Pittsburgh Press, pp. 38–54.

Carrion, Julio F. (1998), 'Partisan Decline and Presidential Popularity: The Politics and Economics of Representation in Peru, 1980–1993', in Kurt Von Mettenheim and James Malloy (eds), *Deepening Democracy in Latin America*, Pittsburgh, PA: University of Pittsburgh Press, pp. 55–70.

Corrales, Javier (2002), *Presidents without Parties: The Politics of Economic Reform in Argentina and Venezuela in the 1990s*, University Park, PA: Pennsylvania State University Press.

Davoodi, Hamid and Heng-fu Zou (1998), 'Fiscal Decentralization and Economic Growth: A Cross-Country Study', *Journal of Urban Economics*, **43** (2), 244–57.

De Luca, Miguel, Mark P. Jones and Maria Ines Tula (2002), 'Back Rooms or Ballot Boxes: Candidate Nomination in Argentina', *Comparative Political Studies*, **35** (4), 413–36.

de Mello, Luiz and Mathis Barenstein (2001), 'Fiscal Decentralization and Governance: A Cross-Country Analysis', Washington, DC, IMF Working Paper No. 01/71.

Eaton, Kent H. (2004), 'Designing Subnational Institutions: Regional and Municipal Reforms in Post-authoritarian Chile', *Comparative Political Studies*, **37** (2), 218–44.

Economist (2005), 'The Greening of China', 22 October.

Fisman, Raymond and Roberta Gatti (2002), 'Decentralization and Corruption: Evidence across Countries', *Journal of Public Economics*, **83** (3), 325–46.

Garman, Christopher, Stephan Haggard and Eliza Willis (2001), 'Fiscal Decentralization: A Political Theory with Latin American Cases', *World Politics*, **53** (2), 205–36.

Gennaioli, Nicola and Ilia Rainer (2004), 'The Modern Impact of Pre-colonial Centralization in Africa', Cambridge, MA, Harvard University, Center for Economic and Financial Research, unpublished paper.

Hayek, Friedrich A. (1948), *Individualism and Economic Order*, Chicago: University of Chicago Press.

Hicken, Allen (2004), 'The Politics of Economic Reform in Thailand: Crisis and Compromise', Ann Arbor, MI, William Davidson Institute Working Paper No. 638.

Huang, Yasheng (2002), 'Managing Chinese Bureaucrats: An Institutional Economics Perspective', *Political Studies*, **50** (1), 61–79.

Huntington, Samuel P. (1968), *Political Order in Changing Societies*, New Haven, CT: Yale University Press.

Jin, Hehui, Yingyi Qian and Barry Weingast (2005), 'Regional Decentralization and Fiscal Incentives: Federalism Chinese Style', *Journal of Public Economics*, **89** (9–10), 1719–42.

Jones, Mark P. and David J. Samuels (2005), 'The Future of Federalism in Mexico: Lessons from Argentina and Brazil', paper presented at the conference 'Democratic Institutions in Latin America: Implications for Mexico's Evolving Democracy', University of California – San Diego, La Jolla, CA, 5–6 March.

Jones, Mark P., Sebastian Saiegh, Pablo T. Spiller and Mariano Tommasi (2002), 'Amateur Legislators – Professional Politicians: The Consequences of Party-Centered Electoral Rules in a Federal System', *American Journal of Political Science*, **46** (3), 656–69.

Kaufmann, Daniel, Aart Kraay and Pablo Zoido-Lobatón (2002), 'Governance Matters II: Updated Indicators for 2000–01', Washington DC, World Bank, Policy Research Working Paper No. 2772.

La Porta, Rafael, Florencio Lopez-de-Silanes, Andrei Shleifer and Robert Vishny (1999), 'The Quality of Government', *Journal of Law, Economics and Organization*, **15** (1), 222–79.

Lin, Justin Yifu and Zhiqiang Liu (2000), 'Fiscal Decentralization and Economic Growth in China', *Economic Development and Cultural Change*, **49** (1), 1–22.

Londregan, John B. (2000), *Legislative Institutions and Ideology in Chile's Democratic Tradition*, New York: Cambridge University Press.

Maskin, Eric, Yingyi Qian and Chenggang Xu (2000), 'Incentives, Information and Organizational Form', *Review of Economic Studies*, **67** (2), 359–78.

Musgrave, Richard A. (1969), 'Theories of Fiscal Federalism', *Public Finances/ Finances Publiques*, **4** (24), 521–32.

Nickson, R. Andrew (1995), *Local Government in Latin America*, Boulder, CO: Lynne Rienner.

Oates, Wallace E. (1972), *Fiscal Federalism*, New York: Harcourt.

Panizza, Ugo (1999), 'On the Determinants of Fiscal Centralization: Theory and Evidence', *Journal of Public Economics*, **74** (1), 97–139.

Parry, Taryn Rounds (1997), 'Achieving Balance in Decentralization: A Case Study of Education Decentralization in Chile', *World Development*, **25** (2), 211–25.

Persson, Torsten and Guido Tabellini (2003), *The Economic Effects of Constitutions*, Cambridge, MA: MIT Press.

Qian, Yingyi and Gérard Roland (1998), 'Federalism and the Soft Budget Constraint', *American Economic Review*, **88** (5), 1143–62.

Qian, Yingyi and Barry Weingast (1996), 'China's Transition to Markets: Market-

Preserving Federalism, Chinese Style', *Journal of Policy Reform*, **1**, 149–85.

Riker, William (1964), *Federalism: Origins, Operation, Significance*, Boston, MA: Little, Brown and Co.

Robalino, David, Oscar Picazo and Albertus Voetberg (2001), 'Does Fiscal Decentralization Improve Health Outcomes? Evidence from Cross-Country Analysis', Washington, DC, World Bank, Policy Research Working Paper No. 2565.

Roland, Gérard and Juan Gonzala Zapata (2005), 'Colombia's Electoral and Party System: Possible Paths for Reform', in Alberto Alesina (ed.), *Institutional Reforms: The Case of Colombia*, Cambridge, MA: MIT Press, pp. 103–30.

Scully, Timothy R. (1995), 'Reconstituting Party Politics in Chile', in Scott Mainwaring and Timothy R. Scully (eds), *Building Democratic Institutions: Party Systems in Latin America*, Stanford, CA: Stanford University Press, pp. 100–137.

Seabright, Paul (1996), 'Accountability and Decentralization in Government: An Incomplete Contract Model', *European Economic Review*, **40** (1), 61–89.

Shleifer, Andrei and Daniel Treisman (2000), *Without a Map: Political Tactics and Economic Reform in Russia*, Cambridge, MA: MIT Press.

Sonin, Konstanin (2003),'Provincial Protectionism', Ann Arbor, MI, William Davidson Institute, Working Paper No. 157.

Spiller, Pablo and Mariano Tommasi (2003), 'The Institutional Foundations of Public Policy: A Transaction Theory and an Application to Argentina', *Journal of Law, Economics and Organization*, **19** (2), 281–306.

Strumpf, Koleman and Felix Oberholzer-Gee (2002), 'Endogenous Policy Decentralization: Testing the Central Tenet of Economic Federalism', *Journal of Political Economy*, **110** (1), 1–36.

Tanzi, Vito (1996), 'Fiscal Federalism and Decentralization: A Review of Some Efficiency and Macroeconomic Aspects', in Michael Bruno and Boris Pleskovich (eds), *Annual World Bank Conference on Development Economics, 1995*, Washington, DC: World Bank, pp. 295–316.

Tiebout, Charles M. (1956), 'A Pure Theory of Local Expenditures', *Journal of Political Economy*, **64** (5), 416–24.

Tommasi, Mariano, Sebastian Saiegh and Pablo Sanguinetti (2001), 'Fiscal Federalism in Argentina: Policies, Politics, and Institutional Reform', *Economia: Journal of the Latin American and the Caribbean Economic Association*, **1** (2), 157–211.

Treisman, Daniel (2000), 'Decentralization and the Quality of Government', Los Angeles, CA, University of California – Los Angeles, Department of Economics, unpublished paper.

Uslaner, Eric (2000), 'Strong Institutions, Weak Parties: The Paradox of Canadian Political Parties', mimeo, College Park, MD, University of Maryland, Department of Government and Politics, unpublished paper.

Winkler, Donald R. and Taryn Rounds (1996), 'Municipal and Private Sector Response to Decentralization and School Choice – Chile', *Economics of Education Review*, **15** (4), 365–76.

Woller, Gary M. and Kerk L. Phillips (1998), 'Fiscal Decentralization and LDC Economic Growth: An Empirical Investigation', *Journal of Development Studies*, **34** (4), 139–48.

Xie, Danyang, Heng-fu Zou and Hamid Davoodi (1999), 'Fiscal Decentralization and

Economic Growth in the United States', *Journal of Urban Economics*, **45** (2), 228–39.

Yakovlev, Evgeny and Ekaterina Zhuravskaya (2006), 'Lobbying in a Federation', Moscow, New Economic School, unpublished paper.

Zhang, Tao and Heng-fu Zou (1998), 'Fiscal Decentralization, Public Spending and Economic Growth in China', *Journal of Public Economics*, **67** (2), 221–40.

Zhuravskaya, Ekaterina (2000), 'Incentives to Provide Local Public Goods: Fiscal Federalism Russian Style', *Journal of Public Economics*, **76** (3), 337–68.

APPENDIX

Table 4A.1   Countries Included in the Sample

Albania*	ALB	Fiji*	FJI	Panama	PAN
Argentina	ARG	Gambia*	GMB	Papua N. Guinea*	PNG
Armenia*	ARM	Georgia*	GEO	Paraguay*	PRY
Azerbaijan	AZE	Guatemala	GTM	Peru	PER
Bahrain*	BHR	Honduras	HND	Philippines	PHL
Banglade	BGD	Hungary	HUN	Poland	POL
Belarus*	BLR	India	IND	Romania	ROM
Benin*†	BEN	Indonesia	IDN	Russia	RUS
Bolivia	BOL	Iran	IRN	Senegal	SEN
Brazil	BRA	Israel	ISR	Slovakia	SVK
Bulgaria	BGR	Jordan	JOR	Slovenia	SVN
Cameroon	CMR	Kazakhstan	KAZ	South Africa	ZAF
Chile	CHL	Kenya	KEN	Sri Lanka*	LKA
China	CHN	South Korea	KOR	Swaziland*†	SWZ
Colombia	COL	Kyrgyzstan*	KGZ	Tajikistan*	TJK
Congo, Republic*	COG	Latvia	LVA	Thailand	THA
Costa Rica	CRI	Madagascar*	MDG	Trinidad & Tobago	TTO
Croatia	HRV	Malawi	MWI	Tunisia	TUN
Cyprus*	CYP	Malaysia	MYS	Turkey	TUR
Czech Republic	CZE	Mauritius	MUS	Uganda	UGA
Dominican Rep.	DOM	Mexico	MEX	Ukraine	UKR
Ecuador	ECU	Moldova	MDA	Uruguay	URY
El Salvador	SLV	Mongolia*	MNG	Venezuela	VEN
Estonia	EST	Nicaragua	NIC	Zambia	ZMB
Ethiopia*	ETH	Pakistan	PAK	Zimbabwe	ZWE

Notes:

*Denotes countries for which the Transparency International index of corruption (one of our outcome variables) is unavailable.

†For Benin and Swaziland the index of control over corruption is unavailable. For Swaziland the index of government effectivenes is unavailable as well. In all regressions, we exclude observations for socialist countries before the beginning of transition because economic institutions in these countries (i.e., central planning systems) were different in nature.

Table 4A.2   Description of the Variables

Variable	Description
Subnational revenue share	Share of revenues of all subnational governments in total revenues of consolidated central budget measured in per cent. Scale from 0 to 100. *Source*: Database on Fiscal Indicators by the World Bank, based on IMF's Government Finance Statistics. Data from Government Finance Statistics 2001 were added. For Armenia, Korea and Pakistan data were added using information from national statistical offices.
Subnational expenditure share	Share of expenditures of all subnational governments (net of transfers to other levels of government) in total expenditures of consolidated central budget measured in per cent. Scale from 0 to 100. *Source*: Database on Fiscal Indicators[1] by the World Bank, based on IMF's Government Finance Statistics. Data from Government Finance Statistics 2001 were added. For Armenia, Korea and Pakistan data were added using information from national statistical offices.
Fractionalization of government parties	The probability that two members of parliament picked at random from among the government parties will be of different parties. Missing if there is no parliament, if there are any government parties where seats are unknown or if there are no parties in the legislature. Scale from 0 to 1. Observations for Thailand prior to 1989 are excluded, because they are inconsistent with the description of the Thai government provided by Hicken (2004). *Source*: Database on Political Institutions, Version 3 (Beck et al. 2001).
Fractionalization of parliament	The probability that two members of parliament picked at random from the legislature will be of different parties. Missing if there is no parliament, if there are no parties in the legislature and if any government or opposition party seats are missing. Scale from 0 to 1. *Source*: Database on Political Institutions, Version 3 (Beck et al. 2001).
Party age	This is the average of the ages of the first government party, second government party and first opposition party, or the subset of these for which age of party is known. The variable is measured in thousands of years. *Source*: Database on Political Institutions, Version 3 (Beck et al. 2001).
Elected municipal executives	Equals one if local executive is locally elected. Equals zero otherwise. No information, or no evidence of municipal governments, is recorded as missing. If one source has information on a specific period, and the other has no information on a different period, we do not extrapolate from one source to another – no information is always recorded as missing. If there are multiple levels of subnational government, we consider the lowest level as the 'municipal' level. *Source*: Database on Political Institutions, Version 3 (Beck et al. 2001), updated using Nickson (1995) and various other sources.

Table 4A.2 (continued)

Elected state/ province executives	Equals one if state/province executive is locally elected. Equals zero otherwise. If there are multiple levels of subnational government, we consider the highest level as the 'state/province' level. Indirectly elected state/province governments, where directly elected municipal bodies elect the state/province level, are not considered locally elected. Indirectly elected state/province governments elected by directly elected state/province bodies are considered locally elected. *Source:* Database on Political Institutions, Version 3 (Beck et al. 2001), updated using Nickson (1995) and various other sources.
Share of Protestants	Identifies the percentage of the population of each country that belonged to the Protestant religion in 1980. Scales from 0 to 100. *Source*: La Porta et al. (1999).
Latitude	The absolute latitude of the country, scaled to take values between 0 and 1. *Source*: La Porta et al. (1999).
Legal origin	Identifies the legal origin of the company law or commercial code of the country. There are five possible origins: (1) English Common Law; (2) French Commercial Code; (3) German Commercial Code; (4) Scandinavian Commercial Code; (5) Socialist/Communist laws. *Source*: La Porta et al. (1999).
Parliamentary system	Systems with unelected executives (those scoring a 2 or 3 on the Executive Index of Political Competitiveness – to be defined below) get a 0. Systems with presidents who are elected directly or by an electoral college (whose only function is to elect the president), in cases where there is no prime minister, also receive a 0. In systems with both a prime minister and a president, we consider the following factors to categorize the system:

(a) Veto power: president can veto legislation and the parliament needs a supermajority to override the veto.
(b) Appoint prime minister: president can appoint and dismiss prime minister and/or other ministers.
(c) Dissolve parliament: president can dissolve parliament and call for new elections.
(d) Mentioning in sources: if the sources mention the president more often than the prime minister then this serves as an additional indicator to call the system presidential (Romania, Kyrgyzstan, Estonia, Yugoslavia).

The system is presidential if (a) is true, or if (b) and (c) are true. If no information or ambiguous information on (a), (b), (c), then (d). Countries in which the legislature elects the chief executive are parliamentary (2). *Source*: Database on Political Institutions, Version 3 (Beck et al. 2001).

Table 4A.2   (continued)

Proportional electoral rule	One if candidates are elected based on the percentage of votes received by their party and/or if our sources specifically call the system 'proportional representation'; zero otherwise. *Source*: Database on Political Institutions, Version 3 (Beck et al. 2001), updated using various other sources.
Control over corruption	Governance indicator reflecting the statistical compilation of perceptions of corruption, conventionally defined as the exercise of public power for private gain, of a large number of survey respondents in industrial and developing countries, as well as non-governmental organizations, commercial risk-rating agencies and think-tanks during 2000 and 2001. Units range from about -2.5 to 2.5, with higher values corresponding to better governance outcomes. *Source*: Kaufmann, Kraay and Zoido-Lobatón (2002).[2]
Government effectiveness	A governance indicator which reflects the statistical compilation of perceptions of the quality of public service provision, the quality of the bureaucracy, the competence of civil servants, the independence of the civil service from political pressures and the credibility of government's commitment to policies of a large number of survey respondents in industrial and developing countries, as well as non-governmental organizations, commercial risk-rating agencies and think-tanks during 2000 and 2001. Units range from about -2.5 to 2.5, with higher values corresponding to better governance outcomes. *Source*: Kaufmann, Kraay and Zoido-Lobatón (2002).
Regulation quality	A governance indicator which reflects the statistical compilation of perceptions of the incidence of market-unfriendly policies such as price controls or inadequate bank supervision, as well as perception of the burdens imposed by excessive regulation in areas such as foreign trade and business development of a large number of survey respondents in industrial and developing countries, as well as non-governmental organizations, commercial risk-rating agencies and think-tanks during 2000 and 2001. Units range from about -2.5 to 2.5, with higher values corresponding to better governance outcomes. *Source*: Kaufmann, Kraay and Zoido-Lobatón (2002).
Rule of law	A governance indicator which reflects the statistical compilation of perceptions of the incidence of both violent and non-violent crime, the effectiveness and predictability of the judiciary, and the enforceability of contracts of a large number of survey respondents in industrial and developing countries, as well as non-governmental organizations, commercial risk-rating agencies and think-tanks during 2000 and 2001. Units range from about -2.5 to 2.5, with higher values corresponding to better governance outcomes. *Source*: Kaufmann, Kraay and Zoido-Lobatón (2002).

Table 4A.2 *(continued)*

Corruption indices	The Transparency International Corruption Perceptions Indexes for years 2000 and 2001, respectively. Scale from 0 to 10, with higher values corresponding to better governance outcomes. *Source*: Transparency International.[3]
Immunization	Immunization, DPT (percentage of children under 12 months). Child immunization measures the rate of vaccination coverage of children under one year of age. A child is considered adequately immunized against diphtheria, pertussis (whooping cough) and tetanus (DPT) after receiving three doses of vaccine. Scale from 0 to 100. *Source*: World Development Indicators 2001, by the World Bank.
Infant mortality	Infant mortality rate is the number of infants dying before reaching one year of age, per 1,000 live births in a given year. *Source*: World Bank World Development Indicators 2001.
Illiteracy	Adult illiteracy rate is the percentage of people aged 15 and above who cannot, with understanding, read and write a short, simple statement on their everyday life. Scale from 0 to 100. *Source*: World Bank World Development Indicators 2001.
Pupil-to-teacher ratio	Primary school pupil–teacher ratio is the number of pupils enrolled in primary school divided by the number of primary school teachers (regardless of their teaching assignment). *Source*: World Bank World Development Indicators 2001.
Fixed investments	Gross fixed capital formation (per cent of GDP). Gross fixed capital formation (gross domestic fixed investment) includes land improvements (fences, ditches, drains, etc.); plant, machinery and equipment purchases; and the construction of roads, railways and the like, including schools, offices, hospitals, private residential dwellings and commercial and industrial buildings. According to the 1993 System of National Accounts, net acquisitions of valuables are also considered capital formation. *Source*: World Bank World Development Indicators 2001.
GDP per capita, PPP	GDP per capita based on purchasing power parity (PPP). PPP GDP is gross domestic product converted to international dollars using purchasing power parity rates. An international dollar has the same purchasing power over GDP as the U.S. dollar has in the United States. GDP is the sum of gross value added by all resident producers in the economy plus any product taxes and minus any subsidies not included in the value of the products. It is calculated without making deductions for depreciation of fabricated assets or for depletion and degradation of natural resources. Data are in current international dollars. *Source*: World Bank World Development Indicators 2001.

Table 4A.2   (continued)

Population	Total population is based on the de facto definition of population, that counts all residents regardless of legal status or citizenship – except for refugees not permanently settled in the country of asylum, who are generally considered part of the population of their country of origin. *Source*: World Bank World Development Indicators 2001.
Openness	Error term from the linear regression of the share of export and import in GDP (measured in per cent) on the area and population of the country. *Source*: Constructed based on data from World Bank World Development Indicators 2001.
Fertility	Total fertility rate represents the number of children which would be born to a woman if she were to live to the end of her childbearing years and bear children in accordance with prevailing age-specific fertility rates. *Source*: World Bank World Development Indicators 2001.
Current level of democracy	Index of democracy. Scale from 0 to 10 with higher values corresponding to more democratic outcomes. *Source*: Polity IV Dataset.
Democratic traditions	Average index of democracy for the last 50 years. Scale from 0 to 10 with higher values corresponding to more democratic outcomes. *Source*: Constructed based on data from Polity IV Dataset.
Ethnolinguistic fractionalization	Index of ethnolinguistic fractionalization for the year 1985. Its value ranges from 0 to 1. *Source*: Roeder (2001).[4]

Notes:
1. Database can be found at http://www1.worldbank.org/publicsector/de centralization/dataondecen.htm.
2. Paper available at http://www.worldbank.org/wbi/governance/pdf/govmatters2.pdf.
3. Indexes can be found at http://www.gwdg.de/~uwvw/.
4. Philip G. Roeder (2001), 'Ethnolinguistic Fractionalization (ELF) Indices, 1961 and 1985', at http://weber.ucsd.edu/~proeder/elf.htm.

Table 4A.3   Summary Statistics (Over-Time Country Averages)

Variable	# of obs	Mean	SD	Min.	Max.
Share of subnational revenues	75	13.71	12.33	1.07	52.43
Share of subnational expenditures	73	16.46	13.56	1.74	55.16
Municipal executives elected	70	0.58	0.43	0	1
State executives elected	70	0.18	0.33	0	1
Fractionalization of governing parties	73	0.22	0.24	0	1
Average age of main parties	70	0.02	0.03	0	0.15
Proportional electoral rule	75	0.63	0.48	0	1
Parliamentary system	75	0.30	0.43	0	1
Level of DPT immunization	75	72.63	15.98	26.89	99.75
Negative of logarithm of infant mortality	75	−45.67	32.90	−141.59	−7.02
Negative of illiteracy level	68	−23.80	21.06	−76.37	−0.20
Negative of logarithm of pupil to teacher ratio	75	−28.96	11.47	−63.54	−11.23
Transparency International index of corruption	55	3.55	1.36	0.4	7.6
Index of government effectiveness	74	4.52	0.96	1.88	5.85
Index of regulation quality	75	2.91	0.64	1.57	3.79
Index of control over corruption	73	4.90	1.08	1.55	6.52
Index of rule of law	75	4.75	1.09	1.93	6.46

Table 4A.4   Correlation Coefficients (Over-Time Country Averages)

	Municipal executives elected	State executives elected	Fractional- ization of governing parties	Average age of main parties
Share of subnational revenues	0.06	0.13	0.02	0.27***
Municipal executives elected		0.49***	0.08	0.16*
State executives elected			−0.06	0.33***
Fractionalization of governing parties				−0.03

Note: ***Significant at 1 per cent level; *significant at 10 per cent level.

5. Democracy and State Effectiveness

Shaoguang Wang

In the late 1980s and early 1990s, when the 'third wave' of democratization reached its climax, many observers were very optimistic about the future of the unfolding 'worldwide democratic revolution'. Now, a decade and a half later, the optimism has faded. Still, as a legitimate form of government, democracy has become 'the only game in town' in nearly 100 countries. But among those countries, over a dozen have suffered democratic 'breakdowns' or 'reversals', and most transition states remain stuck in what Thomas Carothers calls a 'gray zone'. This is an atmosphere in which the word 'democracy' is often associated with such negative adjectives or prefixes as 'façade', 'phony', 'defective' 'partial', 'incomplete', 'illiberal', 'sham', 'ersatz', 'low intensity', 'semi-' and 'pseudo-' (Carothers 2002). This unexpected development has increasingly directed analytic attention away from explaining democratic transitions and consolidation toward assessing the quality of democracy.

Why does the quality of democracy vary from country to country? Or, more generally, what are the conditions for high-quality democracy? The standard answer to this question normally points to three key variables as preconditions for a stable democracy: a relatively high level of economic development (Lipset 1959; Fukuyama 1992; Barro 1999; Przeworski et al. 2000), a vibrant civil society (Putnam 1993; Linz and Stepan 1996) and a strong civic culture (Almond and Verba 1963; Inglehart 1997; Diamond 1999). There is no doubt that these are in fact attributes which characterize the old and stable democracies but are generally lacking in most of the transition countries. However, they are by no means the only characteristics which are absent in the majority of third-wave countries. Most of those countries also lack a coherent, functioning state.

The countries which once belonged to the Soviet Union or Yugoslavia had no national state institutions before they began transition. Throughout much of Sub-Saharan Africa, states exist but are largely incoherent, dysfunctional and unstable. Most of Latin America embarked on democratic transitions with 'a deep legacy of persistently poor performance of state institutions' (Carothers 2002). Elsewhere in the third world, transition away from authoritarian rule often unfolded in the context of extremely weak state structures. Interestingly, almost all of the countries with non-performing states are stuck in the 'gray zone'. The third-wave countries which faced little challenge regarding state building have made the most headway toward democracy. They are primarily countries in Southern and Central Europe, although there are also a few in South America and East Asia (Linz and Stepan 1996; Carothers 2002).

Based on this observation, a growing number of democracy activists and scholars have concluded that the presence of an effective state is a prerequisite for high-quality democracy (Rose and Shin 2001; Carothers 2002). Indeed, democracy is not only a type of political regime, but also a form of state governance. Democracy differs from other regimes in its distinctive mode of governance, but, as Bagehot (1949, 3–4) pointed out, every political system must gain authority and then use authority, because 'authority has to exist before it can be limited' (Huntington 1968, 8). If a government cannot perform basic state functions, no matter how democratic its form may be, the people of the country would not be able to benefit from it. In this sense, 'the issues pertaining to the state are logically prior to those concerning the political regime' (Przeworski 1995, 13). Without an effective state, no democracy is meaningful (Linz and Stepan 1996, 17).

The close association between the quality of democracy and state effectiveness is borne out by the Bertelsmann Transformation Index (BTI) for 2006. The BTI is a global ranking which evaluates transformation processes in 119 countries. The quantitative data collected are organized in two parallel indexes: the Status Index, that assesses the quality of a country's democracy, and the Management Index, that analyzes the quality of a country's governance. As Figure 5.1 shows, the correlation between the two variables is very strong ($R^2 = 0.8107$).[1]

The problem with the correlation presented in Figure 5.1 is that it remains unclear exactly how state effectiveness and the quality of democracy are interrelated. To date not much attention has been devoted in the literature to the specific channels through which state effectiveness may affect the quality of democracy. This exploratory study ventures to fill this scholarly lacuna. I begin by re-conceptualizing the 'quality of democracy' and 'state effectiveness' variables. Rather than treating them as one-dimensional phenomena, I disaggregate the two concepts. I then use the BTI dataset to investigate precisely how the components of state effectiveness affect different dimensions of the quality of democracy.

Figure 5.1   Bertelsmann Transformation Index, 2006

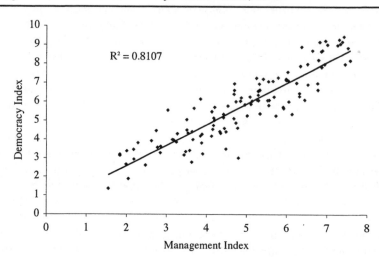

THE QUALITY OF DEMOCRACY

Assessing the quality of democracy first requires a clear definition of what democracy is. Conceptually, the word 'democracy' means a form of government in which the people rule. However, 'rule by the people' is an 'umbrella concept' (Jackman 1985) which contains multiple dimensions and thus is open to multiple understandings. Given the complexity of the concept, I will begin with a basic definition which both captures a set of common core characteristics of all subtypes of contemporary democracy ('democracy with adjectives'), and draws meaningful boundaries between this type of political system and others (Collier and Levitsky 1997).

Schumpeter's notion of electoral democracy provides a good starting point. By Schumpeter's standard, any system can be labeled as 'democratic' if there are recurring, free, competitive and fair elections for the country's most important officeholders (Schumpeter 1942). One consequence of using such a minimalist definition of democracy, however, is that many countries qualify as 'democracies'.[2] It provides no standard for distinguishing the more democratic cases from the less democratic ones.

A thicker version of democracy would be Robert Dahl's notion of 'polyarchy', the most frequently cited working definition of democracy in the last three decades. Dahl's concept of polyarchy has two dimensions: 'inclusiveness' and 'public contestation' (Dahl 1971, 4). Inclusiveness refers to participation, or more precisely, the right and opportunities for virtually all adults to vote and contest for office, while public contestation refers to opposition rights, or creating institutionalized channels for meaningful opposition by those who are adversely affected by government policies. According to Dahl, a political system cannot be considered a 'polyarchy' unless both inclusive participation and political competition are present. Notably, Dahl's notion of inclusiveness reflects the right to participate, not the actual degree of participation. Similarly, Dahl's notion of contestation allows for regular and open competition in – and between – elections, but it never implies that effective competition has to occur. Clearly, Dahl's polyarchy still is a minimalist or proceduralist definition of democracy. A political system which meets his two criteria is not necessarily a high-quality democracy.

Dahl's notion of polyarchy presupposes the existence of a third dimension, namely a set of legal conditions which safeguard basic civil and political liberties, because citizens' rights to articulate and organize around their political beliefs and interests must be guaranteed if participation and contestation are to be truly meaningful. In a strict sense, this is a dimension of liberalism rather than democracy. Nevertheless, such a dimension is indispensable to make a distinction between liberal and illiberal democracies (Zakaria 2003).

For Dahl, polyarchy is a relatively, but incompletely, democratized regime. Polyarchy at best is a necessary, but not a sufficient, condition for a high-quality democracy. He reserves the term 'democracy' for a political system characterized in part by 'the continuing responsiveness of the government to the preferences of its citizens, considered as political equals' (1971, 1). Even if such an ideal system does not actually exist, it can serve as 'a basis for estimating the degree to which various systems approach this theoretical limit' (1971, 2). If rulers are politically accountable to citizens, then the quality of democracy will be higher. This constitutes yet another dimension of democracy, one that concerns the extent to which any given democracy actualizes its potential as a political regime. This is a dimension which looks beyond institutional settings and formal procedures and instead measures the performance of those institutions in terms of their outcomes. This definition takes into account the notion that institutions and procedures are only the means to democracy, not the end. The presence of electoral competitiveness and civil and political freedom is no guarantee of democratic quality. There are countless cases where politicians, once elected, are only minimally responsive to citizen preferences.

In sum, Dahl effectively proposes a framework of four dimensions on which democracies can be evaluated in terms of quality.

Legal Conditions

Legal conditions measure the extent to which citizens, associations and communities enjoy civil and political freedoms on a more or less equal plane. The lack of such conditions makes opposition to the ruling elite and mass participation impossible. Even if all such conditions are present, however, a political system might be constitutionally liberal, but not democratic (Zakaria 2003, 19–20).

Competition

Competition measures 'the extent of permissible opposition, public contestation or political competition' (Dahl 1971, 4). Since a regime might permit opposition to either a very small or a very large proportion of the population to oppose the government, an additional dimension is needed as a supplementary component of democracy.

Participation

Participation measures the extent to which legal opportunities for mass participation are translated into tangible patterns of citizen behavior. Mass participation is important because it puts pressure on the government to be responsive and accountable. Equal political rights, however, only create the potential for citizen participation. In many countries, citizen apathy significantly hinders the realization of this potential. Wherever a large segment of the population is effectively disenfranchised, the system cannot be a high-quality democracy.

Responsiveness

Responsiveness measures the extent to which government policies correspond to citizen demands and preferences. This is indirectly indicated by the degree of citizen satisfaction with the quality of governance. Focusing on the 'input' side of the political system, the preceding dimensions neglect the actual performance and effectiveness of a system which comprises the 'output' side. Performance is crucial for the endurance of a democracy and must be considered when evaluating a system.

The main question underlying any assessment of the quality of democracy is how to differentiate between good and bad democracies. If democracies are rated along a single dimension, very different systems may be lumped together only because their scores are identical.[3] Building on Dahl's concept of democracy/polyarchy, I identify four dimensions of the quality of democracy. By disaggregating democracy into separate components, this framework allows for the development of more transparent conceptualization and more precise assessment of democracy.

Of course, these four dimensions might densely interact and reinforce one another. When this happens, it makes sense to assemble a summary index of democracy in a clear and meaningful way from the separate components. However, the four dimensions might also move in different directions. If this were the case, a single composite measure of democratic quality would not serve as a very useful analytical tool, because democracies which receive identical scores might consist of very different component parts. As long as the four variables do not always overlap, it is better to depict the quality of democracy as a multidimensional phenomenon and to assess the level of democratic development of each dimension individually. Thus, a high-quality democracy may not be high in every dimension of democracy. Conversely, different types of lower-quality democracies may be deficient along different dimensions.

Viewed from this perspective, perhaps all democracies suffer somewhat from uneven performance, although in different ways and in different degrees. Hence, there really can be no perfect democracy. All existing democracies are at best incomplete approximations of the democratic ideal. When the cutoff point is indistinct, a dichotomy of democracy/no democracy makes little sense. For this reason, the best strategy for assessing democratic quality is to examine in detail the extent to which various features of democracy are present, rather than insisting on the presence of certain features. By revealing the possibility of variable and sometimes inconsistent performance within a democratic polity, this disaggregated framework provides a basis for more accurate comparisons across different political systems.

STATE EFFECTIVENESS

To define state effectiveness first requires defining 'state'. In the Weberian sense, the state is a set of institutions which monopolize the legitimate use of force and rule making within a given territory. The monopolization of physical force is the very foundation of the state's existence, endowing the state with power to make authoritative, binding decisions and to perform other functions. Without power, a state cannot be effective.

Power, of course, has many faces. Following Mann, it is useful to distinguish two types of state power: despotic and infrastructural. Despotic refers to the power state elites can exercise 'without routine negotiation with civil society groups' (Mann 1993, 59). State despotic power is measured by the intrusiveness or extensiveness of state intervention. While such power is broad and sometimes unlimited in non-democratic settings, it is more constrained, albeit in different aspects and in varying degrees, in democratic systems. Infrastructural power, on the other hand, is measured by the effectiveness of state intervention. According to Mann, 'infrastructural power refers to the capacity of the state actually to penetrate civil society, and to implement logistically political decisions throughout the realm' (1986, 114). In terms of infrastructure, most powerful states are found in today's Western democracies, where the state's capacity to penetrate everyday life surpasses that of any historical or contemporary third world state. States in other times and other places may be intrusive and ruthless, but they often encounter enormous difficulties in penetrating people's social and economic lives. State infrastructural power in Western democracies, however, is so pervasive that their citizens cannot even find a 'hiding place from the infrastructural reach of the modern state' (Mann 1986, 114).

Despotic power and infrastructural power are analytically two independent aspects of state power. While the former designates the nature of the state (or regime type), the latter determines state effectiveness, defined as the state's capacity to perform its core functions for the majority of its people. Given the broad and growing scope of state activities, state effectiveness obviously is a complex and multidimensional phenomenon. No single index seems able to capture all aspects of state effectiveness. However, I believe that any effective states should possess the capacity to perform the following critical state functions (Pye 1966; Binder et al. 1971; Grew 1978).

Coercive Capacity: Monopolizing the Legitimate Use of Violence

By Weber's definition, the basic test of the existence of a state is whether or not its national government can lay claim to a monopoly of force in the territory under its jurisdiction. Obviously, the monopoly of force is a 'means' rather than an 'end' for the state. The end goal is to ward off external threats to the sovereignty and internal threats to social order. To achieve this goal, all states must build up and deploy armed forces and police, to defend against possible foreign invasion and to prevent and punish deviant conduct and repress social unrest, respectively. Clearly, if the territory of a country is carved up by foreign forces, its government cannot claim to be an effective state. Similarly, if several internal rival groups coexist in a country and all possess organized violence, then none would be in a position to establish permanent control over the contested territory. This situation is best described as 'statelessness'.

It is extremely important to develop a professional, resourceful, dedicated, disciplined and uniformed police. Repressive regimes are often called 'police states', but this is actually the wrong label. In fact, the ratio of police to population tends to be low in so-called police states, while it is much higher in so-called free countries (Shi 2001).

Extractive Capacity: Extracting Resources

A state monopoly on physical force does not come cheap. In order to do so, states needed to 'extract from the population a share of the yearly product of its economic activities' (Poggi 1990, 66). As early as the sixteenth century, when the modern nation-state had just begun to emerge, Jean Bodin had already realized, 'Financial means are the nerves of the state' (cited in Kugler and Domke 1986, 45).

In the last century or so, the scope of state operations has expanded considerably. It is the availability of resources which permits the state to carry out its new tasks. To finance bigger governments, states need to explore more productive extractive devices. In the past, states raised revenue mainly through such mechanisms as military or colonial ventures, the sale of offices, tax farming, monopolies, donations and even drawing on state elites' private wealth (Poggi 1978, 97). Now, 'the regular, unobtrusive levying of taxes on various phases and aspects of the modernized economic process' has largely replaced those less efficient instruments (Poggi 1990, 66). As a result, in Western democracies government spending typically tripled, quintupled or grew even further in the twentieth century (Poggi 1990, 109–10). At present, it commonly accounts for one-third to one-half of the gross domestic products (GDP) in those countries.

Elsewhere, state extractive capacity varies greatly from country to country and generally is much weaker. Nevertheless, an effective state has to be fiscally viable. A state which is unable to generate sufficient resources for realizing its policy goals cannot be effective.

Assimilative Capacity: Shaping National Identity

Backed by extractive capacity, coercive capacity is the most basic aspect of state power. But it would be extremely costly to maintain domestic peace by coercion alone. For any political system to operate effectively there must be some shared identities among its population. This is especially true in diverse societies.

In the early phases of state development in the West, and in the third world today, the state has been one among many autonomous power centers which compete for people's loyalty. Thus, the construction of state coercive and extractive capacities must be followed by rationalization of authority and nation building. Rationalizing authority refers to the centralization of political power, involving the replacement of traditional familial, local, religious and ethnic authorities by a single, secular, national authority. Nation building means 'internal homogenization' (Tilly 1975, 661), involving the transformation of peoples' 'commitment and loyalty from smaller tribes, villages, or petty principalities to the larger central political system, creating a common national culture of loyalty and commitment' (Almond and Powell 1966, 36). The breakup of the Soviet Union, Yugoslavia and Czechoslovakia and ethnic conflicts in Indonesia, Sri Lanka and many African countries vividly demonstrate how the absence of national identity can be a powerful centrifugal force.

It is true that multiethnic and multicultural states normally have greater difficulties in winning and maintaining the allegiance of diverse populations. But this observation should not lead to the conclusion that ethnic, cultural, religious or linguistic identity is primordially given, and thereby any effort to shape a national identity in such diverse societies is doomed to failure. Since almost all nations started out as very diverse culturally, linguistically, religiously or ethnically, the presence of strong national identities in some but not others suggests that identity is amendable. In other words, the formation of national identity is best understood as an outcome of purposeful state efforts to overcome heterogeneity in the society, although some exogenous historical accidents may also affect the outcome. If a society is fragmented, opportunistic politicians might choose to exacerbate minuscule differences to pursue their personal interests. This is 'more likely a consequence of institutional failure rather than a cause of it' (Przeworski 1995, 21). If states are unable to mold national identity, they are unlikely to be effective, because a great deal more resources and energy would have to be diverted to fighting against centrifugal forces.

Regulatory Capacity: Regulating Society and Economy

Regulative capacity is defined as the ability of the state to change and subordinate the behavior of individuals and groups away from their own inclination and in favor of the behavior prescribed by the state.

Regulations are necessary because modern societies are full of hazards engendered from industrialization, commercialization, urbanization and asymmetrical distributions of power and information. To protect people and nature, the state needs to regulate not only such clearly deviant social activities as murder and assault, but also many aspects of economic and social life, such as weights and measures, contracts, road construction, public utilities, food and drug quality, garbage collection, mail delivery, labor–management relations, safety standards, traffic, welfare, environmental protection, health, education, sports, marriage, the arts and even parental responsibilities.

It is not easy for the state to regulate society and the economy. To facilitate effective regulation, for example, the state must collect and store a massive amount of information about everyone living and working in the country. In developed countries, this is not a problem. The state constantly monitors numerous aspects of daily life, including births, education, marriages, divorces, occupation, income, deeds and titles, immigration and even deaths. Nothing seems to escape state screening. In the developing world, however, even statistics on such basic items as population size and distribution are often deficient, not to mention information about mobile tax bases or food-handling practices. For countries which are not capable of monitoring the whereabouts and behaviors of their populations, it is unrealistic to expect their states to possess much regulatory capacity.

In today's world, well-ordered societies, whether democratic or not, are highly regulated. Where governments lack adequate regulatory capacity, again whether democratic or not, people there typically have to put up with frequent industrial accidents, environmental disasters, foul water, inadequate sewage systems, chaotic traffic, appalling work conditions, tense labor–management relations, shoddy consumer products, horrendous medical services and the like. The contrast between the two types of countries clearly points to the significance of regulatory capacity for any modern state.

Steering Capacity: Maintaining Internal Coherence of State Institutions

The state relies upon its bureaucracy to perform the above four key functions. To be effective in those areas, the state has to make the bureaucracy professionalized and meritocratic, so that its recruits have the technical talent and requisite training to be competent for tasks assigned to them. Just as important from the perspective of the state is maintenance of the internal coherence of bureaucratic institutions. The modern bureaucracy is a complex and sophisticated organization made up of multiple, yet minute organs. Although all the activities of the bureaucracy are, in theory, directed from a single center, system coherence can be undercut by the departmentalism of government agencies, and the particularism and corruption of individual government officials.

There are many cases where political executives' policymaking efforts are thwarted by the bureaucracy not so much because it intends deliberately to sabotage those political leaders as because large organizations tend to proceed from inertia and to persist in their routine unless stopped. In addition, bureaucrats and their organizations tend to believe that they understand the policy area in question better than the political leaders (Peters 1987). A more acute problem with bureaucracy, however, is that each agency 'seeks to maximize the state resources it commands, and to assign priority to its own concerns over all others' (Poggi 1990, 30–31). This kind of desire may motivate bureaucratic agencies to intentionally hinder or block the collection of vital information for centralized decision making and to involve agencies in pointless competition against each other. As a result, the ultimate authority of the state may find it difficult, if not impossible, to enforce its policy agenda and to prevent its agents from deserting their strictly implementary role. The corporate coherence of the state then becomes the casualty of 'bureaucratic free enterprise' (Tullock 1965).

The more detrimental problem with the bureaucracy, especially among third world countries, is particularism and corruption. Rather than dehumanize the administrative process, as expected by Max Weber (1946, 215–16), officials who practice particularism allow love, hatred and other personal factors to affect decisions made in the name of the state. Corrupt officials also give preferentiality to people related to them in the execution of state directives, not out of emotion, but out of careful calculation of potential gains and risks (Rose-Ackerman 1999). Despite the difference in motive, both particularism and corruption impair the impartiality of public administration, breed a distrust of public authorities, set off political alienation and, in extreme cases, may even lead to system breakdowns (Klitgaard 1988).

A well-functioning state is supposed to operate as a machine 'propelled by energy and directed by information flowing from a single center in the service of a plurality of coordinated tasks'(Poggi 1978, 98). Where government institutions do not mesh with each other and particularism and corruption are rampant, intrastate and state–society conflicts are bound to increase, thus undercutting the ability of the whole system to control the flow of tax resources and to achieve other policy goals.

Redistributive Capacity: Distributing Resources

The redistributive capacity refers to the authoritative redistribution of scarce resources among different social groups. The purpose of redistribution is to provide the least fortunate members of the society with economic security, as well as to reduce inequality in income and wealth distribution. Urbanization, high literacy levels and the demonstration effect from Western welfare states have all increased the volume and intensity of pressures on governments everywhere to mitigate social risks and to narrow the gaps between the 'haves' and 'have nots' through some forms of redistribution. Some analysts contend that, since the welfare state is primarily a Western luxury which only rich countries can afford, the effectiveness of a state should not be measured by its redistributive capacity (Gros 1996). To the extent that inequality often increases the probability of political instability (Alesina et al. 1996; Alesina and Perotti 1996), redistributive capacity helps maintain domestic public order and enhance its legitimacy. Given the importance of public order and legitimacy for any regime, the instrumental value of redistribution should not be underestimated.

The first two sets of functions mentioned above can define any state. Even pre-modern states were characterized by the creation of regular armies and a taxation system (Weber 1978, I: 54–6). The other four functions are features of the modern nation-state, that create broad 'routine, formalized, rationalized institutions' which affect not only its citizens, but also to a very large extent all actions taking place in the areas of its jurisdiction (Mann 1993, 56). If a state is capable of performing all of those functions well, it is an effective state. If a state is only capable of performing some of the functions, it is a weak or fragile state. When a state is incapable of performing any of those functions, it can legitimately be classified as a failed state.

RELATIONSHIPS BETWEEN STATE EFFECTIVENESS AND THE QUALITY OF DEMOCRACY

Since both state effectiveness and the quality of democracy are multidimensional concepts, the statement that an effective state is a prerequisite of high-quality democracy appears to be elusive. The real question becomes which state capacity is fatal to which dimension of democratic quality. Based upon a set of data on 119 countries, this section intends to delve into this issue. My data are drawn from a wide range of sources (see Appendix 5A.1). The dataset covers the majority of the world's 193 independent states, but excludes two groups of countries; namely full-fledged industrialized democracies in Europe and North America and mini-states with a population of less than three million inhabitants.

Measuring the Quality of Democracy

The most serious difficulty related to a cross-country study of democratic quality is how to measure properly the four dimensions discussed above. Time and financial constraints preclude constructing a new dataset from a massive data collection effort. However, many other empirical studies of democratic quality have successfully used pre-existing datasets.

The quantitative measures of democratic performance started with Dahl's seminal work *Polyarchy* (1971), which measured the performance of 114 states against his two minimalist criteria: political contestation and the right to electoral participation. Since then, a variety of instruments for measuring democracy have been developed and widely used. Examples include the Vanhanen Index, the Polity Index by Jaggers and Gurr, and the Freedom House Index.[4] Covering over 150 countries, these indexes all presume two-dimensionality. Regardless of differences in their particular ways of conceptualization and operationalization, the indexes share at least one key feature: they do not go much beyond Dahl's concept of polyarchy (rather than his more demanding definition of democracy) and focus almost exclusively on institutional and procedural aspects of democracy.

Recently, Germany's Bertelsmann Foundation and its academic partner, the Center for Applied Policy Research at Munich University, have developed a Transformation Index (BTI).[5] The BTI first decomposes the democratization process into five separate dimensions (stateness, political participation, rule of law, institutional stability, and political and social integration) and then recomposes them into a single composite index which they call the 'Status Index (democracy)'. Although the BTI provides a detailed profile of each country's performance along the five dimensions and thus enables readers to reconstruct their own ranking of all countries, its framework of disaggregated criteria nevertheless differs from what is needed here.

Only the Economist Intelligence Unit's democracy index (Economist Intelligence Unit 2007) comes close to the understanding of what makes up democracy which is presented here. The index is based on five categories: civil liberties, electoral process and pluralism, political participation, the functioning of government and political culture. The first four bear a resemblance to the four dimensions identified earlier as the essential components of democracy; namely legal conditions, competition, participation and responsiveness.

Excluding the category of political culture, the calculation of the Economist Intelligence Unit's index relies upon ratings for 52 indicators. The number of indicators included in each category varies, ranging from 9 in political participation to 12 in electoral process and pluralism, to 14 in functioning of government and 17 in civil liberties.

A crucial aspect of the Economist Intelligence Unit's index is that it combines the advantages of both qualitative and quantitative methods. While scores on most indicators are based on expert coding of narrative reports, it also uses, wherever available, public opinion surveys, including the World Values Survey, the Eurobarometer surveys, the Latin American Barometer, Gallup polls and national surveys.

The 'political participation' category is a good example. Participation is not merely measured by the right to electoral participation, but by voter turnout rates, adult literacy rates, adult citizens' interest in political issues, the extent of membership in political parties, non-governmental organizations and social movements, the degree of citizen engagement with politics, the percentage of women in parliament and the government's effort to promote political participation. Participation in these respects is intimately related to political equality, because, even if formal rights of participation are upheld for all, inequalities in the distribution of resources can make it much more difficult for lower-status individuals to exercise their democratic rights of participation.

Similarly, the category of 'functioning of government' includes three groups of indicators of government responsiveness. The first group measures the extent to which elected representatives can make and enforce government policy free of undue influence by foreign countries, domestic regional power centers, the military or security services, bureaucrats and special pressure groups. The second group of indicators focuses on horizontal accountability or, more specifically, whether there is an effective system of checks and balances on the exercise of public authority by different government institutions. The last group measures vertical accountability, or government responsiveness to the expectations, interests, needs and demands of citizens. On top of the three groups of indicators, the category of 'functioning of government' also measures government responsiveness by using survey data to examine how many people have a 'great deal' or 'quite a lot' of confidence in the government. Presumably, a high-quality democracy features high levels of citizen trust in democratic rule, while a low-quality democracy features low levels of such trust.

For all categories, each indicator of the Economist Intelligence Unit's index is first rated on a two- or three-point scale. Then the individual indicator scores in a category are aggregated into a category index, converted to a scale of zero to ten. The higher the aggregate score in a category, presumably, the higher the quality of democracy along this dimension.

I use the resulting indexes of the four categories in the Economist Intelligence Unit's democracy index as the proxy measures for my four dimensions of the quality of democracy: legal conditions (CONDITIONS), competition (COMPETITION), participation (PARTICIPATION) and responsiveness (RESPONSIVENESS). Together, they help reveal how and to what degree each dimension is present in different countries. A country which has high scores in one dimension may fall in others, and vice versa. This means that I can shift from a single verdict on whether or not a whole regime can legitimately be called democratic to a pluralist judgment which allows the possibility of varying degrees of democracy in its different parts.

Independent Variables: State Effectiveness

None of the six dimensions of state effectiveness discussed in the previous section is directly observable. Therefore, I use the following six indicators as their proxies.

Coercive capacity is measured by age-standardized death rates (per 100,000) caused by interpersonal violence in 2002 (VIOLENCE). This is a substitute for murder rates. There are currently three main sources of global homicide data: the International Criminal Police Organization (Interpol), the United Nations and the World Health Organization (Marshall and Block 2004). I use the WHO data (2004). Although interpersonal-violence-related mortality includes deaths due to homicide, sexual assault, neglect and abandonment and other forms of maltreatment, this measure is highly correlated ($R^2 = 0.6482$) with the UN's data on murder rates (UNODC 2001). In 2000 an estimated 520,000 people worldwide died as a result of interpersonal violence. Among them, 95 per cent of homicides occurred in the low- and middle-income countries (WHO 2002). Apparently, the lower a country's coercive capacity is, the higher its murder rate tends to be.

Extractive capacity is calculated as the proportion of total GDP extracted as revenue by all levels of government in 2003 (REVENUE).

Assimilative capacity is indicated via the BTI 'stateness' index (CONSENSUS), which measures the extent to which people accept the statehood of their country and reach fundamental agreement about who qualifies as a citizen of the state (Bertelsmann Foundation 2006). The index is differentiated into ten different levels, with one representing the worst rating and ten representing the best.

The indicator of regulatory capacity is road traffic deaths per 100,000 persons in 2002 (TRAFFICDEATH) (WHO 2004). In 2000 an estimated 1.26 million people worldwide died as a result of road traffic injuries. Approximately 90 per cent of all road traffic injury deaths occurred in the low- and middle-income countries (WHO 2002). Although there are other determinants of traffic death rates (e.g., weather, geography and the number of vehicles), a government's ability to enforce its traffic regulations concerning road conditions, speed limits, license requirements, drunk driving, seat belt usage and vehicle quality is definitely one of the most important reasons for differences in death rates between countries. Regulatory quality in this area may very well reflect a system's overall regulatory capacity.

The indicator of steering capacity is the World Bank Institute's 2006 Control of Corruption Index (CONTROCOR), which provides country scores ranging between −2.5 and 2.5, with higher scores corresponding to greater perceived control of corruption (World Bank 2006a). Rampant corruption is certainly a symptom of weak steering capacity. Conversely, a state with strong steering capacity would be able to detect, punish and minimize corruption in its political, administrative and judicial branches. There are now a variety of alternative corruption measures available. They are highly correlated. For example, the correlation between the World Bank's corruption measure and Transparency International's measure for 2006 (Transparency International 2006) is as high as 0.89. The World Bank Institute's data have the advantage of including more countries and relying on more corruption perception surveys than the Transparency International data.

Finally, redistributive capacity is calculated using the UNDP Human Development Index (HDI) for 2003; it measures the average achievements in a country in three basic dimensions of human well-being: a long and healthy life, knowledge and a decent standard of living (UNDP 2006). Based upon these criteria, nations are given scores from zero to one. Those countries which are closest to one have the best quality of life in the world. By definition, human development involves an improvement in the relative access to resources of excluded groups, implying redistribution. In other words, human development is impossible to achieve unless there is redistribution.

In order to minimize possible omitted variable bias in our analysis, I also include four control variables:

AREA	the land area of the country in thousands of square kilometers;
POPULATION	the size of a country's population in millions in 2003;
FRACTIONALIZATION	an ethnolinguistic fractionalization index measuring the probability that two randomly selected persons from a given country will not belong to the same ethnolinguistic group. The higher the number, the more fractionalized the society; and
PCGNI	Per capita gross national income at purchasing power parities (PPP) for 2004, this serves as an aggregate indicator of socioeconomic development.

Theoretically, there are strong reasons to believe that each of these controls influences the quality of democracy directly or indirectly. Country size, for instance, may have some bearing on state effectiveness. The larger the geographical area and the population size, the more difficult vertical integration and horizontal coordination become. Moreover, if a country encompasses many religious, racial, ethnic and linguistic groups, it would be more difficult for the people to consider themselves as the members of the same community, and for the state to govern. Finally, according to a very substantial and convincing literature, the level of socioeconomic development is strongly correlated with democracy (Lipset 1959).

FINDINGS

Having operationalized dependent and independent variables, it is time to answer the question regarding the relationships between state effectiveness and the quality of democracy. I address this question by running multivariate regression analysis of the dependent variables on all the independent variables identified above. Table 5.1 presents the results from four regression models, that employ, respectively, legal conditions, competition, participation and responsiveness as the dependent variables. The coefficients reported in the table are standardized ones (β) and may be interpreted as showing the net contribution or effect of each of the independent variables listed at the left, holding constant all other factors.

Due to the interrelated nature of the set of variables included in the analyses (e.g. VIOLENCE and TRAFFICDEATH, HDI and PCGNI), I also examine variance inflation factors (VIFs) for all of the independent variables appearing in the models to assess potential multicollinearity problems. The VIFs take values in the numerical range. The higher the value of the VIF, the stronger the evidence of multicollinearity. A generally accepted rule of thumb is to avoid VIFs bigger than ten (Hamilton 1992; Neter et al. 1996; Hair et al. 1998; Miles and Shevlin 2001), although some authors suggest that a value over five is already a symptom of undesirable multicollinearity effects (Judge et al. 1988). Table 5.1 reveals that the maximum VIF is 4.74, which is nowhere near the rule-of-thumb cutoff of ten. Multicollinearity problems, therefore, are not severe for any of the models discussed below.

Among the explanatory variables, the strongest and most consistent association with all dimensions of the quality of democracy is found in the case of CONSENSUS, the proxy for state assimilative capacity. The coefficients on this variable are universally positive and sizable and statistically significant at the level of 0.01.

Such results indicate support for Dahl's thesis that a democracy presupposes a well-defined territorial–social unit and population and a shared identity associated with the land among the people, because democratic methods 'cannot solve the problem of the proper scope and domain of democratic units' (Dahl 1989, 207). The majority principle, for example, would not work without knowing where the boundary of the political community is and who qualifies as a member of the community. Thus, if large segments of the population in a territorial–social unit refuse to accept the unit as an appropriate entity to

Table 5.1   Results of Four Regression Models

	CONDITIONS	COMPETITION	PARTICIPATION	RESPONSIVENESS
	(a)	(b)	(c)	(d)
Control variables				
AREA	−.052	−.007	−.044	−.067
POPULATION	−.011	−.028	.081	.198**
FRACTIONALIZATION	−.005	−.028	.032	−.009
PCGNI	−.113	−.172	.003	−.132
Explanatory variables				
VIOLENCE	.276***	.234**	.187**	.155*
REVENUE	−.061	−.040	.150*	.008
CONSENSUS	.331***	.347***	.323***	.306***
TRAFFICDEATH	−.339***	−.292***	−.194*	−.255***
CONTROCOR	.374***	.294*	.075	.512***
HDI	.144	.180	.305**	.104
Model F	8.517***	6.120***	6.759***	11.108***
Adjusted R^2	.404	.316	.342	.477
VIF (maximum)	4.74	4.74	4.74	4.74
No. of observations	112	112	112	112

Notes: t-ratios *$p < 0.1$; **$p < 0.05$; ***$p < 0.01$ (all two-sided). VIF refers to variance inflation factor and values above 10 are indications of multicollinearity inflating the R-square.

make legitimate decisions and desire to create their independent states or to merge with other states, democratic procedure can neither work nor solve the problem of identity. Here the key challenge for the state is to cultivate a strong identification with the territorial–social unit. Whatever the means used to resolve the stateness problem,[6] only when the vast majority of people 'have no doubt or mental reservations as to which political community they belong to' (Rustow 1970, 351) is it possible for them to craft democratic norms, establish democratic institutions and organize their life in a democratic fashion.

TRAFFICDEATH has negative coefficients across all four regressions. Since TRAFFICDEATH is measured by death rates related to road traffic, higher rates denote weak, rather than strong, state regulatory capacity. Hence, these negative signs mean that regulatory capacity is positively associated with all four dimensions of the quality of democracy, albeit the level of significance for PARTICIPATION ($p < 0.1$) being lower than that for the other three dimensions ($p < 0.01$).

The results are not surprising. Democracy is a rule-intensive polity. It is hard to imagine how democracy could operate if there were no rules with regard to citizenship, elections, distribution of power, relationships among different branches of government, etc. The guidance provided by those rules enables political actors to coordinate their behavior, thus helping reduce uncertainty and create order in human interactions. Without a set of elaborate, clear and non-contingent rules, democracy cannot function. However, it is unrealistic to expect rules to be self-enforceable. The threat of state sanction is imperative to ensure compliance. The legal provision of civil rights provides a useful example. As the cases of Russia and many other transition and developing countries have made excruciatingly clear, liberties could be threatened just as thoroughly by state incapacity as by repressive state apparatus. This observation leads Stephen Holmes to conclude, 'Liberal rights depend essentially on the competent exercise of a certain kind of legitimate public power'. State power is needed to guard property rights, to prevent harm, to repress force, to contain fraud and, above all, to extend its protection to the vulnerable. Viewed from this angle, rather than a threat to personal freedoms, a liberal state is 'the largest and most reliable human rights organization' and 'a non-performing state cannot be a liberal state' (Holmes 1997).

CONTROCOR is the proxy for state steering capacity. A state with strong steering capacity should be able to detect and punish corrupt officials and government employees peremptorily and harshly. Scholars have long debated the impact of democracy on perceived national levels of corruption. While some find that democracy has no significant effect on corruption (Ades and Di Tella 1999), others conclude that democracy can help inhibit corruption (Sandholtz and Koetzle 2000; Montinola and Jackman 2002; Shen and Williamson 2005). Yet other studies discover that the relationship is not straightforward but contingent on a variety of conditions (Treisman 2000). In this study it is clear that the quality of democracy tends to be higher in countries where the state possesses strong steering capacity. This is the case if the quality of democracy is measured by CONDITIONS, COMPETITION and RESPONSIVENESS. Only in the area of PARTICIPATION does the steering capacity have no significant effect on the quality of democracy.

REVENUE is a proxy for state extractive capacity. Interestingly, extractive capacity seems to be negatively associated with two formal and procedural dimensions of democracy (CONDITIONS and COMPETITION), even though both relationships are not statistically significant. In the case of RESPONSIVENESS, the coefficient carries the right positive sign, but again is not statistically significant. PARTICIPATION is the only exception where state extractive capacity appears to have strengthened the quality of democracy, albeit marginally.

Why does state extractive capacity not matter as much as we expected? First, recall that the purpose of resource extraction is to 'lubricate' the state machine so that it can function properly. All states need to extract material resources, but the amount should be restrained rather than excessive. That is why nobody has ever suggested that higher extraction is always better. There must be a sort of threshold, beyond which further extraction would only make things worse rather than better. Second, much of what the state does costs nothing or very little, especially in the areas that concern the operation of democracy. Third, the state may choose to offload many of its responsibilities to private or semi-private agencies. Fourth, some states may make more efficient use of resources than others may. Thus, two countries extracting the same proportion of resources from their populations may be very different in terms of real capacity. Finally, and perhaps most importantly, since other state functions have already been controlled for in the models, it is possible that extractive capacity by itself has no independent effect on certain dimensions of the quality of democracy.

State redistributive capacity is gauged with the measure of HDI. The four coefficients associated with the variable all bear positive signs, suggesting that countries with strong redistributive capacity tend to have high-quality democracy, although statistical significance is not obtained as far as the dimensions of CONDITIONS, COMPETITION and RESPONSIVENESS are concerned. Only in the case of PARTICIPATION are the size and significance of the effect indubitably clear. This, of course, makes sense. Here PARTICIPATION refers to the real extent to which ordinary citizens involve themselves in politics, not just the legal rights to do so. It is a well-established fact that material welfare influences whether and how citizens participate in democratic politics. For example, individuals who are below the median income in society have been repeatedly found less likely to participate in elections, while those above the median income are more likely to do so. For that reason, countries with high levels of socioeconomic inequality tend to have lower levels of political participation (Franzese 1998; La Ferrara 2002; Solt 2004). Redistribution may narrow socioeconomic gaps between classes and thereby help overcome the resources problem for the least advantaged at the bottom of society. Consequently, countries which decouple the connection between work and welfare tend to have higher rates of political participation (Anderson and Beramendi 2005). That is why, unlike the other aspects of democratic quality, political participation can be increased when redistribution brings people closer to the middle from either extreme of the spectrum.

The most surprising outcome in this analysis is that all four dimensions of the quality of democracy are positively affected by the level of VIOLENCE. As pointed out above, VIOLENCE stands for death rates caused by interpersonal violence. High rates are a symptom of weak state coercive capacity. It is therefore expected that lower levels of VIOLENCE will be associated with a higher quality of democracy. The actual relationships, however, turn out to be positive and statistically significant, implying that strong coercive capacity is counterproductive to increases in democracy scores. It is hard to be sure what this means, but there are two possibilities.

First, perhaps coercive capacity is a double-edged sword. A state which is strong in containing violent crime may also be capable of repressing people's democratic desire. Conversely, when state coercive capacity is weak or has become weaker, a democratic system is more likely to survive, but violent crime may run rampant. There is at least some indirect evidence to support this conjecture. For example, a growing number of empirical studies have shown that rapid increases in violent crime appear to have coincided with democratization in many regions of the world. Examples include Eastern Europe and the republics of the former Soviet Union (Hraba et al. 1998; Barak 2000; Backman 1998; Savelsberg 1995), Latin America (Fajnzylber, Lederman and Loayza 1998; Mendez, O'Donnell and Pinheiro 1999) and Sub-Saharan Africa (Reza, Mercy and Krug 2000; Daniel, Southall and Lutchman 2005). It is possible that the two parallel trends can both be attributed to the demise of autocratic regimes and the collateral damage done to state coercive capacity.

Second, homicide rates may not be a good indicator of state coercive capacity in the first place. Perhaps state coercive capacity is but one determinant of violence. Besides the government, the criminal justice system and the police, demographic, economic, social and cultural factors may play equally important or more important roles in crime control (Kelling 1998; Neild 1999). There is also indirect evidence to hold up this conjecture. One study observes, 'By the 1960s, the long-term decline of violent crime rates in many of the established Western democracies had stalled. In fact, in recent decades, several Western democracies have experienced abrupt and serious increases in street crime rates' (Karstedt and Lafree 2006, 8). Another study even finds, '[T]he longer a country remains democratic, the higher its homicide rates' (Lafree and Tseloni 2006, 43). If both claims are true, we have to question if homicide rates (or their proxy) can really serve as a gauge of state coercive capacity, because those industrialized countries certainly have no problem in monopolizing the legitimate use of violence and their overall coercive capacity has not crumbled in the past 45 years.

Unfortunately, the data do not permit a confident judgment regarding which conjecture is right.

Regarding the controls, the physical size of a country is found to be negatively associated with all dimensions of the quality of democracy, but the association is never statistically significant at conventional confidence levels. As for the size of population, the effects are not consistent. The parameter estimates for this variable are negative and insignificant for the two formal and procedural dimensions – CONDITIONS and COMPETITION, but positive for the more substantive dimensions – PARTICIPATION and RESPONSIVENESS. In the case of PARTICIPATION, the coefficient is even statistically significant. There does not seem to be much evidence to bear out a hypothesis that has interested some scholars: large countries, other things being equal, tend to be inferior in terms of democratic quality.

The variable FRACTIONALIZATION is not significant for any of the four regressions regardless of the signs of its estimated coefficients. This implies that the heterogeneity of the population has no independent impact on the quality of democracy once the variables measuring state effectiveness, especially the one that measure stateness, are controlled.

Similar observations can be made for PCGNI, the measure of the level of socioeconomic development, that is not significantly correlated with any dimension of the quality of democracy. This suggests that economic prosperity as such does not affect the quality of democracy one way or another, a finding that contradicts the standard modernization hypothesis.

CONCLUSION

This study starts with an emerging consensus that the presence of an effective state is a prerequisite for high-quality democracy (Rose and Shin 2001). As the so-called third wave demonstrates, democratization can occur anywhere, including 'the most unlikely and unexpected places' such as Albania and Mauritania, but consolidated and high-quality democracies are much harder to find because many of the third-wave countries do not have effective governments (Carothers 2002). This study contributes to the growing literature on the quality of democracy by offering an extended analysis on how exactly different dimensions of state effectiveness affect different dimensions of democracy.

To summarize the findings here, the quality of democracy tends to be higher in countries where the states possess strong assimilative capacity (CONSENSUS), regulatory capacity (TRAFFICDEATH) and steering capacity (CONTROCOR). It does not seem to matter which dimension of democracy is considered or whether these countries are large or small (in terms of geographical or population size), homogeneous or heterogeneous and developed or developing. Extractive capacity (REVENUE) and redistributive capacity (HDI) are, in general, not related to the quality of democracy, once the other dimensions of state effectiveness are controlled for. However, they are essential for the PARTICIPATION dimension of democracy. Finally, the regressions on the indicator of state coercive capacity (VIOLENCE) produce results that stand in sharp contrast with expectations and deserve further attention.

In conclusion, the results of this analysis confirm that state effectiveness has a positive effect on democratic performance, but the impacts of different dimensions of state effectiveness vary across different attributes of democracy, suggesting it is imperative to avoid a single-dimensional composite measure of either democracy or state effectiveness.[7]

If these findings are valid, then it would be foolish, if not suicidal, for democratic reformers intentionally or unintentionally to undermine or weaken state institutions in the process of democratization, especially in those countries where states are nonexistent or extremely weak to begin with. Of course, during the democratic transition, the ways state power is exercised must change, but state power itself should not be impaired. Rather than single-mindedly trying to restrain state power, democratic reformers should make more efforts to build national state institutions where none existed before and to strengthen state capacities wherever they are weak.

NOTES

1. The composition of the Status Index in Figure 5.1 is elaborated below. Indeed, the correlation in Figure 5.1 seems too strong, calling into question both the conceptualization of variables and the devices used to measure them. Since the Bertelsmann group used the same experts to arrive at both scores, it was possible for these 'objective observers' instinctively to assume that 'all good things must go together' (Schmitter 2005).
2. For instance, Freedom House assigned the designation 'electoral democracy' to 123 countries in its 2006 ranking. See http://www.freedomhouse.org/template.cfm?page=269andyear=200.
3. For example, in 2006 Freedom House assigned its highest rating (1.0) to countries as diverse as Barbados, Cyprus, Dominica, Finland, Switzerland and Uruguay. See http://www.freedomhouse.org/template.cfm?page=267andyear=2006.
4. For a detailed introduction of, and comment on, the three indices, please see National Centres of Competence in Research (2005).
5. All country reports and ranking results are freely accessible on the internet at www.bertelsmann-transformation-index.de.
6. In Western Europe, the process of nation building was generally guided by coercive governments, which used a wide range of instruments to repress and eliminate multilingualism and multiculturalism in their territories. The resultant nation-states defined the political communities within which democratization could take place (Linz and Stepan 1996, 33–7). Although those methods are not acceptable by today's moral standards, the lesson from the first wave of democratization is that nation building should precede democratization.
7. Since this is an exploratory study which is based upon limited data, whatever conclusions this study may draw, they should be seen as tentative rather than as conclusive. I only hope that the findings point to a new avenue of inquiry in the empirical study of the relationship between state effectiveness and the quality of democracy.

BIBLIOGRAPHY

Ades, Alberto and Rafael Di Tella (1999), 'Rents, Competition, and Corruption', *American Economic Review*, **89** (4), 982–3.

Alesina, Alberto and Roberto Perotti (1996), 'Income Distribution, Political Instability and Investment', *European Economic Review*, **40** (6), 1203–28.

Alesina, Alberto, Sule Ozler, Nouriel Roubini and Philip Swagel (1996), 'Political Instability and Economic Growth', *Journal of Economic Growth*, **1** (2), 189–211.

Almond, Gabriel and G. Bingham Powell, Jr (1966), *Comparative Politics: A Developmental Approach*, Boston: Little, Brown and Company.

Almond, Gabriel and Sidney Verba (1963), *The Civic Culture: Political Attitudes and Democracy in Five Nations*, Princeton: Princeton University Press.

Anderson, Christopher J. and Pablo Beramendi (2005), 'Economic Inequality, Redistribution, and Political Inequality', paper presented at the Syracuse University, Maxwell School of Citizenship and Public Affairs conference 'Income Inequality, Representation, and Democracy: Europe in Comparative Perspective', Syracuse, NY, 6–7 May.

Backman, Johan (1998), *The Inflation of Crime in Russia: The Social Danger of the Emerging Markets*, Helsinki, Finland: National Research Institute of Legal Policy.

Bagehot, Walter (1949), *The English Constitution*, London: Oxford World's Classics.

Barak, Gregg (ed.) (2000), Crime and Crime Control: A Global View, Westport, CT: Greenwood.

Barro, Robert (1999), 'Determinants of Democracy', *Journal of Political Economy*, **107** (6), 158–83.

Bertelsmann Foundation (2006), 'The Bertelsmann Transformation Index (BTI) at http://www.bertelsmann-transformation-index.de.

Binder, Leonard, James S. Coleman, Joseph LaPalombara, Lucian W. Pye, Sidney Verba and Myron Weiner (1971), *Crisis and Sequences in Political Development*, Princeton: Princeton University Press.

Carothers, Thomas (2002), 'The End of the Transition Paradigm', *Journal of Democracy*, **13** (1), 5–21.

Collier, David and Steven Levitsky (1997), 'Democracy with Adjectives: Conceptual Innovation in Comparative Research', *World Politics*, **49** (3), 430–51.

Dahl, Robert A. (1971), *Polyarchy: Participation and Opposition*, New Haven, CT: Yale University Press.

——(1989), *Democracy and Its Critics*, New Haven, CT: Yale University Press.

Daniel, John, Roger Southall and Jessica Lutchman (eds.) (2005), *State of the Nation: South Africa 2004–2005*, Cape Town, South Africa: Human Sciences Research Council.

Diamond, Larry (1999), *Developing Democracy toward Consolidation*, Baltimore, MD: Johns Hopkins University Press.

Economist Intelligence Unit (2007), 'The Economist Intelligence Unit's index of democracy', at http://www.economist.com/media/pdf/DEMOCRACY_INDEX_2007_v3.pdf.

Fajnzylber, Pablo, Daniel Lederman and Norman Loayza (1998), *Determinants of Crime Rates in Latin America and the World: An Empirical Assessment*, Washington, DC: World Bank.

Franzese, Robert (1998), 'Political Participation, Income Distribution, and Public

Transfers in Developed Democracies', paper presented at the annual meeting of the American Political Science Association, Boston, MA, 3–6 September.

Fukuyama, Francis (1992), 'Capitalism and Democracy: The Missing Link', *Journal of Democracy*, 3 (3), 100–110.

Grew, Raymond (ed.) (1978), *Crises of Political Development in Europe and the United States*, Princeton: Princeton University Press.

Gros, Jean-Germain (1996), 'Towards a Taxonomy of Failed States in the New World Order: Decaying Somalia, Liberia, Rwanda and Haiti', *Third World Quarterly*, **17** (3), 455–71.

Hair, Joseph F., Rolph E. Anderson, Ronald L. Tatham and Bill Black (1998), *Multivariate Data Analysis*, Upper Saddle River, NJ: Prentice-Hall.

Hamilton, Lawrence C. (1992), *Regression with Graphics*, Belmont, CA: Brooks/ Cole.

Holmes, Stephen (1997), 'What Russia Teaches Us Now: How Weak States Threaten Freedom', *American Prospect*, **8** (33), at http://www.theprospect.com.

Hraba, Joseph, Wan-ning Bao, Frederick O. Lorentz and Zdenka Pechacova (1998), 'Perceived Risk of Crime in the Czech Republic', *Journal of Research in Crime and Delinquency*, **35** (2), 225–43.

Huntington, Samuel P. (1968), *Political Order in Changing Societies*, New Haven: Yale University Press.

Inglehart, Ronald (1997), *Modernization and Postmodernization: Culture, Economic, and Political Change in Forty-Three Societies*, Princeton: Princeton University Press.

Jackman, Robert (1985), 'Cross-National Statistical Research and the Study of Comparative Politics', *American Journal of Political Science*, **29** (1), 161–82.

Judge, George, R. Carter Hill, William Griffiths, Helmut Lütkepohl and Tsong-Chao Lee (1988), *Introduction to the Theory and Practice of Econometrics*, 2nd edn., New York: John Wiley and Sons.

Karstedt, Susanne and Gary Lafree (2006), 'Democracy, Crime, and Justice', *ANNALS of the American Academy of Political and Social Sciences*, **605** (1), 6–23.

Kelling, George L. (1998), 'Crime Control, the Police and Culture Wars: Broken Windows and Cultural Pluralism', *Perspectives on Crime and Justice: 1997–1998 Lecture Series*, 1–28.

Klitgaard, Robert (1988), *Controlling Corruption*, Berkeley: University of California Press.

Kugler, Jacek and William Domke (1986), 'Comparing the Strength of Nations', *Comparative Political Studies*, **19** (1), 39–69.

La Ferrara, Eliana (2002), 'Inequality and Group Participation: Theory and Evidence from Rural Tanzania', *Journal of Public Economics*, **85** (2), 235–73.

Lafree, Gary and Andromachi Tseloni (2006), 'Democracy and Crime: A Multilevel Analysis of Homicide Trends in Forty-Four Countries, 1950–2000', *ANNALS of the American Academy of Political and Social Sciences*, **605** (1), 26–49.

Linz, Juan J. and Alfred C. Stepan (1996), *Problems of Democratic Transition and Consolidation in Southern Europe, South America, and Post-Communist Europe*, Baltimore, MD: Johns Hopkins University Press.

Lipset, Seymour Martin (1959), 'Some Social Requisites of Democracy: Economic Development and Political Legitimacy', *American Political Science Review*, **53** (1), 69–105.

Mann, Michael (1986), 'The Autonomous Power of the State: Its Origins, Mechanisms and Results', in John A. Hall (ed.), *States in History*, London: Basil Blackwell, pp. 109–36.

—— (1993), *The Sources of Social Power: The Rise of Classes and Nation-States, 1760–1914*, New York: Cambridge University Press.

Marshall, Ineke Haen and Carolyn Rebecca Block (2004), 'Maximizing the Availability of Cross-National Data on Homicide', *Homicide Studies*, **8** (3), 267–310.

Mendez, Juan E., Guillermo O'Donnell and Paulo Sergio Pinheiro (1999), *The (Un)rule of Law and the Underprivileged in Latin America*, South Bend, IN: University of Notre Dame Press.

Miles, Jeremy and Mark Shevlin (2001), *Applying Regression and Correlation: A Guide for Students and Researchers*, London: Sage.

Montinola, Gabriella R. and Robert W. Jackman (2002), 'Sources of Corruption: A Cross-Country Study', *British Journal of Political Science*, **32** (1), 147–70.

National Centres of Competence in Research (2005), 'Quality of Democracy – Democracy Barometer for Established Democracies', at http://www.nccr-democracy.unizh.ch/nccr/knowledge_transfer/ip14/Project%2014.pdf.

Neild, Rachel (1999), 'Technical Note 9: The Role of the Police in Crime Prevention', Washington, DC, Inter-American Development Bank.

Neter, John, Michael Kutner, Christopher Nachtsheim and William Wasserman (1996), *Applied Linear Regression Models*, Chicago: McGraw-Hill.

Peters, B. Guy (1987), 'Politicians and Bureaucrats in the Politics of Policy-Making', in Jan-Erik Lane (ed.), *Bureaucracy and Public Choice*, London: Sage Publications, pp. 256–82.

Poggi, Gianfranco (1978), *The Development of the Modern State: A Sociological Introduction*, Stanford: Stanford University Press.

—— (1990), *The State: Its Nature, Development and Prospects*, Stanford: Stanford University Press.

Przeworski, Adam (1995), *Sustainable Democracy*, New York: Cambridge University Press.

Przeworski, Adam, Michael Alvarez, Jose Cheibub and Fernando Limongi (2000), *Democracy and Development: Political Institutions and Well-Being in the World, 1950–1990*, New York: Cambridge University Press.

Putnam, Robert D. (1993), *Making Democracy Work: Civic Traditions in Modern Italy*, Princeton: Princeton University Press.

Pye, Lucian W. (1966), *Aspects of Political Development*, Boston: Little, Brown.

Reza, Avid, James Mercy and Etienne Krug (2000), 'A Global Concern: The Impact of Violence-Related Deaths throughout the World', Atlanta, GA, National Center for Injury Prevention and Control, Division of Violence Prevention.

Rose, Richard and Doh Chull Shin (2001), 'Democratization Backward: The Problem of Third Wave Democracies', *British Journal of Political Science*, **31** (2), 331–54.

Rose-Ackerman, Susan (1999), *Corruption and Government*, New York: Cambridge University Press.

Rustow, Dankwart (1970), 'Transitions to Democracy: Towards a Dynamic Model', *Comparative Politics*, **2** (3), 337–63.

Sandholtz, Wayne and William Koetzle (2000), 'Accounting for Corruption: Economic Structure, Democracy, and Trade', *International Studies Quarterly*, **44** (1), 31–50.

Savelsberg, Joachim J. (1995), 'Crime, Inequality, and Justice in Eastern Europe: Anomie, Domination, and Revolutionary Change', in John Hagan and Ruth Peterson (eds), *Crime and Inequality*, Stanford, CA: Stanford University Press, pp. 206–24.

Schmitter, Philippe C. (2005), 'Democratization and State Capacity', paper presented at the 10th international congress of the Internacional del CLAD sobre la Reforma del Estado y de la Administración Pública, Santiago, Chile, 18–21 October.

Schumpeter, Joseph A. (1942), *Capitalism, Socialism and Democracy*, New York: Harper and Row.

Shen, Ce and John B. Williamson (2005), 'Corruption, Democracy, Economic Freedom and State Strength: A Cross-National Analysis', *International Journal of Comparative Sociology*, **46** (4), 327–45.

Shi, Tianjian (2001), 'State-building and Democratization: Some Basic Theoretical Issues', Duke University, unpublished paper.

Solt, Frederick (2004), 'Economic Inequality and Democratic Political Engagement', Syracuse University, Maxwell School of Citizenship and Public Affairs, Luxembourg Income Study Working Paper No. 385.

Tilly, Charles (1975), 'Reflections on the History of European State-Making', in Charles Tilly and Gabriel Ardant (eds), *The Formation of National States in Western Europe*, Princeton, NJ: Princeton University Press, chapter 1.

Transparency International (2006), 'Corruption Perceptions Index 2006', at http://www.transparency.org/policy_research/surveys_indices/cpi/2006.

Treisman, Daniel (2000), 'The Causes of Corruption: A Cross-National Study', *Journal of Public Economics*, **76** (3), 399–457.

Tullock, Gordon (1965), *The Politics of Public Bureaucracy*, Cambridge, MA: Harvard University Press.

United Nations Development Programme (2006), 'Human Development Report' 2006', at http://hdr.undp.org/hdr2006/statistics/.

United Nations Office on Drugs and Crime (2001), 'The Seventh United Nations Survey on Crime Trends and the Operations of Criminal Justice Systems (1998–2000)', at http://www.unodc.org/unodc/en/crime_cicp_survey_seventh.html.

Weber, Max (1946), *From Max Weber: Essays in Sociology*, ed. and trans. H.H. Gerth and C. Wright Mills, New York: Oxford University Press.

—— (1978), *Economy and Society*, 2 vols., Berkeley, CA: University of California Press.

World Bank (2006a), 'Governance Matters V: Governance Indicators for 1996–2005', at http://info.worldbank.org/governance/kkz2005/pdf/2005kkdata.xls.

—— (2006b), *World Development Indicators 2006*, at http://devdata.worldbank.org/wdi2006/contents/TOC.htm.

World Health Organization (2002), *The Injury Chart Book: A Graphical Overview of the Global Burden of Injuries*, Geneva: WHO.

—— (2004), 'Causes of Death: Estimates', at http://www.who.int/entity/healthinfo/statistics/bodgbddeathdalyestimates.xls.

Zakaria, Fareed (2003), *The Future of Freedom: Illiberal Democracy at Home and Abroad*, New York: W.W. Norton.

APPENDIX

Appendix 5A.1 Data Sources

	Source
Dependent variables	
CONDITIONS	http://www.economist.com/media/pdf/DEMOCRACY_INDEX_2007_v3.pdf
COMPETITION	http://www.economist.com/media/pdf/DEMOCRACY_INDEX_2007_v3.pdf
PARTICIPATION	http://www.economist.com/media/pdf/DEMOCRACY_INDEX_2007_v3.pdf
RESPONSIVENESS	http://www.economist.com/media/pdf/DEMOCRACY_INDEX_2007_v3.pdf
Explanatory variables	
VIOLENCE	http://www.who.int/entity/healthinfo/statistics/bodgbddeathdalyestimates.xls
REVENUE	http://devdata.worldbank.org/wdi2006/contents/TOC.htm
CONSENSUS	http://www.bertelsmann-transformation-index.de/11.0.html?&L=1
TRAFFICDEATH	http://www.who.int/entity/healthinfo/statistics/bodgbddeathdalyestimates.xls
CONTROCOR	http://info.worldbank.org/governance/kkz2005/pdf/2005kkdata.xls
HDI	http://hdr.undp.org/hdr2006/statistics/
Control variables	
AREA	http://devdata.worldbank.org/wdi2006/contents/TOC.htm
POPULATION	http://devdata.worldbank.org/wdi2006/contents/TOC.htm
FRACTIONALIZATION	http://www.stanford.edu/~wacziarg/downloads/fractionalization.xls
PCGNI	http://devdata.worldbank.org/wdi2006/contents/TOC.htm

167

PART TWO

Participation and Governance at the Local Level:
Successes and Failures

6. Has Forest Co-management in Malawi Benefited the Poor?

Charles B.L. Jumbe and Arild Angelsen

Forests 'grow' on institutions as much as they grow on the soil. The soil provides nutrients for trees to grow and generate different environmental goods and services for use by mankind, while institutions shape the behavior of forest users to ensure sustainable forest utilization and management. After years of stringent government control over forest resources which restricted the flow of benefits to the surrounding communities, many governments worldwide have developed policies to devolve responsibility for forest management to local bodies such as forest user groups. This forest management system is known as joint forest management in India, community forest management in Nepal, forest co-management in Malawi and community-based forest management in the Philippines (Edmunds and Wollenberg 2003; Jumbe and Angelsen 2007). In one way or another, they all involve the transfer of responsibility and authority over forest resources from the state to local bodies which, to various degrees, are guided by the local governance structures. Devolution of forest management is seen as a rural development strategy to enhance the contribution of forests to poverty reduction and to promote village-level economic development and biodiversity conservation (Ribot 1995, 2001; Fisher 1999; Agrawal and Gibson 1999; Agrawal and Ostrom 2001; Kumar 2002; Edmunds and Wollenberg 2003; Adhikari, Falco and Lovett 2004).

When analyzing local or community forest management (CFM), it is useful to distinguish between CFM which originated locally and has existed for some time (traditional CFM), and CFM which is introduced as an integral part of the devolution or decentralization process whereby rights and obligations are transferred from the state to local communities (introduced CFM). Nevertheless, to be successful, CFM policies must be built on traditional institutions while transferring and formally recognizing community rights and obligations through decentralization. Malawi's co-management program falls primarily in the second category, although it is strongly backed by well-established local institutions, particularly for the co-management program in Chimaliro forest reserve, as will be discussed later in this chapter.

A number of studies have been conducted to assess the impact of devolution programs on resource productivity, organizational stability and environmental sustainability. These studies have demonstrated that the success of devolution programs depends, inter alia, on the effectiveness of institutions at the local level and the conduciveness of the policy environment (Meinzen-Dick, Knox and Gregorio 1999). In particular, case studies have generated some evidence that devolution policies have expanded local decision-making authority in forest management and have enhanced the capacity of village-level organizations to halt or slow down natural resource degradation (e.g., Jodha 1995; Baland and Platteau 1996; Agrawal and Yadama 1997; Saxena 1997; Chakraborty 2001). According to Edmunds and Wollenberg (2003), devolution gives the largest number of poor people who live in or near forests a larger voice in decisions about the management and utilization of local forest resources.

In a meta-study of 69 CFM cases by Pagdee, Kim and Daugherty (2006), 58 per cent of the cases studied were considered successful, based on an ecological sustainability criterion (the most typical measure was 'improved forest condition'). The income, livelihoods and distributional criteria were more diverse and therefore more difficult to compare. But in general, the livelihood outcomes were more mixed and less favorable than the conservation outcomes. The study by Behera and Engel (Chapter 7) in this volume finds that despite the concerted efforts by policymakers to empower the poorer and weaker sections of villages through joint forest management in India, the richer and better-educated people in the community influence most decisions.

However, few studies have tried to quantify rigorously the net benefits of devolution programs and their effects on poverty alleviation and equity among different groups of users (Meinzen-Dick, Gregorio and McCarthy 2004). Using household-level data from the Chimaliro and Liwonde forest reserves under the pilot forest co-management program in Malawi, this chapter seeks to address the following questions: Do the poor benefit from participating in the forest co-management program as intended? Are there any biases in the distribution of forest income among different participants and, if so, what are the sources of inequality?

Addressing such questions is important for a variety of reasons. First, evidence from this analysis helps to assess the effectiveness of forest co-management programs as a pro-poor strategy for enhancing the contribution of forests to rural livelihood. Second, with the high priority given to poverty reduction by the government, it is vital to assess whether the poorest and most vulnerable households actually benefit from participating in the program. This analysis therefore helps to identify which people are negatively impacted by the program in order to design suitable policy prescriptions or compensatory mechanisms to mitigate the negative effects from the programs. Lastly, results from this study yield important insights and lessons necessary for designing better interventions in the future.

This chapter applies the propensity score matching and decomposition techniques to measure how participation in the co-management program affects the forest earnings of vulnerable households, especially female-headed and low-income households. Matching techniques are commonly applied in evaluating social and training programs (e.g., Heckman 1997; Heckman and Smith 1999; Dehejia and Wahba 2002; Hirsch and Mehay 2003). Similarly, decomposition techniques are commonly applied in labor market studies to assess the impact of discrimination on the wage rates or earnings of different groups of people defined by gender (Oaxaca 1973; Liu, Zhang and Chong 2004; Jolliffe and Campos 2005), ethnicity (Blinder 1973; Darity, Gullkey and Winfrey 1995; Trejo 1997) or union membership (Andrews et al. 1998; Arbache and Carneiro 1999). This is the first study to combine these econometric techniques to assess the impact of participation in the forest co-management program using household survey data from a developing African country.

In addition, most impact studies of forest devolution programs have not controlled for unobserved heterogeneity and sample selection bias. In this chapter, we use an endogenous switching regression model to adjust the estimates of forest earnings for different groups for sample selection bias.[1] These estimates are subsequently used in the propensity score matching and decomposition analyses. Heckman and Li (2004) show that failure to adjust for unobserved heterogeneity and sample selection effects may lead to incorrect inference as estimates from such analyses may be potentially biased. This is indeed demonstrated in this chapter, as the direction of the effects is often reversed when moving from a simple comparison of averages of forest income between participants and non-participants to the more advanced methods.

FOREST MANAGEMENT IN MALAWI

Malawi has a long history of involving local people in managing forests. Prior to 1891, during the pre-colonial period, informal institutions governing the utilization and management of indigenous forest resources existed as a set of unwritten rules which catered for the needs of the society at that time, mainly to regulate the use of forests for poles, medicines, hunting and fuel wood (Jumbe, Kachule and Mataya 2000). The control over the use of natural resources was vested in the local chiefs, who made decisions regarding the use of different forest products and instituted some controls over the use of forest patches which were preserved as places of worship or as graveyards, while some forest species were protected for their medicinal values.

Forest policies and institutions have evolved from unwritten records to some formal institutions which competed with the informal institutions. During the colonial period (1891–1963), the British colonial administration appropriated large chunks of land in Malawi for large-scale farming (Jumbe, Kachule and Mataya 2000). Most forests were declared protected forest areas by the mid-1920s (Kayambazinthu 2000). The colonial administration further outlawed the cutting or harvesting of indigenous trees on both customary and public land against the ravages of the people who lived on the fringes of these resources (Mayers et al. 2001). However, due to conflicts between the state and the local communities over land, the colonial government established the Communal Forest Scheme, managed by the central government (District Administration). Under the scheme, approximately 2.7 million hectares of forest land were allocated to communities whereby residents decided on their use and management, referred to as the village forest areas (VFAs) (Kayambazinthu 2000). These VFAs were managed by the Village Forest Committees (VFCs), led by village heads. However, the scheme only lasted one decade, when the policy focus of the colonial administration shifted from community forestry to plantation forestry for commercial forest exploitation.

After the country attained independence in 1964, Malawian officials adopted the colonial model of forestry sector management which emphasized forest protection. All forest-related matters on customary land[2] were placed under the responsibility of the local government (District Councils). During this period, the VFCs were mandated to oversee the use, control and management of forests on customary land. In 1985 management responsibility reverted to the central government (Forestry Department). By that time, the authority of village heads to control the VFAs had been usurped by the political influence which dictated the composition and operations of the VFCs. The number of active VFAs dropped from 5,108 in 1963 to 1,182 in 1994 (Kayambazinthu and Locke 2002). The key feature of the government's forestry policy remained that of 'command and control'; most protected areas were heavily guarded and patrolled, and forest products obtained from indigenous forests were confiscated.

Despite the strict controls and significant government investment in forest protection, degradation and deforestation still continued due to forest encroachment and clearing for settlements, opening of new farms, timber extraction and removal of fuel wood (charcoal and firewood) (Malawi Government 2001b). For example, before the 1960s, more than 59 per cent of the total land area of 9.4 million hectares was covered by forests (Jumbe 2006). In the 1970s most forests were cleared to establish large estates for cash crop production, especially tobacco, to boost agricultural exports. As a result, the total forest area had shrunk to 38 per cent by the 1980s (Malawi Government 2001b). Recent estimates indicate that forests now occupy approximately 27 per cent of the total land area (FAO 2005).

As the Malawi government began to formulate the 1996 National Forestry Policy, it took into consideration the continuing forest degradation, the significance of forests to rural livelihood and the 1992 United Nations Earth Summit in Rio de Janeiro. Participants at the Earth Summit had accepted the principle of participatory development as an integral part of the overall rural development strategy. In Malawi, the parliament endorsed the Forestry Act in 1997, that was aimed at better integrating forest utilization and sustainable management. The law removed a number of barriers to people's involvement in the conservation of trees, forests and protected forest areas, and empowered village heads to confiscate forest products illegally obtained from natural woodlands (Sakanda 1996; Malawi Government 1996, 1997). As a framework for implementing the new legislation, the government launched the National Forestry Program (NFP), that specifies forestry sector priorities and strategies to enhance the contribution of forests to rural livelihood, while ensuring sustainable management (Malawi Government 2001a).

THE FOREST CO-MANAGEMENT PROGRAM

In 1996 the World Bank and the British government, through the Department for International Development (DFID), initiated a pilot forest co-management program in Malawi. The program was designed to promote local participation in forest management in exchange for the benefits of long-term sustainable management, such as continued access to fuel wood, poles and non-timber forest products (Kayambazinthu 2000). The Chimaliro and Liwonde forest reserves, located in the North-Central and Southern regions of Malawi, respectively, were selected as pilot research sites. These forest reserves are among the largest in the country, covering approximately 160,000 ha and 274,000 ha, respectively. The woodland in both reserves comprises semi-deciduous and evergreen natural *miombo* woodlands, which are dominated by *Brachystegia, Julbernadia* and *Uapaca* species in the Chimaliro forest reserve; *Uacapa* and *Brachystegia* are the dominant species found in the Liwonde forest reserve (Chanyenga and Kayambazinthu 1999; Makungwa and Kayambazinthu 1999).

These two pilot sites have distinct features. The Chimaliro forest reserve is located in a remote area with underdeveloped forest markets and a relatively more homogeneous society dominated by the Tumbuka tribe. In contrast, the Liwonde forest reserve is closer to the large cities of Blantyre and Zomba. The area is more densely populated and has a more ethnically diverse population. Most households in Liwonde are involved in forest-based businesses such as selling fuel wood, cane baskets and curio products as their main source of livelihood. The average household income in Liwonde is lower than in Chimaliro, where the main source of livelihood is tobacco farming (Jumbe 2006).

Under the program, approximately 210 ha of the Chimaliro forest reserve and 1,172 ha of the Liwonde forest reserve were demarcated into three blocks for joint management between surrounding communities and the government. In Chimaliro, the block sizes are 18 ha, 118 ha and 74 ha, while in Liwonde the sizes are 416 ha, 288 ha and 468 ha. The overall legal framework for the program is guided by a constitution developed and agreed upon by the local communities (Marsland, Henderson and Burn 1999). The rights and obligations of the committees and government, conditions for sharing revenue between government and the community, and the types of forest products which can be legally collected from the forest reserves are clearly detailed in the local constitution. The government's role is mainly to provide guidance, counseling and training to local communities. The program does not provide long-term secure rights to forests and their products, and the forest co-management structures do not have the legal mandate to prosecute violators of forest regulations (Kayambazinthu 2000).

At the heart of the forest co-management program is the implementation of forest management plans, which include boundary marking, firebreak maintenance, controlled early burning, selective harvesting, monitoring of illegal activities such as timber pit-sawing, use of indigenous wood for charcoal production and trafficking in forest products for sale or domestic use. In return, the scheme legitimizes participants' access to and use of the forest reserves to collect various forest products. These include fuel wood, thatch grass, poles, fodder, mushrooms, wild fruits and other non-timber forest products (NTFPs) (Kayambazinthu 2000). These products are important in people's daily livelihood (Campbell and Luckert 2002). In particular, NTFPs such as mushrooms, wild fruits and vegetables help to fill gaps in food supplies during the lean period between November and March, the rainy season when most NTFPs become more abundant (Jumbe 2006).

Within each forest block, a forest management committee with representatives from the designated villages provides leadership in the drafting of the local bylaws and block management plans. The operations of the program differ from block to block and between the two reserves, due to differences in the leadership and the degree of tribal cohesion. Most co-management activities are undertaken during the dry season (July to October), when demand for agricultural labor is relatively low and when forest reserves become more susceptible to wild fires.

Participation in the forest co-management program is voluntary, and members are expected to embrace the principles of forest co-management, abide by the local bylaws and actively participate in the program activities. Members also play a very important policing role by reporting individuals or households who break co-management rules to the local chiefs, government officials or the village forest committees for appropriate disciplinary action. In general, the enforcement of forest regulations hinges on the power and authority of local chiefs and the respect local people have toward their leaders (Jumbe 2006).

This chapter examines whether participation in the program enhances household income. The analysis is based on data from a household survey conducted in 31 villages adjacent to the Chimaliro and Liwonde forest reserves in 2002. Prior to the survey, we conducted focus group discussions and key informant interviews and compiled a list of participating villages and households for sampling purposes. The main survey covered 404 randomly selected households: 205 households from 20 villages in Chimaliro and 199 households from 11 villages in Liwonde.

PROGRAM EVALUATION AND EMPIRICAL STRATEGY

The empirical part of this chapter is based on Jumbe and Angelsen (2006), that gives a detailed theoretical and empirical framework for quantifying the benefits of program participation and how discrimination affects forest earnings for different groups of participants. We hypothesized that participation in the forest co-management program enhances forest-derived income of rural people such that forest earnings of those who participate in the program would have been lower had they not participated. In addition, the model was developed to analyze the net earnings for different groups of participants, classified by gender and poverty class, to assess the sources of unequal distribution of forest earnings.

The model uses different sets of variables to determine factors which influence program participation. These include demographic variables and social capital variables such as past group experience (e.g., farmers' association for tree planting, credit or beekeeping clubs) and tribal cohesion (i.e., whether the respondent belongs to the main ethnic group in the area). The majority of households surrounding the Chimaliro and Liwonde forest reserves belong to the Tumbuka and Yao tribes, respectively. The rest of the variables used are given in Table 6.1 (excluding total monthly income, that is included as background information).

We use the procedure described in Jumbe and Angelsen (2006) to obtain selection-

Table 6.1   Summary Statistics

Variables	Participation status		Gender	
	Yes	No	Male headed	Female headed
Age of household head (years)	44.82*	42.62	46.11	43.28
Education (primary = 1)	0.21	0.16	0.16	0.38
Family size	5.24	4.68	4.68	5.42**
Sex ratio (female to male)	1.27**	1.08	1.12	1.51***
Food insecure months	6.16	6.05	6.17	5.60
Forest business (participate = 1)	0.68	0.68	0.67	0.77*
Own private forest (own = 1)	0.48***	0.36	0.42	0.40
Land per capita (ha/person)	0.34	0.34	0.34	0.34
Ownership of livestock (own = 1)	0.35	0.37	0.36	0.38
Migration status (non-migrant = 1)	0.47	0.56*	0.60	0.51
Duration of residence (years)	29.49	28.68	28.83	32.11
Tribal cohesion (main tribe = 1)	0.61*	0.54	0.57	0.55
Past group experience (yes = 1)	0.36***	0.06	0.19	0.23
Distance to forest market (km)	6.06	7.34***	6.90**	5.70
Distance to forest reserve (km)	0.78	0.87	0.82	0.89
Monthly forest income (MK)	244.58	431.23***	390.06***	218.40
Total monthly income (MK)	2934.97	5174.79***	4680.75***	2620.80
No. of observations	182	222	357	47

bias adjusted estimates of forest income which were subsequently used to assess the impact of participation in the forest co-management program. We use a number of techniques to estimate the impact of program participation. For example, we used the propensity score matching technique proposed by Rosenbaum and Rubin (1983) in which the average forest income of non-participants (selected based on having the same probability of participation) was used as the counterfactual income for participants.[3] We use four matching estimators to estimate the impact of participation in the program: nearest neighbor, radius, kernel and stratification matching. Variables used to estimate the propensity score are listed in Table 6.1 (excluding forest income and total household income).

We employed the decomposition technique as applied in Reimers (1983) to assess whether different groups of participants benefit equally from participating in the program and to identify sources of unequal distribution of benefits. We compared forest incomes between male- and female-headed participants and between high- and low-income households participating in the

Table 6.1   (continued)

Variables	Poverty class	
	High income	Low income
Age of household head (years)	44.66**	41.00
Education (primary = 1)	0.37***	0.19
Family size	4.20	5.79***
Sex ratio (female to male)	1.19	1.16
Food insecure months	4.55***	6.73
Forest business (participate = 1)	0.72	0.66
Own private forest (own = 1)	0.40	0.42
Land per capita (ha/person)	0.48**	0.28
Ownership of livestock (own = 1)	0.46**	0.320
Migration status (non-migrant = 1)	0.60	0.59
Duration of residence (years)	25.78***	30.59
Tribal cohesion (main tribe = 1)	0.53	0.58
Past group experience (yes = 1)	0.16	0.20
Distance to forest market (km)	6.22	6.98*
Distance to forest reserve (km)	0.99	0.76***
Monthly forest income (MK)	619.72***	237.36
Total monthly income (MK)	7436.70***	2848.30
No. of observations	116	288

Notes:

*Significant at 10 per cent level; **significant at 5 per cent level; ***significant at 1 per cent level.

MK = Malawi Kwacha (US$1.00 = MK76.00 in 2002).

program. Low-income households are those which have daily incomes below the national poverty line of MK19.47 ($0.26)[4] per person per day (National Economic Council 2000), while high-income households are those whose daily income is above this poverty line.

In general, the technique decomposes forest earnings of comparison groups (male versus female, poor versus rich participants) by separating how much of the income gap between the two groups is attributable to the differences in the returns to endowments (coefficients), or inter-group differences in characteristics such as age, experience, education or assets (endowments) (see Jones and Kelly 1984). The first effect is defined as (statistical) discrimination,[5] whereas the second is referred to as the endowment effect.[6] We also applied the decomposition techniques based on the standard OLS regression as applied in Oaxaca (1973) to compare the results with those obtained from the methodology of Reimers (1983).

DESCRIPTIVE STATISTICS

Table 6.1 shows that there are statistically significant differences between participants and non-participants in key variables such as age, education, family composition, group experience and tribal cohesion. There are also significant differences between male- and female-headed households in some variables. For example, female-headed households tend to be less educated and have larger families with more female members than male-headed households. We also note that low-income households have larger families and smaller land size per capita (0.28 ha per person compared with 0.48 ha per person for high-income households). As expected, low-income households are exposed to a longer period of food insecurity (seven months). The average monthly forest incomes per household for low- and high-income households are estimated at MK237 ($3.12) and MK620 ($8.15) respectively, which accounts for 8 per cent of their respective average monthly incomes.

Table 6.2 presents pairwise correlations between program participation, forest income and other variables. Age of household head is negatively correlated with forest income, but positively correlated with participation. This may suggest that as people grow older, they may depend less on forests as their main source of income and be more responsive to forest conservation by participating in the program. This corresponds well with the raw data, where 54 per cent of forest entrepreneurs in the sample are below 40 years of age compared with only 20 per cent among those above 55 years. Thus, the young seem to take advantage of the new forest business opportunities at the expense of conservation. The data show that 46 per cent of oldest households (above 55 years of age) participate in co-management, whereas only 25 per cent of youth (below 40 years of age) participate.

From the last row of Table 6.2, we note that forest income is negatively correlated with participation, especially in Liwonde. This indicates that either participation in the co-management program reduces forest revenue for participants or that high forest income reduces the incentive among households to participate in the program. If the latter is correct, this could have negative implications for the long-term sustainability of the program.

Table 6.3 reports the absolute and relative forest income for different groups. Negative figures in the last column imply less forest revenue for program participants. For example, forest income of participants in Chimaliro and Liwonde drops by 53 per cent and 46 per cent, respectively. Among low-income

Table 6.2 Correlations among Forest Income, Participation and Selected Variables

Variable	Overall Participation	Overall Income	Chimaliro Participation	Chimaliro Income	Liwonde Participation	Liwonde Income
Age of household head	0.07	-0.12*	0.05	-0.12*	0.11	-0.06
Formal education	-0.06	0.02	0.06	0.05	-0.13*	0.14*
Household size	-0.04	-0.03	-0.03	-0.08	-0.05	0.04
Sex ratio	0.11*	0.01	0.19*	0.08	0.13*	-0.01
Food insecurity	0.12*	0.07	0.22*	0.10	-0.01	-0.07
Forest business	-0.00	0.19*	-0.07	0.09	-0.13*	0.09
Woodlot ownership	0.12*	-0.19*	0.24*	0.00	0.05	-0.10
Land holding size	0.01	-0.19*	0.01	-0.02	0.08	-0.10
Livestock ownership	-0.02	-0.07	-0.07	-0.01	0.03	-0.02
Migration status	0.06	-0.09*	0.13*	-0.13*	-0.03	-0.19*
Duration of residence	0.02	-0.06	0.16*	-0.01	0.16*	0.08
Social cohesion	0.07	-0.27*	0.02	0.07	0.16*	-0.14*
Group experience	0.38*	-0.15*	0.65*	-0.08	0.02	-0.11
Distance to forest market	-0.13*	-0.29*	-0.36*	-0.15*	0.12	-0.26*
Firewood price	-0.13*	0.38*	-0.05	0.02	-0.15*	0.11
Distance to forest reserve	-0.04	-0.10*	-0.01	-0.01	-0.16*	-0.06
Forest income	-0.13*	1.00	-0.12*	1.00	-0.19*	1.00
Number of observations		404		205		199

Note: *Significant at 10 per cent level.

Table 6.3   Average Monthly Forest Income Differentials (Malawi Kwacha)

Overall	PP (S.E.)	NP (S.E.)	Difference (t-statistic)	Relative income differential (%)
Full sample	244.58	431.23	−186.65***	−43.28
(PP=182, NP=222)	(42.91)	(37.21)	(2.61)	
Chimaliro	37.45	80.18	−42.73**	−53.29
(PP=89, NP=116)	(1.82)	(22.17	(1.92)	
Liwonde	442.80	815.41	−372.60***	−45.69
(PP=93, NP=106)	(78.82)	(105.59)	(2.83)	
Low-income households				
Full sample	173.62	292.05	−118.43***	−40.55
(PP=133, NP=155)	(23.96)	(47.59)	(53.27)	
Chimaliro	38.90	44.11	−5.21	−11.81
(PP=69, NP=82)	(2.13)	(6.25)	(6.80)	
Liwonde	318.86	570.56	−251.70***	−44.11
(PP=64, NP=73)	(42.99)	(90.54)	(100.23)	
Female-headed households				
Full sample	223.55	210.21	13.34	+6.35
(PP=62, NP=39)	(61.26)	(67.33)	(0.15)	
Chimaliro	35.68	43.11	−7.43	−17.23
(PP=31, NP=20)	(2.53)	(8.59)	(0.83)	
Liwonde	411.42	386.11	25.32	+6.56
(P=31, NP=19)	(113.59)	(127.32)	(0.15)	

Notes:

Asterisks indicate that the means are statistically different between participants and non-participants.

PP = program participants; NP = non-program participants.

**Significant at 5 per cent level; ***significant at 1 per cent level.

households, the program appears to reduce forest revenue of participants by 41 per cent. In Chimaliro, the data show that female participants would 'sacrifice' 17 per cent of their forest revenue, while the program would enhance revenues for female participants in Liwonde by 6 per cent, although the difference is not that significant.

Ironically, the raw data presented above seem to indicate that non-participants benefit more from the forest co-management program than participants. While this may imply that the program is not conducive to enhancing forest income of program participants, it may also highlight the weak enforcement of rules to exclude non-participants from obtaining benefits from the co-managed forests. Nonetheless, using the average income of program participants and non-participants to make inferences about the overall program performance may lead to incorrect inferences, as the estimates often suffer from sample (participation) selection biases, as discussed earlier. This calls for methodologies which correct for potential selection bias.

ESTIMATION RESULTS

Table 6.4 displays the results of both selection-bias adjusted and unadjusted estimates of the average treatment effects on the treated (ATET), which is the measure of the impact of program participation derived from the four matching methods as described in Jumbe and Angelsen (2006). The table shows that selection-bias unadjusted estimates of ATET are consistently negative (except for the female subsample) and not statistically significant across subsamples. This suggests that the program does not increase the income of program participants. This is in line with Table 6.3.

After adjusting for selection bias, most estimates are positive and statistically significant across all subsamples, although the sizes of estimated coefficients and their levels of significance differ across matching methods. As Smith and Todd (2005) point out, results from different matching methods are sensitive to the set of variables used in the propensity scores and the sample used to estimate the program impact. Nonetheless, the selection-bias adjusted results differ sharply from the unadjusted ones. This suggests that there are critical selection biases which should be taken into account when assessing the impact of participation in the forest devolution programs. The rest of the discussion, therefore, focuses on the results from selection-bias adjusted estimates.

Overall Impact of Forest Co-management Program

The estimates from the nearest neighbor and kernel matching methods for the full sample are statistically significant, while those from the radius and stratification matching methods are not, although they are positive (see Table 6.4). Estimates of the net gains to program participants from the nearest neighbor and kernel matching methods are very close (i.e., MK20 ($0.27) and MK18 ($0.24) per month per household, respectively). This represents an increase of 51 per cent

Table 6.4   Matching Estimates of Income Gains from Forest Co-management (Malawi Kwacha)

A: Bias unadjusted ATET	Nearest neighbor			Radius matching		
	Treated mean	Control mean	Average effect	Treated mean	Control mean	Average effect
Full sample	138.21	139.23	−1.073	138.21	154.09	−15.88
	[93.46]	[103.10]	(15.17)	[93.46]	[111.12]	(8.92)
Chimaliro	37.45	43.62	−6.17	37.45	40.243	−2.79
	[17.17]	[17.72]	(7.80)	[17.17]	[25.86]	(3.40)
Liwonde	442.80	620.02	−177.22	442.80	734.97	−292.17
	[760.19]	[930.99]	(153.40)	[760.19]	[1053.66]	(157.31)
Females	151.08	139.44	11.64	143.92	113.01	30.91
	[113.07]	[98.40]	(22.85)	[111.69]	[83.87]	(23.42)
Low income	118.60	120.43	−1.84	118.59	129.51	−10.91
	[78.47]	[86.84]	(24.29)	[78.47]	[84.50]	(12.52)

B: Adjusted ATET	Nearest neighbor			Radius matching		
	Treated mean	Control mean	Average effect	Treated mean	Control mean	Average effect
Full sample	57.51	37.88	19.63***	57.51	56.52	0.99
	[36.80]	[32.95]	(4.61)	[36.79]	[34.42]	(4.24)
Chimaliro	25.03	12.84	12.19***	25.026	26.19	−0.93
	[11.33]	[10.55]	(2.61)	[11.33]	[11.73]	(5.13)
Liwonde	144.14	312.61	−168.47***	144.14	446.75	−302.61***
	[91.10]	[267.92]	(37.30)	[91.10]	[277.18]	(29.11)
Females	87.03	76.30	10.73	80.84	71.46	18.38***
	[73.90]	[90.73]	[32.36]	[72.26]	[93.98]	(9.38)
Low income	51.77	26.15	25.62***	51.77	37.73	14.04***
	[27.77]	[19.00]	(2.98)	[27.77]	[16.19]	(2.66)

Table 6.4   *(continued)*

A: Bias unadjusted ATET	Kernel matching			Stratification		
	Treated mean	Control mean	Average effect	Treated mean	Control mean	Average effect
Full sample	138.21	141.50	−3.291	142.03	140.24	−2.027
	[93.46]	[103.22]	(10.77)	(103.22)	[102.7]	(11.07)
Chimaliro	37.45	42.42	−4.97	61.62	65.10	−3.47
	[17.17]	[19.55]	(6.98)	[180.86]	[26.11]	(6.06)
Liwonde	442.80	552.50	−109.69	641.28	722.82	−81.54
	[760.19]	[897.54]	(118.01)	[964.36]	[956.12]	(104.34)
Females	151.08	140.82	10.25	120.43	108.78	11.65
	[113.07]	(89.09)	(19.94)	[97.20]	[90.74]	(19.98)
Low income	118.59	122.62	−4.026	119.76	120.75	−2.16
	[78.47]	[67.12]	(12.68)	[80.89]	[74.57]	(11.35)

B: Adjusted ATET	Kernel matching			Stratification		
	Treated mean	Control mean	Average effect	Treated mean	Control mean	Average effect
Full sample	57.51	39.16	18.34***	56.80	60.80	3.29
	[36.79]	[5.88]	(3.75)	(35.22)	[35.23]	(3.37)
Chimaliro	25.03	13.03	11.99***	30.62	31.52	−0.90
	[11.33]	[6.57]	(2.74)	[14.01]	[13.12]	(1.92)
Liwonde	144.14	344.84	−200.71***	339.16	620.91	−281.76***
	[91.10]	[167.97]	(29.27)	[306.79]	[306.79]	(32.27)
Females	87.03	71.34	15.69*	74.42	45.06	29.36***
	[73.90]	[98.12]	(8.33)	(78.58)	[87.53]	(11.73)
Low income	51.77	26.76	25.01***	44.39	38.25	13.52***
	[27.77]	[14.34]	(3.45)	[23.15]	[11.91]	(3.12)

Notes:

ATET: average treatment effect on the treated.

*Significant at the 10 per cent level; ***significant at the 1 per cent level.

Standard deviations shown in brackets and bootstrapped standard errors in parentheses.

and 47 per cent, respectively, of what they would earn had they not participated in the program. These results suggest that the surrounding communities are generally better off by participating in the program.

Similarly, in Chimaliro results from both the nearest neighbor and kernel matching methods show marginal income gains of approximately MK12 ($0.16) per month per household to program participants, an increase of more than 90 per cent of what they would have earned had they not participated in the program. While past studies describe the forest co-management program in Chimaliro as one of 'the most up-to-date' forest devolution programs in Southern Africa from both institutional and ecological perspectives (Kayambazinthu 2000; Shackleton and Campbell 2001), these results indicate that the program has only a minor impact on household income, at least in the short run. However, it must be stressed that most of these households are so poor that even the small cash income and subsistence goods they obtain from forests represent an important component of their livelihood strategies. Moreover, the local chiefs in Chimaliro command deep respect from local villagers and are actively involved in the program (Jumbe 2006). This implies that households are compelled to participate in the program partly for social benefits (e.g., solidarity, social security or self-esteem) and for the inherent fear of social reprisal and exclusion. These are important factors for understanding the relative success of the program in Chimaliro compared with Liwonde.

In contrast, the estimates from all four matching methods in Liwonde are consistently negative and highly significant, suggesting that the forest co-management program does not adequately reward participants by enhancing their income. Results from different matching methods suggest that the forest co-management program reduces forest revenue of participants by between MK168 ($2.22) and MK302 ($3.98) per month per household, a drop in forest revenue of between 54 per cent and 68 per cent of what they would have obtained without participating in the program but illegally obtaining forest products from co-managed forest areas. Thus, households in Liwonde sacrifice their forest income to participate in the program. These findings support other qualitative studies in Africa and Asia which find that sometimes devolution policies can make some groups of forest users worse off (Shackleton et al. 2002; Edmunds and Wollenberg 2003). In fact, the forest co-management program imposes restrictions on participants in terms of the frequency, quantity and type of forest products they can collect from the reserves. These are significant, considering that more than 80 per cent of the households in Liwonde rely on forest-based businesses as their primary source of livelihood (Jumbe and Angelsen 2007).

A methodological reminder is in order here. Our methodology measures the impact of participation in the forest co-management program rather than the general local impact of the program, that would require quantifying all the benefits from sustainable forest management and utilization, such as the preservation of nature, scenery, biodiversity conservation and carbon sequestration. In Liwonde, for example, results suggest that non-participants free ride on the benefits of the program (better forest management). Thus, the correct interpretation of these results is that participation in the program by the households in Liwonde is costly, as it lowers their forest income.

Since the program does not have effective enforcement mechanisms in place to stop free riding and illegal forest use, we can therefore conclude that the socioeconomic and ecological sustainability of the program in Liwonde is at risk, both due to the high costs imposed on participants as well as the high degree of forest exploitation and dependence, where forest income accounts for 23 per cent of their total income (Jumbe and Angelsen 2007).

The results for Liwonde point out the need to address the short-term needs of local people, such as by increasing the share of forest revenue retained by local communities which can be used for village development projects or shared among participants. Currently, 70 per cent of the revenue from sales of forest products from co-managed forests is supposed to be remitted to government, while only 30 per cent is retained by the community (Kayambazinthu 2000). This rule applies to joint bulk sale of forest products from the co-management forest areas, and such sales are not very common. This high 'taxation' serves as a disincentive for people's participation in the program, considering that forest products have substantial commercial values in Liwonde.

Another strategy is to design parallel interventions alongside forest co-management programs to provide forest-dependent households with supplementary sources of income. This may create the incentives among households to participate in the program, to comply with forest regulations and to reduce pressure on the forest reserves.

Does the Program Help Vulnerable Households?

Other analyses were conducted to examine the extent to which the livelihood of vulnerable households, namely female-headed and low-income households, is enhanced by participating in the program. In general, the results from Table 6.4 suggest that the program generates positive income gains to female participants ranging from MK11 ($0.14) to MK29 ($0.39) per month per household, representing an increase in forest income of between 13 per cent and 65 per cent of what they would have earned had they not participated in the program. During the fieldwork, we noted that most fuel wood traders were women who were involved in the day-to-day selling of fuel wood along the main roads. Similarly, empirical results from all the matching methods in Table 6.4 indicate that low-income participants earn more forest income by participating in the program. Income gains to low-income participants are estimated at between MK13 ($0.18) and MK26 ($0.34) per month per household, an increase in forest income of between 35 per cent and 98 per cent of what they would have earned without participating in the program.

Taken together, this analysis suggests that the forest co-management program protects vulnerable households from extreme poverty. We can therefore conclude that the livelihood of both female-headed and low-income households would have declined if they had not participated in the program. In other words, the forest co-management program helps to improve the living standards of vulnerable households which participate in the program, but is not a long-term solution out of poverty. These results are more consistent with the safety-net and gap-filling roles of forests (Byron and Arnold 1999; Angelsen and Wunder 2003).

THE IMPACT OF DISCRIMINATION ON FOREST INCOME

This section discusses the results from the decomposition analysis to assess how the benefits of forest co-management programs are distributed among different groups of participants.

Male–Female Decomposition Results

Table 6.5 presents the results of linear decomposition of forest income for male and female participants. OLS-based decomposition (selection-bias unadjusted) results and their respective standard errors are reported in the first two columns for comparisons, while those based on the switching regression model (selection-bias adjusted estimates from Reimers' [1983] decomposition technique) are displayed in the last two columns. Section A of the table presents predicted values of forest income for male and female participants, while Section B indicates how simultaneous changes in endowments and coefficients affect male–female income disparity.

From Section A, the natural logs of mean forest income for male and female participants are statistically significant from both the selection-bias adjusted and unadjusted decomposition techniques. The difference in average income between male and female participants is highly significant from the bias adjusted, but not from the bias unadjusted estimates (third row). It is, however, interesting to note that the difference between the antilog of average income for male and female participants shows a small positive premium of about MK8 ($0.11) per month per household for male participants. This implies that

Table 6.5   Results of Linear Decomposition of Log of Forest Income

	OLS based (bias unadjusted)		Switching regression based (bias adjusted)	
A: Mean prediction	Mean	Standard error	Mean	Standard error
Male participants	4.582	0.098***	3.925	0.037***
Female participants	4.495	0.126***	3.748	0.053***
Male–female income differential	0.087	0.160	0.177	0.065***
B: Simultaneous change in endowments and coefficients				
Three-fold endowments	−0.160	0.069*	−0.100	0.029***
Coefficients	0.108	0.165	0.179	0.068***
Interaction	0.139	0.081*	0.099	0.033***

Note: *Significant at 10 per cent level; ***significant at 1 per cet level.

income for female participants would increase slightly if they earned like their male counterparts, i.e., without statistical discrimination.

From Section B, endowment coefficients are negative and significant (first row), suggesting that female participants would earn more than their male counterparts if females retained their coefficients, but had the endowments as for males. However, the positive sign for the coefficients in the second row indicates that male participants would still earn more than their female counterparts if female participants retained their endowments, but had similar coefficients to male participants. Similarly, the positive and significant sign for the interaction (last row) indicates that females would still earn less than males even if females had similar coefficients and endowments to their male counterparts.

Table 6.6 presents a summary of male–female income decomposition results. The first column reports the OLS-based decomposition results (selection-bias unadjusted) using average forest income for male participants as a non-discriminatory benchmark. The last column presents bias adjusted decomposition results based on the switching regression estimates of forest income (selection-bias adjusted).

The selection-bias unadjusted results show that 24 per cent of the male–female income differential is attributable to the differences in endowments in

Table 6.6   Summary of Male–Female Income Decomposition

Decomposition summary	OLS based (bias unadjusted)	Switching regression based (bias adjusted)
Predicted income differential (MK/month/household)[a]	8.15	8.22
Proportion of total differential (per cent)		
Total attributable to endowments (variables) (E + C)	60.42	29.91
due to differences in variable means (E)	−2.11	−0.15
due to differences in variable coefficients (C)	62.53	30.05
Unexplained part due to differences in model intercepts (U)	−51.72	−12.71
Unadjusted total differential {(E + C + U) = R}	8.70	17.71
Adjusted total differential[b] {(C + U) = D}	10.81	17.68
Endowments as % of total differential (E/R)	−24.24	−0.83

Notes:

[a]Difference between antilog of earnings of male and female income.

[b]Part of total differential due to discrimination. Positive number indicates advantage to males; negative number indicates advantage to females.

favor of female participants (ninth row, first column). However, results from the last row in the first column indicate that the entire male–female income disparity is due to larger coefficients for male participants or 'discrimination' against the female counterparts, accounting for 124 per cent of the income disparity.

After adjusting for sample selection, the difference in the endowments between male and female participants (fourth row, second column) accounts for only 0.15 per cent of the forest income differential. This minor difference is reflected in the small figure for endowments of just 0.83 per cent (ninth row, second column). From the last row in the second column, results indicate that the main source of income disparity is statistical 'discrimination', that accounts for 100 per cent of the total differential against female participants. Thus, the sizes of the estimated coefficients for variables in the income equation for the male subsample such as age, education and household assets are larger than those for the female subsample. In other words, the difference in forest income between male and female participants reflects how the program functions, and not necessarily that the female participants are more resource poor.

Table 6.7   Results of Linear Decomposition of Log of Forest Income

	OLS based (bias unadjusted)		Switching regression based (bias adjusted)	
A: Mean predictions	Mean	Standard error	Mean	Standard error
High-income participants	4.769	0.177***	3.985	0.051***
Low-income participants	4.473	0.084***	3.721	0.086***
High–low-income differential	0.296	0.196	0.265	0.100***
B: Simultaneous change in endowments and coefficients				
Three-fold endowments	−0.021	0.101	0.155	0.158
Coefficients	0.512	0.376	0.118	0.083*
Interaction	−0.196	0.336	0.023	0.168

Note: *Significant at 10 per cent level; ***significant at 1 per cent level.

High- and Low-Income Decomposition

Table 6.7 presents results from a similar analysis as above to determine the extent of forest income disparity between high- and low-income participants. From Section A, both estimates for the natural log of forest income for high- and low-income participants are highly significant from both the OLS and Reimers (1983) decomposition methods (first and second rows). However, the difference between forest income for the two groups is highly significant from the bias-adjusted decomposition (third row) but not from the unadjusted decomposition. The differences in the antilog of the low- and high-income differentials are MK30 ($0.40) and MK13 ($0.16) per month per household for the bias unadjusted and adjusted decomposition, respectively.

From Section B, endowments, coefficients and the interaction terms from OLS-based decomposition estimates are not statistically significant (first three rows, first column). However, from the bias adjusted decomposition results (second row, second column), only the coefficient is positive and statistically significant. This suggests that low-income households would earn more if they had similar coefficients to the high-income households, i.e., in the absence of 'discrimination'.

Table 6.8 gives a summary of decomposition results, i.e., how much of the differential is attributable to the differences in endowments and statistical 'discrimination' (i.e., differences in the estimated coefficients). Overall, the results suggest that inter-group differences in characteristics (endowments)

Table 6.8　Summary of High–Low Income Decomposition

Decomposition summary	OLS based (bias unadjusted)	Switching regression based (bias adjusted)
High–low-income differential (MK/month/household)[a]	30.20	12.50
Proportion of total differential (per cent)		
Total attributable to endowments (variables) (E + C)	−52.39	−10.83
due to differences in variable means (E)	−21.62	−15.77
due to differences in variable coefficients (C)	−30.77	4.94
Unexplained part due to differences in model intercepts (U)	82.01	−15.62
Unadjusted total differential {(E + C + U) = R}	29.62	−26.45
Adjusted total differential[b] {(C + U) = D}	51.24	−10.68
Endowments as % of total differential (E/R)	−72.99	59.64

Notes:

[a]Difference between antilog of earnings of male and female income.

[b]Part of total differential due to discrimination. Positive number indicates advantage to males; negative number indicates advantage to females.

account for 73 per cent of the total income differential in favor of the low-income participants, while statistical 'discrimination' accounts for 173 per cent of the income differential in favor of the high-income group (last two rows, first column). After adjusting for sample selection bias, 'discrimination' and inter-group differences in endowments between high- and low-income households account for only 40 per cent and 60 per cent of the income disparity, respectively, in favor of high-income participants.

From the decomposition analyses, our empirical results show that statistical 'discrimination' is the source of income disparity between male and female participants, accounting for 100 per cent of the total income differential, while the income disparity between high- and low-income participants is mainly due to the differences in endowments. This is consistent with the descriptive data, where high-income households have better endowments than low-income households in terms of age, education and household assets (land, livestock and private woodlots) which affect forest income. Endowment differences are more structural and difficult to address with the forest co-management program, e.g., a skewed asset distribution. The differences due to 'discrimination', however, can more directly be attributed to the operation of the program.

Thus, these findings highlight problems with the design and/or operation of the program which particularly discriminate against female participants as well as the low-income group. The study did not dig deeply into the nature of this discrimination, but it is likely to reflect the more general norms and structures of the society. And this is not limited to Malawi. These results are in line with the findings of Behera and Engel (Chapter 7): minority groups are de facto kept out of the decision-making processes in India's joint forest management (JFM) programs. As such, they are also less likely to benefit from the program despite the fact that poorer households were more likely to attend JFM meetings.

CONCLUSION

This chapter investigates the impact of participation in the co-management program and the effect of discrimination on household forest income by applying the propensity score matching and decomposition techniques to survey data from the Chimaliro and Liwonde forest reserves in Malawi. After controlling for sample selection bias, there is some evidence from different matching methods that program participation leads to increases in forest income by approximately 50 per cent, using pooled data from both sites.

We find, however, contrasting evidence of the impact of participation between the two sites. While these results indicate that the program enhances forest income of participants at Chimaliro by 90 per cent, the results for Liwonde suggest that participation in the forest co-management program drastically reduces forest revenue of participants by approximately 60 per cent. Due to the very low forest income share in total income of households in Chimaliro, the gain in absolute terms is quite modest, just MK12.00 ($0.16) per month per household. It is, however, worth pointing out that although families earn very small amounts of cash income and subsistence goods from forests, most of these families are so poor that these amounts make a significant contribution to their overall welfare. Again, there are also other benefits in terms of village development projects, environmental benefits from forest productivity through sustainable management, and utilization of forests which have not been captured by this analysis.

The results for Liwonde suggest that participation in the program imposes costly restrictions, in a setting where forest-based businesses (i.e., sale of different forest products) are the main source of livelihood. More generally, these findings are in line with other qualitative studies in other African and Asian countries which suggest that devolution policies can serve as a tool for strengthening the state's control over the management of local resources at a lower cost to the state and can make previous resource users worse off (e.g.,

Shackleton et al. 2002; Edmunds and Wollenberg 2003).

At the heart of many forest management programs is the fact that previous levels of resource use were unsustainable. Restricting access and limiting resource use are therefore necessary to halt the degradation of – and possibly boost – the resource base. Thus, the jury should take a long-term perspective, and a key hypothesis deriving from this analysis is that forest users in Chimaliro eventually will be rewarded for their better management, while those in Liwonde will suffer from continuing forest degradation. A follow-up study of the same households which participated in the 2002 survey currently (2007) being undertaken will test this prediction.

These results also point to the fact that high forest dependency can make it more difficult for the local communities to achieve compliance with forest regulations, as the opportunity costs of following forest rules and regulations are higher. Thus, the forest co-management program is least successful in Liwonde, where the pressure on forests is higher, and therefore calls for alternative management regimes. This also raises questions about the long-term ecological and socioeconomic sustainability of the program if it cannot cope with higher resource pressure.

Another general lesson of the program concerns the role of social capital and social pressure in enhancing participation and compliance. Chimaliro differs from Liwonde by being more socially and culturally homogeneous. The program is also more integrated into the traditional institutions through the active participation of the chiefs in the program. Thus, non-participation and non-compliance are more socially costly in Chimaliro.

Another lesson concerns the design of the program. The results suggest that the livelihood of women would have worsened without the program. However, decomposition results suggest that female participants derive relatively smaller benefits from the program than their male counterparts due to 'discrimination', that accounts for the male–female income differential. In other words, the program would contribute even more to the livelihoods of female participants if they had similar opportunities to their male counterparts. It is therefore vital for the government and development agencies to design gender-focused devolution programs in order to eliminate 'discrimination' and to boost their income, which would at the same time create better incentives for women's increased participation in the program.

The analysis provides some evidence that the livelihood of low-income households would have worsened without participation in the program. Estimation results suggest that low-income households get between 35 per cent and 98 per cent more forest income compared to what they would have earned had they not participated in the program. However, decomposition results show that high-income participants capture more benefits from the program due to 'discrimination' and differences in endowments, that account for 40 per cent and 60 per cent of the income differential, respectively. These results point to the need to implement complementary interventions alongside forest co-management programs to provide poor households with supplementary sources of income. This may reduce pressure on forests and stimulate greater participation among forest-dependent households.

Lastly, the results of this analysis point to the need for policymakers to address the short-term needs of rural households when designing future co-management programs, for example by increasing the proportion of forest revenue from the forest co-management programs which is retained by the community. Currently the government takes 70 per cent of the cash income from joint sales of forest products from co-managed forests, while only 30 per cent is left to the community. Increasing the share of revenue retained by the community will increase the amount of disposable income which can be invested in village development projects or shared among participants to improve their livelihood, while at the same time increasing the incentives for greater participation in the program and avoiding free riding.

NOTES

We thank Ian Watson, Monica Fisher, David Kaimowitz, D. Andrew Wardell, Ragnar Øygard, Olvar Bergland, Gerald Shively, Steinar Strøm and the editors of this volume for constructive comments on earlier versions of this chapter.

1. For a detailed discussion about selection bias refer to Heckman, Ichimura and Todd (1997) and Heckman and Li (2004).
2. With the exception of land explicitly registered as private land, or registered as 'government land', all the remaining land falling within the jurisdiction of a recognized Traditional Authority granted to a person or group and used exclusively for the benefit of a specific community is referred to as customary land (Malawi Government 2002).
3. For details about the propensity score matching, refer to Heckman, Ichimura and Todd (1997), Smith and Todd (2001, 2005) and Dehejia and Wahba (2002).
4. US$1.00 = MK70.00 in 2002.
5. Discrimination refers to the differences in the magnitude of the coefficients of the estimated equation for the two groups of interest. For example, after running the income equations using the male and female subsamples, 'discrimination' refers to the situation where the estimated coefficients in the income equations for the male subsample for some variables, say 'level of education', are higher than those for the income equation for the female subsample.
6. 'Endowment effects' refers to differences in the averages of household characteristics and other variables which determine income. For example, years of experience in fuel wood selling is an endowment, in that a person with many years of experience as a fuel wood seller may earn more income than the newcomer, due to better communication and bargaining skills.

BIBLIOGRAPHY

Adhikari, Bhim, Salavatore D. Falco and Jon C. Lovett (2004), 'Household Characteristics and Forest Dependency: Evidence from Common Property Forest Management in Nepal', *Ecological Economics*, **48** (2), 245–57.

Agrawal, Arun and Clark C. Gibson (1999), 'Enchantment and Disenchantment: The Role of Community in Natural Resource Conservation', *World Development*, **27** (4), 629–49.

Agrawal, Arun and Elinor Ostrom (2001), 'Collective Action, Property Rights and Decentralization in Resource Use in India and Nepal', *Politics and Society*, **29** (4), 485–514.

Agrawal, Arun and Gautam N. Yadama (1997), 'How do Local Institutions Mediate Market and Population Pressures on Resources? Forest *Panchayats* in Kumaon, India', *Development and Change*, **28** (3), 435–65.

Andrews, Martyn J., Mark B. Stewart, Joanna K. Swaffield and Richard Upward (1998), 'The Estimation of Union Wage Differentials and the Impact of Methodological Choices', *Labour Economics*, **5** (4), 449–74.

Angelsen, Arild and Sven Wunder (2003), 'Exploring the Forestry–Poverty Link: Key Concepts, Issues and Research Implications', Jakarta, Center for International Forestry Research (CIFOR) Occasional Paper No. 40.

Arbache, Jorge S. and Francisco G. Carneiro (1999), 'Unions and Interindustry Wage Differentials', *World Development*, **27** (10), 1875–83.

Baland, Jean-Marie and Jean-Philippe Platteau (1996), *Halting Degradation of Natural Resources: Is There a Role for Local Communities?*, New York: Oxford University Press.

Behera, Bhagirath and Stefanie Engel (2007), 'Participation and Joint Forest Management in Andhra Pradesh, India,' in Natalia Dinello and Victor Popov (eds), *Political Institutions and Development: Failed Expectations and Renewed Hopes*, Camberley, UK: Edward Elgar, pp. 200–227.

Blinder, Alan S. (1973), 'Wage Discrimination: Reduced Form and Structural Estimates', *Journal of Human Resources*, **8** (4), 436–55.

Byron, Neil and Michael Arnold (1999), 'What Futures for the People of the Tropical Forests?', *World Development*, **27** (5), 789–805.

Campbell, Bruce M. and Michael C. Luckert (eds) (2002), *Uncovering the Hidden Harvest: Valuation Methods for Woodland and Forest Resources*, Sterling, VA: Earthscan.

Chakraborty, Rabindra N. (2001), 'Stability and Outcomes of Common Property Institutions in Forestry: Evidence from the Terai Region of Nepal', *Ecological Economics*, **36** (2), 341–53.

Chanyenga, T.F. and D. Kayambazinthu (1999), 'Monitoring and Evaluating Productivity in Miombo Woodlands under Co-management Arrangements: The Case of Liwonde Forest Reserve', in Mzoma R. Ngulube, Lusayo Mwabumba and Paxie Chirwa (eds), *Community-Based Management of Miombo Woodlands: Proceedings of a National Workshop, Sun and Sand Holiday Resort, Mangochi, Malawi, 27–29 September 1999*, Zomba, Malawi: Forestry Research Institute of Malawi.

Darity, William Jr., David Gullkey and William Winfrey (1995), 'Ethnicity, Race, and Earnings', *Economics Letters*, **47** (3–4), 401–8.

Dehejia, Rajeev H. and Sadek Wahba (2002), 'Propensity Score Matching Methods for Non-Experimental Causal Studies', *Review of Economics and Statistics*, **84** (1), 151–61.

Edmunds, David and Eva Wollenberg (eds) (2003), *Local Forest Management: The Impacts of Devolution Policies*, Sterling, VA: Earthscan.

Fisher, Robert J. (1999), 'Devolution and Decentralization of Forest Management in Asia and the Pacific', *Unasylva*, **50** (4), 1–5.

Food and Agriculture Organization (FAO) (2005), *State of the World's Forests, 2005*, Rome: Food and Agriculture Organization of the United Nations.

Heckman, James J. (1997), 'Instrumental Variables: A Study of Implicit Behavioral Assumptions Used in Making Program Evaluations', *Journal of Human Resources*, **32** (3), 441–62.

Heckman, James J. and Xuesong Li (2004), 'Selection Bias, Comparative Advantage and Heterogeneous Returns to Education: Evidence from China in 2000', *Pacific Economic Review*, **9** (3), 155–71.

Heckman, James J. and Jeffrey A. Smith (1999), 'The Pre-programme Income Dip and the Determinants of Participation in a Social Programme: Implications for Simple Programme Evaluation Strategies', *Economic Journal*, **109** (457), 313–48.

Heckman, James J., Hidehiko Ichimura and Petra E. Todd (1997), 'Matching as an Econometric Evaluation Estimator: Evidence from Evaluating a Job Training Programme', *Review of Economic Studies*, **64** (4), 605–54.

Hirsch, Barry T. and Stephen L. Mehay (2003), 'Evaluating the Labor Market Performance of Veterans using a Matched Comparison Group Design', *Journal of Human Resources*, **38** (3), 673–700.

Jodha, N.S. (1995), 'Common Property Resources: A Missing Dimension of Development Strategies', Washington, DC, World Bank Discussion Paper No. 169.

Jolliffe, Dean and Nauro F. Campos (2005), 'Does Market Liberalisation Reduce Gender Discrimination? Econometric Evidence from Hungary, 1986–1998', *Labour Economics*, **12** (1), 1–22.

Jones, F.L. and Jonathan Kelly (1984), 'Decomposing Differences between Groups: A Cautionary Note on Measuring Discrimination', *Sociological Methods and Research*, **12** (3), 323–43.

Jumbe, C.B.L. (2006), 'Local Forest Management, Poverty and Energy Use in Malawi', Ph.D. diss., Norwegian University of Life Sciences, Norway.

Jumbe, Charles and Arild Angelsen (2006), 'Do the Poor Benefit from Devolution Policies? Evidence from Forest Co-management in Malawi', *Land Economics*, **82** (4), 562–81.

Jumbe, Charles and Arild Angelsen (2007), 'Forest Dependence and Participation in CPR Management: Empirical Evidence from Forest Co-management in Malawi', *Ecological Economics*, **62** (3–4), 661–72.

Jumbe, Charles B.L., Richard N. Kachule and Charles Mataya (2000), 'Evolution of Forestry Policies in Malawi with Reference to the Miombo Woodlands', *UNISWA Research Journal of Agriculture, Science and Technology*, **4** (1), 69–76.

Kayambazinthu, Dennis (2000), 'Empowering Communities to Manage Natural Resources: Where Does Power Lie? The Case of Malawi', in Sheona Shackleton and Bruce Campbell (eds), *Empowering Communities to Manage Natural Resources. Case Studies from Southern Africa*, Jakarta: Center for International Forestry Research, pp. 53–79.

Kayambazinthu, Dennis and Catherine Locke (2002), 'Malawi Forest Management and

Diverse Livelihoods in Malawi', Norwich, UK, University of East Anglia, Ladder Working Paper No. 24.

Kowero, Godwin, Bruce M. Campbell and Ussif R. Sumaila (2001), *Policies and Governance Structures in Woodlands of Southern Africa*, Jakarta: Center for International Forestry Research.

Kumar, Sanjay (2002), 'Does "Participation" in Common Pool Resource Management Help the Poor? A Social Cost–Benefit Analysis of Joint Forest Management in Jharkhand, India', *World Development*, **30** (5), 763–82.

Liu, Pak-Wai, Junsen Zhang and Shu-Chuen Chong (2004), 'Occupational Segregation and Wage Differentials between Natives and Immigrants: Evidence from Hong Kong', *Journal of Development Economics*, **73** (1), 395–413.

Makungwa, Stephen and Dennis Kayambazinthu (1999), 'Monitoring and Evaluating Productivity in Miombo Woodlands under Co-management Arrangements: The Case of Liwonde Forest Reserve', in Mzoma R. Ngulube, Lusayo Mwabumba and Paxie Chirwa (eds), *Community-Based Management of Miombo Woodlands: Proceedings of a National Workshop, Sun and Sand Holiday Resort, Mangochi, Malawi, 27–29 September 1999*, Zomba, Malawi: Forestry Research Institute of Malawi.

Malawi, Government of (1996), *National Forestry Policy of Malawi*, Lilongwe: Ministry of Natural Resources.

—— (1997), *Forestry Act 1997*, Lilongwe: Ministry of Forestry, Fisheries and Environmental Affairs.

——(2001a), *Malawi's National Forestry Program, Priorities for Improving Forestry and Livelihood*, Lilongwe: NFP Coordination Unit.

——(2001b), *State of the Environment Report, 2001*, Lilongwe: Ministry of Natural Resources and Environmental Affairs.

—— (2002), *Malawi National Land Policy*, Lilongwe: Ministry of Lands, Physical Planning and Surveys.

Marsland, Neil, Simon Henderson and Bob Burn (1999), *On-going Evaluation of FRP Project: Sustainable Management of Miombo Woodland by Local Communities in Malawi*, Reading, UK: University of Reading, Natural Resources Institute.

Mayers, James, John Ngalande, Pippa Bird and Bright Sibale (2001), 'Forestry Tactics: Lessons Learned from Malawi's National Forestry Program', London, International Institute for Environment and Development (IIED) Policy that Works for Forests and People No. 11.

Meinzen-Dick, Ruth, Anna Knox and Monica D. Gregorio (1999), Collective Action, Property Rights and Devolution of Natural Resource Management – Exchange of Knowledge and Implications for Policy; Proceedings of the International Conference, Feldafing, Germany: Deutsche Stiftung für Internationale Entwicklung/ Zentralstelle für Ernährung und Landwirtschaft.

Meinzen-Dick, Ruth, Monica D. Gregorio and Nancy McCarthy (2004), 'Methods for Studying Collective Action in Rural Development', Washington, DC, Systemwide Program on Collective Action and Property Rights (CAPRi) Working Paper No. 33.

National Economic Council (2000), *Profile of Poverty in Malawi, 1998: Poverty Analysis of the Malawi Integrated Household Survey, 1997–98*, Lilongwe: Government of Malawi.

Oaxaca, Ronald (1973), 'Male–Female Wage Differentials in Urban Labor Markets', *International Economic Review*, **14** (3), 693–709.

Pagdee, A., Y. Kim and P.J. Daugherty (2006), 'What Makes Community Forest Management Successful: A Meta-Study From Community Forests Throughout the World', *Society and Natural Resources*, **19**, 33–52.

Reimers, Cordelia W. (1983), 'Labor Market Discrimination against Hispanic and Black Men', *Review of Economics and Statistics*, **65** (4), 570–79.

Ribot, Jesse C. (1995), 'From Exclusion to Participation: Turning Senegal's Forestry Policy Around?', *World Development*, **23** (9),1587–99.

——(2001), 'Integral Local Development: Accommodating Multiple Interests through Entrustment and Accountable Representation', *International Journal of Agriculture, Resources, Governance and Ecology*, **1** (3–4), 327–50.

Rosenbaum, Paul R. and Donald B. Rubin (1983), 'The Central Role of the Propensity Score in Observational Studies for Causal Effects', *Biometrika*, **70** (1), 41–55.

Sakanda, G.P. (1996), 'National Report on the Forestry Policy in Malawi', in Food and Agriculture Organization (ed.), *Forestry Policies of Selected Countries in Africa*, Rome: FAO, pp. 321–41.

Saxena, N.C. (1997), *Saga of Participatory Forest Management in India*, Bogor, Indonesia: Center for International Forestry Research.

Shackleton, Sheona and Bruce Campbell (2001), *Devolution in Natural Resource Management, Institutional Arrangements and Shifts. A Synthesis of Case Studies for Southern Africa*, Bogor, Indonesia: Center for International Forestry Research.

Shackleton, Sheona, Bruce Campbell, Eva Wollenberg and David Edmunds (2002), 'Devolution and Community-Based Natural Resource Management: Creating Space for Local People to Participate and Benefit', *Natural Resource Perspectives*, **76** (March),1–6.

Smith, Jeffrey A. and Petra E. Todd (2001), 'Reconciling Conflicting Evidence on the Performance of the Propensity-Score Matching Methods', *American Economic Review*, **91** (2), 112–18.

—— (2005), 'Does Matching Overcome LaLonde's Critique of Nonexperimental Estimators?', *Journal of Econometrics*, **125** (1–2), 305–53.

Trejo, Stephen J. (1997), 'Why Do Mexican Americans Earn Low Wages?', *Journal of Political Economy*, **105** (6), 1235–68.

7. Participation and Joint Forest Management in Andhra Pradesh, India

Bhagirath Behera and Stefanie Engel

One important reason for the massive degradation of natural resources in developing countries is the lack of well-defined, secure property rights (Panayotou 1993; Pearce and Warford 1993). It is now clear that technological solutions alone will not be sufficient for achieving sustainable development; institutional and governance issues play a fundamental role (World Bank 2003). Institutions are the formal and informal rules of a society. They set the limits of individual action and crucially determine the incentives faced by individual resource users. However, these institutions change in parallel with changes in government policies and social structure. Forest management programs typically adopt one of two arrangements: formal state-controlled forest management institutions or a blend of formal and informal community forest management institutions.

Under the predominant state-controlled forest management regime, the governments of most developing countries nationalized their forests in the belief that forest-dependent people were the main cause of forest degradation and deforestation, and that an exclusionary, state-controlled, top-down forest management approach is required to achieve sustainable forest management (Kumar and Kant 2005). The state-controlled forest management approach is based on the assumption that the government is capable of enforcing its property rights over forests (Saxena 1997). However, these assumptions often do not hold in developing countries, due to ineffective law enforcement, slow legal systems and large, forest-dependent populations. It is now widely accepted that state-controlled forest management frequently gives rise to violent conflicts and severe distrust between forest dwellers and forest bureaucrats (Bulte and Engel 2006). Violations of forest law in the form of grazing and firewood collection were widespread. Central authorities frequently ignored or tolerated incidences of illegal forest use, resulting in unabated forest degradation and negative impacts on local livelihoods.

Over the last two decades, many developing countries have opted to devolve forest resource management and access rights to local communities as a response to failed state policies and shrinking government budgets (Edmonds 2002; Larson and Ribot 2004). This shift has involved either power-sharing arrangements with the state, greater legal access for local communities to forest resources or decentralization within government institutions to ensure more power for local communities. In principle, devolution of forest management responsibilities from central government agencies to the local communities implies a transfer of some important decision-making authorities and benefits in order to make local user groups more active in the management of forests. Devolution is fueled by the idea that community-level organizations can establish and enforce micro-level institutions which promote sustainable development and enhance local livelihoods by building a social barrier to protect forests from grazing, fire and illegal logging (Kolavalli 1995). Moreover, local communities can manage forests at lower costs, as they may rely on existing informal monitoring and sanctioning institutions (Baland and Platteau 1996). Devolution can also remove the information gap between the state forest department and local users (Bardhan 1996); locally devised management institutions are often better able to adapt to changes in local conditions (Bulte and Engel 2006). Previous studies have documented the conceptual advantages of resource management by users (e.g., Bromley 1992; Ostrom 1992; Bardhan 1993). Experience with community-based forest management suggests that these institutions may, in principle, be successful not only in promoting effective management of forests, but also in contributing to an equitable distribution of benefits derived from the managed forests (Ostrom 1990).

India has been at the forefront of efforts to devolve natural resource management to the community level, particularly in the forestry sector. Its 1988 forest policy was a landmark, because for the first time it recognized the importance of local involvement in forest management for improving community livelihood and for protecting forest resources. In a follow-up document issued in 1990, the central government issued guidelines to all state governments to implement 'Joint Forest Management Systems' (JFM) by transferring everyday forest use and management rights to local forest protection committees (FPCs), while keeping the de jure rights over forests in the hands of the state (co-management). Accordingly, all Indian states have formally resolved to implement JFM, making it one of the largest programs of its kind in the world (Kumar 2002). More than 50 million people partner with forest departments (FDs) to regenerate and manage around 17 million hectares of forests (India 2004). Key features of the JFM policy include the mutual acceptance of responsibilities, rights and accountability for forest management between the state forest departments (FDs) and local communities (Kolavalli 1995).

The success of the JFM program, and participatory resource management approaches in general, depends on the active participation of local forest users. However, after more than a decade of JFM implementation in India, it is still unclear to what extent the program has been successful in securing local forest users' participation in the management and protection of forests. JFM agreements assign several important decision-making powers to local users, empowering them to formulate and enforce rules which will most suit their interests. There is growing empirical evidence, however, that more powerful actors in the communities may manipulate resource management policies to favor their own interests to the detriment of poor and marginalized groups and the environment (Shackleton et al. 2002; Agarwal 2001; Platteau 2003; Kumar 2002). The fundamental issue, therefore, is to identify which members of local communities attend meetings where crucial decisions on forest management are taken and, more importantly, who influences decisions at these meetings.

In this study, we contribute to the current literature on the determinants of household participation by explicitly distinguishing different levels of participation in JFM institutions and their explanatory factors. In particular, the levels considered include attendance of JFM meetings, membership in executive committees and influence on decisions taken at the meetings. We present a conceptual model and empirical analysis linking the various levels of participation. This allows us to analyze the barriers to participation of the poor in more detail. The analysis is based on an in-depth study conducted in 55 local communities in the Indian state of Andhra Pradesh.

INFORMAL RULES AND NORMS

Institutions can broadly be divided into informal and formal ones (North 1990). Informal institutions are rules, norms and customs which typically have been practiced for centuries. These are generally found to have a strong underpinning in the religion, culture and tradition of a community. Several studies from India's states have highlighted the importance of informal rules and norms for understanding differential outcomes of joint forest management (Heltberg 2001; Saxena 1997; Sarin 1999).

The creation of forest protection committees imposes new institutions on the traditional system, potentially leading to new conflicts and problems. Most importantly, the FPCs defined under joint forest management schemes frequently exclude some of the individuals and/or communities which hold customary and traditional rights to forest usage and resources (Bathla 1999; Kumar 2000). This has created inter- and intra-village conflicts and tenure insecurity on the part of traditional users excluded from FPCs. For example, specific sections of forest are frequently allotted to a nearby village community, while villagers living farther away from the forest areas are deprived of the fuel wood and fodder on which their livelihood depends.

Depriving communities living far from the forest – but who claim traditional rights – is a highly sensitive issue. In Orissa, inter-village rivalry and clashes arose when neighboring villages demanded a share in the usufructs, i.e. the rights to use forests for extraction of products (Nayak 2002). Similarly, many parts of Jammu, Kashmir and Rajasthan experienced serious problems in implementing the JFM program when nomads, a tribal group with traditional rights to graze their cattle in forests which does not belong to the local communities, were excluded from the decision-making process (Bathla 1999).

Several empirical studies on devolution in natural resource management have shown that households within a given community differ widely in their actual use of natural resources, as well as their level of participation in collective management activities and decision-making processes (Baland and Platteau 1996; Sarin 1999, 1996; Agarwal 2001; Engel, Iskandarani and Useche 2005; Jumbe and Angelsen 2007). Previous studies have shown that devolution may lead to rent-seeking activities by community elites (Abraham and Platteau 2002; Agrawal and Ostrom 2001; Platteau and Gaspart 2003) and that more powerful actors in the communities may manipulate devolution outcomes in their own favor (Shackleton et al. 2002) if the poor are not empowered enough to oppose pressures from the local elite (Platteau 2003). Agarwal (2001) discusses how seemingly participatory institutions often exclude significant sections of the community, such as women. Studying the Indian state of Jharkhand, Kumar (2002) shows that wealthier sections of the communities benefit from the JFM program at the expense of the poor.

After receiving a share of the total benefits from state timber extraction, communities have tended to adopt rules which favor long-run timber benefits through forest closure and planting high-value species. As a consequence poor, forest-dependent households suffered from the reduced availability of – and access to – non-timber forest products (NTFPs). However, these results are not easy to generalize. Karmacharya, Karna and Ostrom (2003) found that in Nepal some communities using community forestry programs have successfully created specific pro-poor rules and incentives. But they also found that parallel programs of leasehold forestry, that explicitly assign rights over degraded forest only to groups of poor households, have led to serious enforcement problems because other community members do not recognize these rights. The authors conclude that the government should share information about existing pro-poor provisions and encourage user groups to adopt similar rules. The more favorable equity outcomes in the Nepalese case may be due to the fact that timber production for revenue plays less of a role in Nepal. Where community-based forest management involves financial transfers from donor agencies, NGOs or the government, sequential and conditional release of funds may be a useful approach to discipline local leaders (Platteau 2003). However, for this approach to be effective, funding or implementing agencies need to cooperate to avoid competition among themselves which benefits local leaders. One possible remedy would be systematic reporting of cases of failure, that stands in contrast to current practice by funding agencies.

Several recent empirical studies aim to shed further light on the determinants of household participation in decentralized development programs. Many found that the socioeconomic indicators of the participants are the main factors which determine the degree to which a household participates in the local institutional decision-making process (Lise 2000; Weinberger and Jütting 2001; Maskey, Gebremedhin and Dalton 2003; Engel, Iskandarani and Useche 2005; Agrawal and Gupta 2005). Social hierarchies in the form of religion and caste are also critical explanatory factors (Shackleton et al. 2002; Deshingkar, Johnson and Farrington 2005). Indian society is characterized by a highly unequal distribution of wealth and is largely divided based on the age-old caste system (Borooah 2002). Hence, empowering the poor, lower castes and other weaker sections of the population in a largely divided society becomes a challenge to both policymakers and donor agencies.

In a study of factors influencing people's participation in forest management in the Indian states of Bihar, Hariyana and Uttar Pradesh, Lise (2000) found that the first consideration for people's participation in forest management is social indicators, followed by economic indicators. The study also notes that high dependency on forests and good forest quality enhance people's participation. It argues that when people are highly dependent on forests, their interest in forests is likely to be greater, inducing people to participate in forest management and protection activities. Maskey, Gebremedhin and Dalton (2003) and Agrawal (2000) report similar findings in case studies from Nepal and India, respectively. Using econometric models to study a protected area in Nepal's Terai region, Agrawal and Gupta (2005) found that the likelihood of participation in community-level user groups is greater for those who are economically and socially better off. They also found that individuals who have greater access to – and who more frequently visit – government offices related to decentralization policies are more likely to participate in user groups created by the state officials. Their measure of participation is, however, based on several different levels of participation combined into one single index. Moreover, their econometric analysis suffers from the weakness of using endogenous variables such as firewood and fodder collection as independent variables. Our analysis explicitly distinguishes different levels of participation and accounts for endogeneities.

One of the reasons for the lack of poor people's participation is that poor households have high opportunity costs related to participation, as the time spent on JFM affairs could be used as labor for cash income. Behera and Engel (2004) point out that high transaction costs may discourage the participation of poorer segments of forest communities in forest protection committees, thereby freeing the way for richer segments to adopt rules which are biased towards their own interests.

Weinberger and Jütting (2001) have analyzed the determinants of participation in local development groups in Chad and Pakistan. Their results suggest that middle-income households are more likely to participate than poorer and richer segments of the community due to the high opportunity costs of joining the group. They also find that an existing social network and bargaining power are important determinants of participation.

All of these studies have focused on attendance at meetings or membership in organizations as indicators of participation. As we will show, mere attendance does not automatically assure that a given household actually influences the outcomes of community decision making. Moreover, it is important to note that household participation under a co-management system not only depends on the socioeconomic and political attributes of the households but also, crucially, on how the government agency implementing the co-management program deals with local residents (Arora 1994). With the exception of Agrawal and Gupta's (2005) study, the issue has been grossly neglected in studies on participation, while the main emphasis has been put on household and community characteristics.

JFM is a co-management system where the government agency (here the forest department) which owns the forest resources seeks the cooperation of local people living in and around the forest for forest regeneration and protection. The relationship between the FD and local people in India has historically been one of mistrust and plagued with conflicts (Kumar and Kant 2005). As a consequence, the role of the FD in influencing people's participation in the JFM program cannot be ignored. Although the 1988 forest policy and subsequent JFM guidelines recognized the importance of people's participation in the success of JFM (India 1990), very little has been mentioned about the change in behavior of the forest bureaucrats.

Finally, a famous and widely cited success story within India's JFM program is the Arabari experience in the state of West Bengal. The idea of JFM is believed to have originated here, due to a forest department's effort to unofficially engage people in forest protection efforts in return for shared benefits (Joshi 1999; Ballabh, Balooni and Dave 2002; Kumar 2002; Balooni 2002). The Arabari experience highlights the importance of state–community interactions as a key to attaining local participation in the management and protection of forests. Kumar and Kant (2005) suggest the need for a massive change in the organizational structure, support system and FD culture to match the paradigm of community-based forest management systems.

ANALYZING HOUSEHOLD PARTICIPATION IN JFM

Figure 7.1 presents a conceptual framework of household participation in joint forest management. A household's decision to attend a JFM meeting is likely to depend on the expected net present value of participation. This in turn depends on two factors: the costs of participation (in particular, the opportunity cost of attendance) and the expected returns from participating in the meeting.

Costs of Participation

The opportunity costs of participation differ across households and are influenced by employment opportunities in agricultural activities and off-farm opportunities. When the opportunity costs of a household increase due to the availability of both agricultural and non-agricultural non-forest activities in the region, the household is less likely to show interest in JFM. Having more land and livestock, richer households may not participate in the meetings unless they have a specific interest in village funds and forests. The probability of people being engaged in off-farm employment depends on the skills which they acquire through education.

Returns on Participation

Potential returns on participation include expected present and future forest value, as well as wage income from engaging in forest management activities, community development and other direct benefits. Because landless laborers and marginal and small-scale farmers in rural India depend mostly on common property resources for their fuel and fodder supplies, they have a personal interest in the regeneration of degraded forests under the JFM program. Furthermore, forest products from commons are an important source of employment and income for the rural poor, especially where other opportunities are non-existent (Jodha 1997). One objective of the JFM program is to create employment for underprivileged sections of society, and more than 60 per cent of the expenditure incurred in JFM is paid as wages (Balooni 2002). People attend meetings in order to acquire information about the wage rate provided for forest work. Another important incentive for people to participate in the JFM program is the provision of public and private goods and services. Community

Figure 7.1 Schematic Framework for Analyzing Household Decisions to Participate in JFM

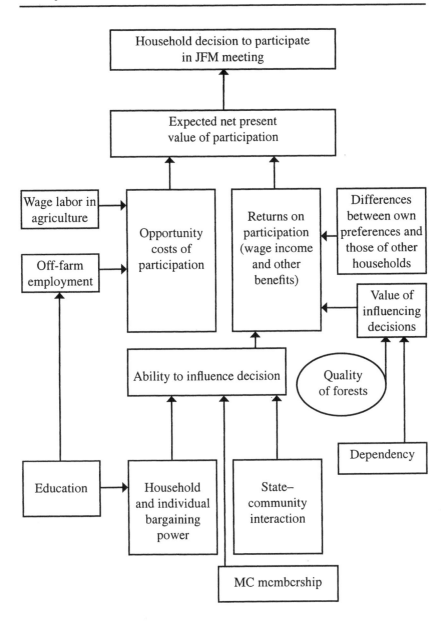

development supports small improvements in village infrastructure and helps communities explore opportunities for income generation using both forests and other options, such as agriculture and animal husbandry (World Bank 2003). Initiatives to improve the economic conditions of poor and backward households include distributing animals, lands and monetary loans. During our fieldwork we discovered that money has often been spent on development activities without prioritizing community needs (Behera and Engel 2006).

A household's expected returns on participating in JFM meetings can be decomposed into three important factors: (1) the household's benefits from influencing decisions in its favor, (2) the household's ability to influence decisions when attending the meeting and (3) the probability that a decision favorable to the household would have been taken anyway, that in turn depends on the difference between the household's own preferences and those of other households in the community.

Benefits from Influencing Decisions

The household's benefits from influencing decisions depend on forest quality and on the extent to which the household depends on the forest for its livelihood. Dependency on the forests for daily livelihood is one of the most important reasons for a household to participate in the JFM program and generally depends on the household's socioeconomic characteristics (e.g., land holding size, caste background). Landless and poor households are more likely to depend on forests in their daily lives. Lower-caste households also generally rely on collecting forest products for their livelihoods. Where forests are of good quality and substantially contribute to household income, households should be more likely to participate in the program.

Ability to Influence Decisions

Household ability to influence decisions is likely to depend on the household's bargaining power, the state–community interaction and on the household's membership in executive committees. While the 1988 forest policy mentions equal participation of all stakeholders in the JFM program, emphasis has been given to underprivileged groups in society such as the landless labor force, marginal and small-scale farmers, schedule castes, tribes and women. To what degree this is represented in actual membership in executive committees remains an empirical question. Bargaining power is likely to depend on the relative strength of the household's social group in the community and other household characteristics, such as education, wealth, age and gender. The forest department's attitude indirectly influences the household's ability to influence decision making in the community by setting the parameters of which decision-making powers are devolved to households.

Benefits from Participating in a Meeting

Finally, the benefits from participating in a meeting also depend on whether the household's interests would already be represented by others from the same socioeconomic stratum. In a heterogeneous community, people's preferences regarding JFM activities will vary according to their basic socioeconomic and cultural needs and strategic interests in the forests. The different groups or individuals which can potentially have different preferences in JFM activities owing to their socioeconomic background can be classified on the basis of caste, land holding, education, etc. For example, lower-caste groups of households are generally engaged in the collection of firewood and other NTFPs, while higher-caste households may show less interest in these products. Similarly, labor-class poor people have more interest in wage labor employment under JFM than richer people with larger land holdings.

THE DATA

Our analysis is based on an in-depth study conducted in 55 forest protection committees in the Indian state of Andhra Pradesh. Both qualitative and quantitative approaches were used to elicit information. Qualitative methods include focus group discussions among different groups of FPC members, such as women, poor and lower-caste groups and peer group discussions. Quantitative information was collected from 660 households of 55 joint forest management communities through community-level and household-level structured questionnaires. Eight communities were excluded from the dataset, as they had conducted no meetings in the village. Detailed information was collected on household participation in those JFM meetings where important issues are discussed and final decisions are taken. These include fixing wage rates for forest work, use of village common funds, selection of tree species for plantation, and other issues related to forest protection (i.e., patrolling forests, employing watchmen, etc.) and management (formulating rules for access and use of forests).

Household participation in the meetings can be classified into four categories: nominal, passive, active and interactive (Agarwal 2001). In our context, nominal participation refers to membership in the general body of the FPC. Passive participation indicates that a household was informed about the decisions taken in the meetings but did not speak up in the meetings (attendance at meetings). Active participation means the participants expressed opinions in the meetings. Interactive participation indicates that a participant feels that he has influenced the decisions taken at the meetings. Some 463 households (82 per cent) attended the most recent forest management plan meeting. Among the households who had attended meetings, around 41 per cent expressed their opinions in these meetings, but only 18 per cent felt that they influenced the decision taken. For the purpose of regression analysis, we focus on two levels of participation: passive (attendance at meetings on most recent forest management plan) and interactive (influencing decisions related to the most recent forest management plan). We now explain in detail the variables which are included in the regression models and the associated hypotheses. Tables 7.1 and 7.2 present the detailed explanations of variables used in the two stages and their hypothesized relationships.

Determinants of Influencing Decisions

We predict that a household's ability to influence decisions in the meetings will mainly depend on three factors: the bargaining power of the participant households, the state/forest department–community interaction and household membership in executive committees.

Bargaining power

The relative bargaining power among the participant households largely depends on their socioeconomic characteristics as well as institutional and community characteristics (Engel, Iskandarani and Useche 2005). Education is generally considered to be a very important determinant of participation, because it enables awareness and a willingness to search information (Verba and Nie 1972, as quoted in Weinberger and Jütting 2001). We hypothesize that more educated members in the community have greater bargaining power and thus are more likely to influence decisions. We also hypothesize that higher-caste members in the community dominate rural life and therefore have more influence in meetings compared with lower-caste groups.

We also predict that members with higher-class wealth status in the community will have more bargaining power compared with landless and labor-class members. We used television ownership as a proxy for wealth/income in the model. There are two advantages of using this proxy. First, it captures the households which receive remittances from household members working in cities and do not own any land or livestock. Second, households often underreport ownership of other assets such as land and livestock, whereas a television is easily noticed. Nevertheless, we also include land ownership as a

Table 7.1 Variables Used in Econometric Analysis of Determinants Influencing Decision in Most Recent Forest Management Plan Preparation

Variable	Definition	Expected effect
Influencing decisions in the meetings	Dummy variable = 1 if household feels that it influenced decision in most recent forest management plan preparation; = 0 otherwise	Dependent variable
Household caste	Dummy variable = 1 if household belongs to Schedule Tribe (ST); 0 = otherwise	−
Years of education of the household head	Years of schooling of household head (years)	+
Land holding size	Square root of land owned by household (acres)	+
Ownership of television	Dummy variable =1 if household owns a TV; 0 = otherwise	+
Sex of household head	Dummy variable = 1 if household head is male; = 0 otherwise	+
Age of household head	Log of household head's age (years)	+
Female–male ratio of the household	Female–male ratio (number of female household members divided by male ones)	+
State–community interaction	Proportion of households in a community that expressed FD attitude as dominant	−
Democratic village	Dummy variable =1 if household belongs to a democratic village (benevolent leadership provided by either NGOs or locals); 0 = otherwise	+
Relative strength of households	Total number of households in a household's caste group as proportion of total households in the community	+

further proxy for household wealth.

We hypothesize that, despite the JFM program's emphasis on empowering marginalized groups, traditional power structures continue to dominate community decision making; thus large farmers in the community are more likely to influence decisions compared with landless, small and marginal farmers. Indian rural society is typically characterized by a high degree of respect towards elders. Hence we hypothesize that older household heads are more likely to influence decisions than younger household heads. In the light of earlier results, we hypothesize that households with female heads have less bargaining power than male-headed households. We also include the female–male ratio of the household to shed further light on gender dynamics.

Moreover, we hypothesize that in a more democratic working environment, decisions are taken on a consensus basis and are less likely to be dictated by top-down influences. Even the poor in those communities may feel that they have influenced decisions. A democratic working environment could be due to benevolent leadership provided by a local NGO or it could originate from within the community (both traditional and modern leaders). Thus we include a 'democratic village' variable (formed in qualitative discussions during the fieldwork) and hypothesize that people belonging to these villages are more likely to influence decisions in the meetings. Finally, to measure the relative strength of households in the community we divided all households into four caste groups: Schedule Tribe (ST), Schedule Caste (SC), Backward Caste (BC) and Upper Caste (UC). A variable was created measuring the proportion of the household's caste group in all households in the community. We hypothesize a positive relationship between the relative strength of the household and its likelihood of influencing decisions.

State–community interaction

We predict that people's ability to influence decisions in the meetings will depend on the forest department's attitude toward JFM. In particular, we include a variable to account for the FD's attitude toward the community by calculating the proportion of households within a community which reported that the FD attitude was dominant. We hypothesize that people are more likely to influence decisions when the FD is cooperative.

Membership in managing committees

One of the important aims of the joint forest management program was to attract poor people's active participation in forest management and protection by electing them to the JFM decision-making body, the managing committee

(MC). However, the selection of MC members is highly endogenous in terms of our analysis and is likely to depend on the same variables included in the analysis of influencing decisions. Therefore, we run a reduced-form analysis of the determinants of influencing decisions. The next section presents an analysis of determinants of membership in the MC. Comparing the results will allow us to draw some conclusions on the success of JFM in including poor and marginalized segments of the community in executive positions and whether this translates into real decision-making powers by these segments.

Determinants of Attendance at Meetings

Probability of influencing decisions

An individual's willingness to attend meetings should depend on his/her ability to influence decisions made during the meetings. To capture the probability of an individual's ability to influence decisions, we have used the predicted probability of influencing decisions from the first-stage regression. Hence we hypothesize that the higher the probability that an individual is likely to influence decisions in the meetings, the higher is the likelihood that he or she will attend JFM meetings.

Unique preferences

In the Indian setting, household interests in the community as well as in the JFM forests can largely be classified along the line of caste background. We hypothesize that a household belonging to a large caste group is less likely to attend meetings, because the household would expect that other households in the same group would attend the meetings and represent similar interests. Therefore, the marginal benefit from attending a meeting would be relatively small for a household belonging to a large caste group.[1] We thus use the ratio of the total number of households in a household's caste group to the total number of households in the community as an explanatory variable in our regression.

Benefits from influencing decisions

The value of attendance at meetings should increase with the quality of the forests protected by the FPC and with the degree of household dependency on the forests. Forest dependency, in turn, is likely to be endogenous and depend on socioeconomic characteristics of the household. We expect that lower-caste households and those with lower levels of education and smaller land holdings, as well as female-headed households and those with high female–male ratios,

Table 7.2 Variables Used in Econometric Analysis of Determinants of Attendance at Meetings on Most Recent Forest Management Plan Preparation or Micro Plan Preparation

Variable	Definition	Expected effect
Attendance at meetings	Dummy variable = 1 if household attended meetings on most recent forest management/micro plan; = 0 otherwise	Dependent variable
Household caste	Dummy variable = 1 if household belongs to Schedule Tribe (ST); 0 = otherwise	−
Years of education of the household head	Years of schooling of household head (years)	−
Land holding size	Square root of land owned by household (acres)	+
Sex of household head	Dummy variable = 1 if household head is male; = 0 otherwise	?
Age of household head	Log of household head age (years)	−
Female–male ratio of the household	Number of female household members divided by male ones	−
State–community interaction	Proportion of households expressing FD attitude as dominant	−
Road	Dummy variable = 1 if village is connected with motorable road; = 0 otherwise	−
Distance to market	Distance to the nearest market (km)	+
Forest quality	Dummy variable =1 if FPC forest cover class and height class are more than 75% and 5 meters respectively; = 0 otherwise	+
Predicted probability of influencing decisions	Predicted probability of influencing the decisions in the most recent forest management	+
Relative strength of households	Relative strength of household in the community calculated on the basis of caste of household. Total number of households of each caste (ST, SC, BC, UC) divided by total households in the community	−

are more dependent on forests for their livelihood than are higher-caste, more educated, land-rich and male-headed households. Dependency on forests may also be higher in communities located far from markets and without access to a motorable road. Finally, the returns from participation may also depend on the forest department's role. The most favorable community rules may not provide real benefits to households if the FD dominates actual management activities or fails to take on important roles such as rule enforcement.

Costs of attending meetings

As stated earlier, the main cost of attending meetings is the opportunity cost of the time spent in the meetings. For people with greater land holdings, the opportunity costs of attending meetings may be higher compared with land-poor people. However, very poor and lower-caste people may struggle to survive, thereby facing very high opportunity costs in real terms. The opportunity costs of attending meetings are likely to be higher if better opportunities are available to work in off-farm activities in the region and in communities located closer to markets and with road access. The potential of a person to work off-farm, and the corresponding opportunity cost, is likely to depend on gender, age and education level. We therefore hypothesize that households with greater land holdings, higher levels of education, those located closer to markets and roads, male-headed households and lower-caste households are less likely to attend JFM meetings.

Several of the socioeconomic variables enter into the participation decision through more than one channel, e.g., by affecting opportunity costs, the benefits from influencing decisions and the probability of influencing decisions. Often effects move in the same direction; where they do not, the overall effect can only be determined through empirical analysis.

RESULTS AND DISCUSSION

Influencing Decisions

Table 7.3 presents the results on the determinants which most influenced decisions during the preparation of the most recent forest management plans. The results are quite robust and generally consistent with theoretical expectations.

The relation between caste and influencing decisions is negative, as expected, but it is highly insignificant. The level of education of household heads, however, is positively related to influencing decisions and is highly significant. Hence level of education is likely to play a very important role in promoting

Table 7.3　Determinants Influencing Decisions in Most Recent Forest Management Plan Meetings

Variable	Coef.	Robust std. err.	t-value	P-value
Household caste	−0.009	0.434	−0.020	0.983
Years of education of household head	1.008	0.297	3.400	0.001
Sex of household head	0.667	0.678	0.980	0.325
Female–male ratio	0.320	0.139	2.300	0.021
Democratic village	0.765	0.324	2.360	0.018
Age of household head	0.835	0.462	1.810	0.071
Relative strength of household	1.406	0.712	1.970	0.048
State–community interaction	−0.316	1.119	−0.280	0.778
Ownership of television	1.522	0.364	4.190	0.000
Land holding size	0.017	0.132	0.130	0.897
Constant	−7.786	1.981	−3.930	0.000
Number of observations	462			
Wald chi2(10)	38.92			
Prob > chi2	0.0000			
Log pseudo-likelihood	−183.205			
Cases correctly predicted	82.90%			

people's participation in a decentralized development program in general and JFM in particular.

The positive sign of the sex of the household head variable indicates that male-headed households are more likely to influence decisions in the meetings. This finding is expected in a male-dominated society like India. Interestingly, the female–male ratio is positive and significant at the 5 per cent level, which indicates households with more female members are more likely to influence the decisions. One possible explanation of this phenomenon is that women are very closely associated with the forests, as they tend to be more involved in the collection of firewood, fodder and other NTFPs for their daily livelihoods in comparison to their male counterparts (see Behera and Engel 2006 for further empirical support of this hypothesis). Being highly dependent on forests for their livelihoods and having detailed information about the forests, these women can make a difference in the meetings by motivating their household head to influence and support the decisions that best suit their interests. Lise (2000) found similar results in the state of Uttar Pradesh, where a higher number of women in the family is positively and significantly linked to the level of participation, but did not provide a convincing explanation for this phenomenon.

The 'democratic village' variable is positive and significant at the 5 per cent level, suggesting that households belonging to democratic villages, irrespective of their socioeconomic status, are more likely to feel that they have influenced decisions in the meetings. This is consistent with our impression from fieldwork, where we found that a truly democratic village, due to benevolent leadership and high accountability, can create an atmosphere in which all sections of the community can participate and be able to influence decisions. In democratic villages, the poor were allowed and even encouraged to speak up in meetings and participate in discussions; important decisions were taken on the basis of mutual consensus, making everybody understand why a particular decision was good for them compared with the other options. However, due to the somewhat subjective and possibly endogenous nature of the democratic village variable, we ran a separate regression excluding this variable to test whether the other results are robust. The signs and significance levels of all the variables remained unchanged (Behera and Engel 2006).

As expected, age of the household head is positive and significant at the 10 per cent level, implying that older people tend to influence decisions more than younger people. The relationship between influencing decisions and relative strength of the household is also as expected. The effect is positive and significant at the 5 per cent level, indicating that households belonging to a larger caste group are more likely to influence decisions. This result suggests that it is important to understand the group dynamics in the community in order to design any institutions which can ensure equal participation from all sections of the local community. The state–community interaction variable displayed the expected negative relationship, indicating that a more dominant FD reduces the ability of any household to influence decisions. The effect is, however, not significant.

The television ownership variable shows a positive effect which is significant at the 1 per cent level, indicating that richer section people in the community are more likely to dominate and influence decisions. This finding corroborates some of the recent literature on decentralization and devolution of natural resources, that argues that local elites at the community level are likely to capture benefits intended for poorer groups (Platteau and Gaspart 2003; Shackleton et al. 2002; Kumar 2002). Similarly, land holding size also showed a positive effect, but was not significant.

Table 7.4   Determinants of Selection of Candidates for Managing Committees

Variable	Coef.	Robust std. err.	t-value	P-value
Household caste	0.434	0.321	1.35	0.18
Years of education of household head	0.624	0.258	2.42	0.02
Sex of household head	−0.445	0.400	−1.11	0.27
Ownership of television	0.350	0.337	1.04	0.30
Land holding size	−0.350	0.143	−2.45	0.01
Age of household head	−0.098	0.385	−0.26	0.80
Relative strength of household	−0.509	0.497	−1.02	0.31
Female–male ratio	0.034	0.141	0.24	0.81
Constant	0.442	1.464	0.3	0.76
Number of observations	545			
Wald chi2(8)	16.28			
Prob > chi2	0.0386			
Log pseudo-likelihood	−348.036			

Managing Committee Membership

One of the important aspects of the JFM program was to attract poor people's active participation in forest management and protection by electing them to the managing committee of local forest protection committees. Since the selection of MC members is endogenously determined and depends on the same variables as does the influencing of decisions, we estimate the determinants of the selection of MC members and compare the individual variables with the regression results from the previous section. Here the dependent variable is a dummy variable which takes the value one if a household has a member in the MC and zero otherwise. Table 7.4 presents the results of determinants of the selection of MC members.

Two variables show significant effects. Education of household head is positive and significant at the 5 per cent level, meaning that educated persons are more likely to become MC members. Size of household land holding turns out to be negative and significant at the 1 per cent level, indicating that landless and marginal farmers are also selected as MC members. In regard to caste, the results indicate that lower-caste people tend to be somewhat more likely to be selected for the MC, but the effect is only significant at the 18 per cent level. The results indicate that while selecting MC members, implementing agencies

Table 7.5 Determinants of Attendance at Meetings in Most Recent Forest Management Plan

Variable	Coef.	Robust std. err.	t-value	P-value
Household caste	0.293	0.322	0.910	0.363
Years of education of household head	−0.513	0.441	−1.160	0.245
Land holding size	−0.231	0.141	−1.640	0.101
Sex of household head	−0.719	0.506	−1.420	0.156
Age of household head	−1.368	0.516	−2.650	0.008
Female–male ratio	−0.348	0.197	−1.770	0.077
State–community interaction	−2.933	0.691	−4.240	0.000
Ownership of television	−2.198	0.698	−3.150	0.002
Road	−0.212	0.358	−0.590	0.553
Distance to market	0.049	0.027	1.800	0.073
Forest quality	0.275	0.280	0.980	0.325
Relative strength of household	−1.818	0.828	−2.200	0.028
Predicted probability of influencing decisions	8.637	2.947	2.930	0.003
Constant	8.435	2.386	3.540	0.000
Number of observations		563		
Wald chi2(13)		45.11		
Prob > chi2		0.0000		
Log pseudo-likelihood		−246.013		
Cases correctly predicted		81.88%		

have made efforts to include members from weaker sections. However, as we saw from the results of determinants of influencing decisions in Table 7.4, decisions are still largely influenced by richer people.

Attendance at Meetings

Table 7.5 presents the results for the parameter estimates of determinants of meeting attendance. As expected, the predicted probability of influencing decisions shows a positive and highly significant effect on meeting attendance. Thus, households which are more likely to influence decisions are also more likely to attend the meetings.

In addition, the positive sign of the caste variable implies that, ceteris paribus, households belonging to lower-caste (Schedule Tribe) groups are more likely to attend meetings. However, this is the direct effect of caste, as opposed to the indirect effect through household bargaining power and MC membership, both of which affect a household's ability to influence decisions and thereby meeting attendance indirectly. The direct effect could be due to the fact that lower-caste households have more to benefit from JFM and also have fewer off-farm opportunities (see Behera and Engel 2006 for further empirical support of this hypothesis).

Similarly, the level of education of the household head is negatively and significantly related to attendance at meetings when only the direct effect is considered. This indicates that less-educated people are more likely to attend meetings than the more educated, which is consistent with our hypothesis that less-educated people are more dependent on the forest and tend to have fewer off-farm opportunities.

Land holding size also has a negative and significant direct effect on attendance at meetings, indicating that landless and land-poor households are more likely to attend meetings. This is again consistent with our expectation that households with less land are more dependent on the forest. In particular, a main attraction of the JFM program is wage labor benefits for poor landless people. In order to qualify for the benefits of employment in forest activities, these people may show more interest in attending meetings in an attempt to lobby for employment and enhance the wage rate. Television ownership also has a negative and significant direct effect on the attendance at meetings, further confirming our arguments. Another interesting result is that of gender participation. The variable 'sex of the household head' is negatively related to attendance at meetings, indicating that women are more likely to attend meetings. This is consistent with our expectation that women are more dependent on the forest and thus have higher benefits from attending a meeting. Moreover, women tend to have fewer off-farm opportunities. The effect of gender on meeting attendance is, however, not significant.

Furthermore, the results indicate that younger people are more likely to attend meetings, as the coefficient for age of the household head is negative and significant at the 1 per cent level. This could be due to the fact that young people are more interested in employment and other issues concerning forests. A similar finding is also reported in a study of community forest management in Nepal (Maskey, Gebremedhin and Dalton 2003). Again, it should be noted that, in addition, there is an indirect effect which discourages attendance by younger people, namely the greater likelihood of older people to influence decisions.

As expected, the variable 'relative strength of the household in the community' shows a negative and significant effect on the attendance of meetings. This supports our hypothesis that households belonging to larger groups in the community may not attend meetings, for they would expect other members of their group to represent and lobby on behalf of their interests. Again, this is in contrast to the indirect effect whereby households from larger groups are more likely to influence decisions, providing them with an incentive to attend meetings. The attitude of the forest department, representing the state–community interaction variable, has negative effects on the attendance of meetings and it is significant at the 1 per cent level. This indicates that when the attitude of the forest department is dominant or indifferent, people are less likely to participate in the meetings. This confirms the idea that people feel that they have less to gain from joint forest management when the forest department fails to take on important roles, such as rule enforcement, or dominates forest management to its own benefit. The effect is reinforced by the indirect effect whereby a dominant FD reduces households' expected probabilities of influencing decisions in the meetings.

Distance to market has a positive effect, significant at the 10 per cent level, on attendance at meetings, indicating that households in communities located far from the local market are more likely to participate in the meetings. This finding confirms the hypothesis that communities located in remote areas have lower opportunity costs and may also be more dependent on forest resources. It also supports the idea that such communities are more likely to be successful in overcoming collective action problems (Ostrom 1990). Similarly, the presence of a road has a negative effect on attendance, although this effect is not significant. Finally, as expected, household participation in JFM meetings is enhanced when people perceive their forest resources as being of good quality. The effect is, however, insignificant.

CONCLUSION AND POLICY IMPLICATIONS

The devolution of management, use and access rights to local communities and user groups has, over the last two decades, become an important policy tool for many developing countries in their efforts to promote more sustainable management of natural resources. It is fueled by the idea that community-level organizations can establish and enforce micro-level institutions which promote sustainable development and enhance local livelihoods. India's JFM program has been at the forefront of this trend. Devolution will only be successful with active participation of all segments of local communities. When powerful actors in the communities manipulate resource management outcomes in their own interest to the detriment of poor and marginalized groups, there is a risk that the resulting micro-level institutions will suffer from a lack of acceptance and compliance. In this study, we contribute to the current literature on the determinants of household participation by explicitly distinguishing different levels of participation in JFM institutions, the links between these levels and their explanatory factors. In particular, we distinguish between attendance at JFM meetings, membership in executive committees and influence on decisions taken. Our results, based on data from the state of Andhra Pradesh, indicate that, despite concerted effort by policymakers to empower poor and marginalized segments of local communities through the JFM program, richer and more-educated people in the community still are significantly more likely to influence the decisions taken. Older people and households belonging to larger caste groups are also more likely to influence decisions. The dominance of wealthier and more-educated segments of the community in the decision-making process is observed despite the fact that policies to include more marginalized groups in forest management committees have been somewhat successful. Our results indicate that being land-poor and from a lower caste increases the likelihood of a household being selected for the management committee. Less-educated people are, however, also less likely to become MC members. Our findings suggest that minority groups in the communities, although they may be formally given some authority in the JFM process, are still de facto kept out of the decision-making process. This reality is likely to have serious repercussions on the distribution of benefits from the JFM forests.

   In a second stage we estimated the determinants of meeting attendance. As hypothesized, the ability of a household to influence decision making is a crucial determinant of the household's decision on whether to attend the meeting. In this sense, our earlier results imply that poorer and less-educated households are discouraged from attending because they have a low ability to affect decision making. This is to some degree offset, however, by the fact that marginalized households have a greater stake in the forest and fewer outside options. We found that wealth has a significant direct effect on meeting attendance specifically that poorer households are more likely to attend JFM meetings. Forest quality also plays an important role in the household decision to participate in meetings or not. Good quality forests tend to encourage households to participate in the meetings. This is rational from the point of view of household cost–benefit analysis. However, it is important to note that the main objective of the JFM was to regenerate degraded forests, and most of the JFM villages were initiated on degraded forest land. Hence we can infer from the fact that good forest quality promotes participation that households failed to see the long-term benefits of forest regeneration. This gap may have serious implications for the long-term sustainability of the JFM program.

   Distance to market was also found to have a significant positive effect on participation in meetings, as households located in more remote areas tend to be more dependent on the forest and have lower opportunity costs in terms of time. We also find a certain 'free-rider effect' with participation, in the sense that households from larger groups within the community tend to participate less in the meetings.

A dominant attitude on the part of the FD not only reduces a household's chances of influencing decisions, but it also directly discourages meeting attendance, as households expect fewer benefits from JFM in an FD-dominated management regime. Therefore, if the JFM program is to succeed, in terms of bringing genuine participation from the community, the forest department must change its attitude by devolving more power and rights to local communities. Perhaps FDs could hand over responsibilities for program implementation to other agencies such as reputable NGOs and other civil society organizations and become an outside observer and facilitator.

Policymakers have made a concerted effort to promote female participation in the decision-making process by implementing quotas in the executive committee and compulsory membership in the general body committee. Our results indicate that there has been some success: female-headed households are somewhat more likely to be MC members and also show a positive direct effect on meeting attendance. Nevertheless, our first-stage results indicate that the policy is thwarted by the existing structure of male-dominated society, as the results clearly show that male members are more likely to influence decisions. This result confirms the findings of several other studies which argue that women were systematically excluded from the main decision-making process, resulting in inefficient management of forests and local institutions (Agarwal 2001; Sarin 2003).

A primary aim of participatory approaches like JFM lies in attracting the most vulnerable segments of society. The most striking finding of this study is that while these approaches seem to be relatively successful in achieving representation of marginalized groups in executive committees and in encouraging attendance at meetings, they are less successful in achieving an actual influence by these groups on the decisions taken in the meetings. This lack of influence discourages poor and marginalized groups from participating in meetings despite having a high stake in the forest. Moreover, even if these groups participate in JFM meetings, community elites continue to dominate actual decision-making processes, putting in question how participatory the programs really are. Our results point to the difficulty of imposing democratic structures on traditional societies characterized by strong hierarchies.

Two important policy implications emerge from our empirical results. First, forest departments must change their attitudes in order for forest users to realize meaningful participation in joint forest management programs. This can be accomplished through training local FD officials. Second, education is a crucial determinant of a household's ability to influence decisions. This points to strong synergies between general policies aimed at improving access to education for poor and marginalized groups and the success of JFM in truly assuring the full participation of these groups in forest management.

NOTE

1.   Of course, if all households think the same way, a problem of free riding may result.

BIBLIOGRAPHY

Abraham, Anita and Jean-Philippe Platteau (2002), 'Participatory Development in the Presence of Endogenous Community Imperfections', *Journal of Development Studies*, **39** (2), 104–36.

Agarwal, Bina (2001), 'Participatory Exclusions, Community Forestry and Gender: An Analysis for South Asia and a Conceptual Framework', *World Development*, **29** (10), 1623–48.

Agrawal, Arun (2000), 'Small is Beautiful, But is Larger Better? Forest Management Institutions in the Kumaon Himalaya, India', in Clark C. Gibson, Margaret A. McKean and Elinor Ostrom (eds), *People and Forest, Communities, Institutions and Governance: Politics, Science and the Environment*, Cambridge, MA: MIT Press, pp. 57–86.

Agrawal, Arun and Krishna Gupta (2005), 'Decentralization and Participation: The Governance of Common Pool Resources in Nepal's Terai', *Word Development*, **33** (7), 1101–14.

Agrawal, Arun and Elinor Ostrom (2001), 'Collective Action, Property Rights and Decentralization in Resource Use in India and Nepal', *Politics and Society*, **29** (4), 485–514.

Andra Pradesh, Government of (2002), Government Order Ms. No. 13, dated: 12 February 2002, 'Environment Forests Science and Technology', Government of Andhra Pradesh, Forest Department, Hyderabad.

Arora, Dolly (1994), 'From State Regulation to People's Participation: The Case of Forest Management in India', *Economic and Political Weekly*, **39** (12), 691–8.

Baland, Jean-Marie and Jean-Philippe Platteau (1996), *Halting Degradation of Natural Resources: Is There a Role for Local Communities?*, New York: Oxford University Press.

Ballabh, Vishwa, Kulbhushan Balooni and Shibani Dave (2002), 'Why Local Resources Management Institutions Decline: A Comparative Analysis of Van (Forest) Panchayats and Forest Protection Committees in India', *World Development*, **30** (12), 2153–67.

Balooni, Kulbhushan (2002), 'Participatory Forest Management in India: An Analysis of Policy Trends Amid Management Change', *Policy Trend Report*, pp. 88–113.

Bardhan, Pranab K. (1993), 'Analytics of Institutions of Informal Cooperation in Rural

Development', *World Development*, **21** (4), 633–9.

——(1996), 'Decentralized Development', *Indian Economic Review*, **31** (2), 139–56.

Bathla, Seema (1999), 'Externalities Impinging on Participatory Forest Management in India', World Wide Fund for Nature – India, Policy and Joint Forest Management Paper No. 4.

Behera, Bhagirath and Stefanie Engel (2004), 'The Four Levels of Institutional Analysis of Evolution of Joint Forest Management (JFM) in India: A New Institutional Economics (NIE) Approach', paper presented at the annual meetings of the International Association for the Study of Common Property, Oaxaca, Mexico, August.

——(2006), 'Who Forms Local Institutions? Levels of Household Participation in India's Joint Forest Management Program', Bonn, Germany, Center for Development Research, ZEF-Discussion Paper on Development Policy No. 103.

Borooah, Vani (2002), 'The Political Economy of Caste in India', paper presented at the annual meetings of the European Public Choice Society, Belgirate, Italy, 4–7 April.

Bromley, Daniel (ed.) (1992), *Making the Commons Work: Theory, Practice and Policy*, San Francisco: Institute for Contemporary Studies.

Bulte, Erwin and Stephanie Engel (2006), 'Conservation of Tropical Forests: Addressing Market Failure', in Ramón López and Michael A. Toman (eds), *Economic Development and Sustainability: New Policy Options*, New York: Oxford University Press, pp. 412–52.

Deshingkar, Priya, Craig Johnson and John Farrington (2005), 'State Transfers to the Poor and Back: The Case of the Food-for-Work Program in India', *World Development*, **33** (4), 575–91.

Edmonds, Eric V. (2002), 'Government-Initiated Community Resource Management and Local Resource Extraction from Nepal's Forests', *Journal of Development Economics*, **68** (1), 89–115.

Engel, Stefanie (2004), 'Designing Institutions for Sustainable Resource Management and Environmental Protection', habilitation thesis, Faculty of Agriculture, University of Bonn, Germany.

Engel, Stefanie, Maria Iskandarani and Maria del Pilar Useche (2005), 'Improved Water Supply in the Ghanaian Volta Basin: Who Uses It and Who Participates in Community Decision Making', Washington, DC, International Food Policy Research Institute (IFPRI), EPT Discussion Paper No. 129.

Gyasi, Osman (2005), *Determinants of Success of Collective Action on Local Commons: An Empirical Analysis of Community Based Irrigation Management in Northern Ghana*, New York: Peter Lang.

Heltberg, Råsmus (2001), 'Determinants and Impacts of Local Institutions for Community Resource Management', *Environment and Development Economics*, **6** (2), 183–208.

India, Government of (1990), 'Involvement of Village Communities and Voluntary Agencies for Regeneration of Degraded Forest Lands', Memorandum to Forest Secretaries of All States and Union Territories, No. 6-21/89-F.P., 1 June, New Delhi Ministry of Environment and Forests.

——(2004), *Annual Report, 2003–2004*, New Delhi: Ministry of Environment and Forests.

Jodha, N.S. (1997), 'Management of Common Property Resources in Selected Dry Areas of India', in John M. Kerr, Dinesh K. Marothia, Katar Singh, C. Ramasamy and

William B. Bentley (eds), *Natural Resource Economics: Theory and Application in India*, New Delhi: Oxford and IBH Publishing, pp. 339–61.

Joshi, Anuradha (1999), 'Progressive Bureaucracy: An Oxymoron? The Case of Joint Forest Management in India', London, Overseas Development Institute, Rural Development Forestry Network Paper No. 24a.

Jumbe, Charles B.L. and Arild Angelsen (2007), 'Has Forest Co-management in Malawi Benefited the Poor?', in Natalia Dinello and Victor Popov (eds), *Political Institutions and Development: Failed Expectations and Renewed Hopes*, Camberley, UK: Edward Elgar, pp. 200–27.

Karmacharya, Mukunda B., Birendra Karna and Elinor Ostrom (2003), 'Rules, Incentives and Enforcement: Livelihood Strategies of Community Forestry and Leasehold Forestry Users in Nepal', paper presented at the conference 'Rural Livelihoods, Forests and Biodiversity', Bonn, Germany, 19–23 May.

Kolavalli, Shashi (1995), 'Joint Forest Management: Superior Property Rights?', *Economic and Political Weekly*, 29 June, 1933–8.

Kumar, N. (2000), 'All is Not Green with JFM in India', *Forest, Trees and People* (42), 46–50.

Kumar, Sanjay (2002), 'Does Participation in Common Pool Resource Management Help the Poor? A Social Cost–Benefit Analysis of Joint Forest Management in Jharkhand, India', *World Development*, **30** (5), 763–82.

Kumar, Sanjay and Shashi Kant (2005), 'Bureaucracy and New Management Paradigms: Modeling Foresters' Perceptions Regarding Community-Based Forest Management in India', *Forest Policy and Economics*, **7** (4), 651–69.

Larson, Anne. M. and Jesse C. Ribot (2004), 'Democratic Decentralisation Through a Natural Resource Lens: An Introduction', *European Journal of Development Research*, **16** (1), 1–25.

Lise, W. (2000), 'Factors Influencing People's Participation in Forest Management in India', *Ecological Economics*, **34** (3), 379–92.

Maskey, Vishakha, Tessa G. Gebremedhin and Timothy J. Dalton (2003), 'A Survey of Analysis of Participation in a Community Forest Management in Nepal', paper presented at the Northeastern Agricultural Resource Economics Association, Portsmouth, New Hampshire, 8–10 June.

Nayak, Prateep K. (2002), 'Community-Based Forest Management in India: The Issue of Tenurial Significance', paper presented at the ninth conference of the International Association for the Study of Common Property, 'The Commons in an Age of Globalisation', Victoria Falls, Zimbabwe, 17–21 June.

North, Douglass C. (1990), *Institutions, Institutional Change and Economic Performance*, New York: Cambridge University Press.

Ostrom, Elinor (1990), *Governing the Commons: The Evolution of Institutions for Collective Action*, New York: Cambridge University Press.

—— (1992), *Crafting Institutions for Self-Governing Irrigation Systems*, San Francisco: Institute of Contemporary Studies.

Panayotou, Theodore (1993), *Green Markets: The Economics of Sustainable Development*, San Francisco: Institute of Contemporary Studies.

Pearce, David W. and Jeremy J. Warford (1993), *World Without End: Economics, Environment and Sustainable Development*, New York: Oxford University Press.

Platteau, Jean-Philippe (2003), 'Decentralized Development as a Strategy to Reduce Poverty?', paper prepared for the Agence Francaise de Développement, Centre de

Recherche en Economie de Développement, University of Namur, Belgium.
Platteau, Jean-Philippe and Frederic Gaspart (2003), 'The Risk of Resource Misappropriation in Community-Driven Development', *World Development*, **31** (10), 1687–1703.
Sarin, Madhu (1996), 'From Conflict to Collaboration: Institutional Issues in Community Management', in Mark Poffenberger and Betsy McGean (eds), *Village Voices, Forest Choices: Joint Forest Management*, Delhi: Oxford University Press, pp. 165–209.
—— (1999), 'Policy Goals and JFM Practice: An Analysis of Institutional Arrangements and Outcomes', World Wide Fund for Nature – India, Policy and Joint Forest Management Paper No. 3.
——(2001), 'Disempowering in the Name of Participatory Forestry? Village Forests Joint Management in Uttarakhand', *Forests, Trees, and People Newsletter*, No. 44.
—— (2003), 'Devolution as a Threat to Democratic Decision-Making in Forestry? Findings from Three States in India', London, Overseas Development Institute Working Paper No. 197.
Saxena, N.C. (1997), *Saga of Participatory Forest Management in India*, Bogor, Indonesia: Center for International Forestry Research.
Shackleton, Sheona, Bruce Campbell, Eva Wollenberg and David Edmunds (2002), 'Devolution and Community-Based Natural Resource Management: Creating Space for Local People to Participate and Benefit', *Natural Resource Perspectives*, **76** (March), 1–6.
Weinberger, Katinka and Johannes Paul Jütting (2001), 'Women's Participation in Local Organizations: Conditions and Constraints', *World Development*, **29** (8), 1391–1404.
World Bank (1994), *The World Bank and Participation*, Washington, DC: World Bank Operations Policy Department.
—— (2003), 'World Bank to Help Community to Take Over Forest Management in Andhra Pradesh: Project Aims to Reduce Rural Poverty Through Community Empowerment', Washington, DC, World Bank, South Asia Region, Press Release No. 2003/022/MNA.

8. Clientelism, Public Workfare and the Emergence of the Piqueteros in Argentina

Lucas Ronconi and Ignacio Franceschelli

Over the last ten years, Argentina has experienced a significant increase in the number of collective protests. This increase was not due to increased militancy by existing organizations. In fact, the average annual number of strikes organized by labor unions decreased from 509 in 1983–96 to only 219 in 1997–2004. Rather, the higher level of social conflict comes from non-institutionalized protesters and forms of protest. This chapter focuses on a new social movement, popularly known as *Piqueteros* (people who block roads or 'the picketers'), that has organized most of these non-traditional demonstrations.[1]

The total number of road blockades between 1997 and 2004 was 7,135, implying an average of 892 per year, more than four times the number of strikes. Curiously, participants in the road blockades tend to be poor, unemployed people not linked together by any previous work experience. This population usually does not have the resources or the network ties to collectively organize. How is that they became the most salient protesters?

Several authors have attempted to explain the origins and growth of the Piqueteros (Camarero, Pozzi and Schneider 1998; Conti and Schneider Mansilla 2003; Farinetti 1999; Galafassi 2003; Isman 2004; Kohan 2002; Laufer and Spiguel 1999; Oviedo 2001; Pozzi 2000; Scribano 1999; Svampa and Pereyra 2003). They argue that the movement emerged mainly as a response to poverty, unemployment, inequality and limited democracy. Structural conditions and a desire for social justice motivated people to create or join the Piqueteros organizations, according to this view. This opinion has some appeal, considering Argentina's recent economic crisis. However, this view contains some weaknesses. 'Social movements are not a simple knee-jerk response to social conditions' (Wilson 1973, 90), and we found that there is not an obvious relationship between grievances and demonstrations, either across time or across provinces in Argentina.

This study focuses on the nature of the goods which participants in the Piquetero movement seek, and how these goods must be produced. The government's decision to implement temporary public works programs – workfare – in 1993 triggered the emergence of the Piqueteros and provided the resources for their growth. Participants in these temporary public works programs would receive a monthly wage in exchange for part-time community service. In particular, we emphasize how the government managed workfare and the intrinsic characteristics of this policy.

First, only a small proportion of the eligible population (less than 10 per cent) actually participated in the workfare program. Most poor and unemployed individuals were aware that filling out an application form did not guarantee their access to benefits. Second, cronyism in the selection of recipients eroded the legitimacy of the government, further inducing individuals to search for alternative channels to obtain these benefits. Third, workfare fostered networking among beneficiaries. Participants were organized into groups of approximately 50 individuals to perform public work. Once participation ended (generally after three to six months) ex-participants interested in another round had stronger networks among themselves, facilitating coordination. Fourth, workfare provided selective material incentives to overcome free riding. Since a workfare benefit (monthly wage) is an excludable good, the Piqueteros organizations had an effective tool to induce people to join them and participate in demonstrations: only members of the organization who actively participate in road blockades receive the workfare benefits which the Piqueteros distribute on behalf of the government.

In game-theory terminology, workfare changed the collective action problem from a prisoner's dilemma into an assurance game, since workfare benefits are selective incentives which remove the temptation to free ride. Moreover, workfare also helped reduce coordination problems (the main barrier to collective action in assurance games) by fostering networking among unemployed people.

Previous research has not ignored the linkage between the Piqueteros and workfare. But it views access to workfare benefits as a mere outcome of the road blockade (Colmegna 2003; Delamata 2004; Ferrara 2003; Svampa and Pereyra 2003). Demanding public goods such as social justice and democratization is, according to this view, the causal reason why aggrieved individuals collectively organize and participate in protests. More importantly, they exclusively see the implementation and expansion of workfare as the government's reaction to the emergence of the movement. While we agree that the government typically reacted to demonstrations by providing workfare funds to the Piqueteros, we stress the opposite causal sequence: road blockades were organized to obtain workfare benefits, and the government's attempt to silence the protests by distributing benefits among the Piqueteros meant more resources for these organizations and actually ended up fueling demonstrations.

We present empirical evidence about a topic which so far has been mainly discussed theoretically, and we assess the merits of the existing models of social movement to account for the Piqueteros' case. Neither system strain, the main explanation according to the classical model, nor cognitive liberation, a necessary condition according to McAdam's formulation of the political process model, are adequate explanations for the development of insurgency. All the evidence we find is consistent with the view that selective material incentives and access to external resources were fundamental for the emergence and growth of the Piqueteros.

THE EMERGENCE OF THE PIQUETEROS

In his study of the black protest movement in the United States, Doug McAdam categorizes theories of social movements into three groups: classical, resource mobilization and political processes. The classical model views social movements as a collective reaction to system strain. Such strain has psychological effects on individuals and, when severe enough, triggers social insurgency. The classical model, particularly when applied to an open and responsive political system, assumes that 'movement participants are not engaged in rational political action. Instead, the rewards they seek are primarily psychological in nature' (1999, 17).

According to the resource mobilization model, social movements 'are not forms of irrational behavior but rather a tactical response to the harsh realities of a closed and coercive political system' (20). A change in the amount of resources available to unorganized but aggrieved groups is the key cause for the emergence of social movements.

Finally, the political process model considers three sets of factors to be crucial in the generation of insurgency. First, shifts occur in the structure of political opportunities which promote insurgency 'only indirectly through a restructuring of existing power relations' (41). Second, the amount of resources of the aggrieved population changes, enabling them to exploit the political opportunities. The third factor is cognitive liberation: 'Before collective protest can get under way, people must collectively define their situation as unjust and subject to change through group action' (51). All three factors are regarded as necessary, but not sufficient, causes of social insurgency.

Previous research attempting to explain the emergence and growth of the Piqueteros generally fits into the classical model.[2] Scribano (1999), for example, argues that the geographical areas with more road blockades tend to be regions where unemployment and inequality are higher, where more privatizations have taken place and where electoral participation is lower. Oviedo (2001) argues that government corruption combined with deteriorating economic conditions explains the emergence of insurgency. The same view is presented by Delamata: 'These organizations [Piqueteros] emerged as a result of people struggling for jobs, on the one hand, and fighting against local Peronist bosses, on the other' (2004, 2). The idea is that the Piquetero movement emerged mainly as a response to social conditions, clientelistic practices and limited democracy. Structural conditions and a desire for social justice motivated people to create and join the Piqueteros organizations.

There are two reasons why we find this view incomplete. First, it is not obvious that political restrictions and social deprivations were at their peak when the Piqueteros emerged.[3] Second, how is it that poor and unemployed people, not linked together by any previous work experience, were able to collectively organize and become the most prominent group of protesters? This is particularly puzzling, considering that this group has few resources and historically has been shut out of the political arena.[4]

While economic grievances and political discontent played a role in the emergence of the Piqueteros, the process was more complex than previously presented. We believe that system strain contributed to the formation of a latent group. However, the mere existence of individuals interested in altering the economic and political system does not necessarily imply that they would be able to collectively organize, because social justice and political rights are public goods. They benefit all (or most) members of society, not only those who work toward achieving them. Additionally, these goods can usually be produced only if large numbers of individuals work together to achieve them. Free riding and coordination are usually formidable barriers to overcome, as pointed out by Olson (1965) and further developed by Chong (1991).[5] We believe that the implementation of public workfare in Argentina, and the method the government used to administer workfare funds, reduced those barriers and triggered the development of the insurgency.

WORKFARE, EXTERNAL RESOURCES AND MATERIAL SELECTIVE INCENTIVES

In 1993 Argentina's federal government began implementing workfare programs with the objective of providing temporary employment and income relief to unemployed and poor workers. The most emblematic of these programs was the *Programa Trabajar* (employment program), implemented in 1996 with financial support from the World Bank. The Trabajar is a successor to the *Programa Intensivo de Trabajo* (intensive labor program) created in 1993.[6] According to the legislation, these programs were targeted toward poor and unemployed individuals, with a priority for heads of households. The federal government allocated workfare funds among provinces and municipalities. Local governments selected workfare recipients and provided them with the necessary materials to perform public service, such as cleaning public areas or making minor repairs to public buildings. Recipients were asked to work between 20 and 40 hours per week on these projects and received, in exchange, a fixed monthly stipend and health coverage.[7]

Table 8.1 shows the evolution of workfare beneficiaries. The monthly average number of participants increased from 26,000 in 1993 to 280,000 in 2001. In May 2002, as a response to a major economic and political crisis, the new government increased dramatically the number of recipients to 1.4 million with the implementation of a workfare program known as *Jefes de Hogar* (heads of households). In 2003 the number of beneficiaries was further increased to approximately two million people, and it remains at that level today.

Given the high rate of unemployment observed during the 1990s, the number of workfare beneficiaries represented only approximately 3.5 per cent of the unemployed population until 1996; it increased to 7 per cent in 1997. It was not until May 2002 – when the Piqueteros were already the most salient group of protesters – that participation became universal. Clearly, meeting the eligibility criteria was insufficient to access workfare benefits in the 1990s.

Workfare participants were gathered in groups of approximately 50 individuals to perform public works, an arrangement which also promoted networking among recipients. Participation – and hence access to the cash benefit – lasted three to six months. While a second round of participation was not legally prohibited, the government sought to allocate the scarce funds to those eligible individuals who had not received the benefit previously. Because the chances of getting a job in the labor market were low in the mid-1990s due to high unemployment, a large fraction of former program participants were interested in re-enrolling. But since they had to compete with eligible applicants who had not participated before, and also because the available benefits could serve only a small fraction of the intended population, these former participants looked for alternative channels to access benefits. The social capital they developed while working in the program could become a valuable asset if the alternative route involved collective action. This networking effect was essential – it makes workfare distinctive from other social programs which also provided excludable goods, such as the PAN and Plan Vida food programs implemented in the 1980s and early 1990s.

Not only was the number of workfare beneficiaries small relative to the needy population, but some recipients did not even meet the eligibility requirements. Ronconi, Sanguinetti and Fachelli (2006) find that approximately one-third of

Table 8.1   Number of Workfare Beneficiaries

| Year | Number of participants (monthly average) | | Total |
	Federal workfare programs	Provincial workfare programs	
1993	26,236	na	26,236
1994	27,716	1,071	28,787
1995	48,909	377	49,286
1996	62,084	11,438	73,522
1997	129,508	23,938	153,446
1998	116,196	69,064	185,260
1999	107,466	56,831	164,297
2000	85,894	110,988	196,882
2001	88,145	192,002	280,147
2002	1,294,777	118,150	1,412,927
2003	2,173,572	157,738	2,331,310

Source: Argentine Ministry of the Economy (2001, 2002, 2004); Argentine Ministry of Labor (1998, 2001, 2002).

workfare participants were members of households located in the top 50 per cent of the per capita income distribution. Furthermore, anecdotal evidence, such as media reports, suggests other forms of corrupt practices were at work.[8] Some participants were coerced into participating in political events supporting the ruling party[9] or hand over a percentage of the cash benefit to local political bosses.[10]

Such manipulation made it very clear to the people that workfare funds were not allocated according to fair and objective rules, eroding the legitimacy of the government. Eligible individuals realized that being poor and unemployed were not sufficient conditions to access the benefit. They could appeal to local political bosses, and if they were lucky enough to receive payments, to accept the shady strings attached. They could also try to become politically powerful in order to obtain workfare benefits by themselves and impose their own terms when bargaining with the government. But these aggrieved individuals faced coordination and motivation challenges which made it difficult to pursue the second option. To be politically powerful they needed a certain number of individuals to participate in a demonstration, and individuals are more likely to participate if they expect that participation will bring them some reward. Workfare benefits are excludable goods, allowing organizations controlling benefits to discriminate between those aggrieved individuals who participate in protests from those who do not. Only those who participate in road blockades have access to the benefits the Piqueteros obtained from the government.

In addition, since 1996 NGOs formally registered in Argentina have been allowed to apply for workfare funds. They had to submit a public work project proposal to the government, including the names, IDs, addresses and socioeconomic characteristics of the prospective participants. If the project was selected, the government provided a monthly stipend directly to participants, and the NGO had to provide the materials needed to carry out the proposed project. While in theory the option of accessing workfare benefits through NGOs – an alternative channel to corrupt local party bosses – might have impeded the emergence of the Piqueteros, it actually had the contrary effect, in part because only a small proportion of workfare funds were allocated to NGOs.

Political entrepreneurs such as Luis D'Elia and Juan Carlos Alderete – the actual leaders of the two major Piqueteros organizations – were able to harness the large demand for workfare benefits by realizing that access to workfare was a matter of political strength, not of fulfilling formal requirements. They began organizing road blockades in 1996 and 1997, demanding benefits by presenting themselves as organizations of unemployed workers, even if their groups were not formally registered as NGOs and without presenting the required project description. Every individual willing to actively participate in road blockades was allowed to do so, regardless of his or her personal background. Several groups which were given low priority or even not allowed to participate in workfare according to the eligibility requirements, such as low-income self-employed workers, poor women (usually not heads of households) or ex-workfare participants, plus all the eligible applicants who could not access benefits through local political bosses or formally registered NGOs, found these incipient organizations of unemployed workers an attractive option.

Joining a Piquetero organization was neither cost free nor risk free, since protesters have to spend days blocking roads, and there was a possibility of police harassment or simply not succeeding at the bargaining table. But Piqueteros were also the only option for citizens who could not access benefits through existing institutional channels. Furthermore, several events which had occurred a few years before the emergence of the Piqueteros organizations improved people's expectations about the efficacy of road blockades.

In the early 1990s there were several demonstrations, particularly in Salta and Neuquén, organized by unionized workers who had recently been fired from their jobs due to the privatization of public companies, mainly the petroleum company Yacimientos Petrolíficos Fiscales (YPF). These unionized workers decided to block roads, a quite creative form of protest at the time, and usually received workfare benefits from the government in exchange for demobilization.[11] Then in 1997 the government again reacted positively, providing workfare benefits to the first road blockades carried out by small groups of poor individuals with no formal organizational framework or previous experience in labor unions.

Obtaining workfare benefits improved the strength of these incipient organizations of poor and unemployed people. Not only did these groups gain reputations as effective channels to access workfare, inducing aggrieved individuals to join them, but this access translated into human and monetary resources. The government did not provide the workfare benefits (monthly wages) directly to beneficiaries, as the program required, but to the leaders of these incipient Piqueteros organizations, who used the funds mainly to reward those who had participated in the initial road blockades and also to cover organizational costs.[12] Rewarded individuals are asked to continue participating in road blockades, not only to renew their stipends but also to obtain additional benefits from the government, such as free food, which the organizations use to increase membership.[13] The Piqueteros not only organize road blockades, but they also run several communitarian projects which are financed through workfare funds. Not surprisingly, their membership increased from less than 1,000 in 1997 to more than 300,000 in 2004.

THE GOVERNMENT: WORKFARE IN A PATRONAGE-BASED SYSTEM

This overview raises many questions about the behavior of Argentina's government. Why did it introduce workfare in the first place and why did it select beneficiaries in a clientelistic manner? Why did it reward protestors? We consider the emergence and growth of the Piqueteros to be an unintended consequence of a clientelistic government, particularly when operating under tight budget constraints and with low political support.

When President Carlos Menem introduced a currency board in 1991, the government, to a large extent, lost the ability to finance social policies via decreed increases in private-sector wages, fiscal deficits or expansionary monetary policy. Furthermore, a law passed in the early 1990s prevented the federal government from increasing public employment. Targeted social programs controlled by the executive branch, such as workfare, were implemented in part to soften the shock of the economic reforms, but also because they were among the few instruments which incumbent politicians had to buy votes. The government – more interested in the next election than in promoting long-term development – usually reacted to road blockades by fulfilling the demands of the protesters in a belief that it could thereby reduce conflict, at least until the next election. Moreover, ignoring or repressing protests organized by poor and unemployed people was usually a politically inconvenient option for these democratically elected governments, that tried to differentiate themselves from previous dictatorships by satisfying social demands instead of repressing them.

Low political support also explains why the government increased workfare expenditures and ended up fueling the growth of the Piqueteros. The Peronist party was in power from 1989 to 1999.[14] It remained quite united during the early 1990s, but lost cohesion, particularly when President Menem sought reelection for a third consecutive term in 1999 and was confronted by Buenos Aires' governor Eduardo Duhalde, who held considerable power in the party. In order to gain political support from local political bosses, the executive branch increased the distribution of workfare benefits. The next administration also used workfare funds to gain political support. In 2000 the governing coalition (*Alianza*) divided when Vice President Carlos Alvarez resigned. Immediately after, President Fernando de la Rúa signed a fiscal pact with the governors, agreeing to the transfer of $225 million in federal funds to the provinces during 2001 – earmarked to finance provincial workfare programs – in order to gain support in Congress and ensure political stability (Tommasi 2002).

MEMBERSHIP AND CONTROL OVER WORKFARE BENEFITS

Precise data about the total number of Piqueteros organizations are not available, but estimates indicate that there are more than 100 organizations nationwide.[15] The fact that most organizations are not formally registered and frequent mergers and separations further complicate obtaining a precise figure. Five organizations, however, contain the most members and organize most of the blockades:

1. Federación de Tierra, Vivienda y Hábitat (FTV),
2. Corriente Clasista Combativa vertiente Desocupados (CCCD),
3. Coordinadora Aníbal Verón,[16]
4. Movimiento Integrado de Jubilados y Desocupados (MIJD) and
5. Polo Obrero.

In 2004 they claimed about 300,000 members and controlled more than 150,000 workfare benefits.

An historical account of these organizations suggests that in the mid-1990s they were very small groups of poor and unemployed neighbors with no formal organization or ties with labor unions or political parties.[17] They began organizing road blockades in 1996–97, demanding access to workfare benefits and obtained some from the government (usually for fewer than 100 people). These benefits were used to reward protesters, attract new members and organize more road blockades. The groups grew fast over time, thanks to the growing amount of workfare benefits under their control. Eventually they evolved into the organizations now popularly called Piqueteros. Some of these organizations later joined existing labor unions.[18] The Polo Obrero is the only major Piquetero organization which began as an initiative of a traditional political party (Partido Obrero) but it is relatively young compared with the others.[19] The political entrepreneurs who organized the first protests are now the actual leaders of these Piqueteros organizations (D'Elia in FTV, Alderete in CCCD and Raúl Castells in MIJD).

The fact that the initial road blockades and the emergence of the Piqueteros organizations occurred a few years after public workfare programs were first introduced in 1993 is consistent with our argument. The implementation of workfare was clearly not a government reaction to the Piqueteros. Rather, the expectation of receiving workfare benefits induced aggrieved individuals to organize road blockades in the first place. According to the self-history of the Piqueteros, access to workfare and other material benefits provided the motivation for collective action. The following account, extracted from one Piquetero organization website, is illustrative:

> In August 1997, due to lack of jobs and poverty, as a group of neighbors from Solano we began gathering together to improve our own situation, tired of the unfulfilled promises of the government, and the manipulation of workfare benefits, which were given by the politicians to their friends and relatives. We began gathering together in the local church. ... After useless meetings with the municipal authorities, we decided to organize our initial road blockade on November 11, 1997 ... we obtained 120 workfare benefits and 150 boxes of food.[20]

Another way to test our hypothesis is to go back to the mid-1990s and find a group of neighbors identical to one which later became a Piquetero organization in every way except that it did not receive workfare benefits. If access to workfare effectively played a key role in the emergence and growth of the Piqueteros organizations as we claim, then we should observe that the group which did not receive workfare benefits remained small and politically insignificant.

One case in point is the MTD La Matanza (also known as Cooperativa La Juanita), which was created in 1995 by a group of poor and unemployed neighbors demanding jobs. This cooperative shared many characteristics with the two cooperatives which later became the FTV and CCCD, the largest

Piqueteros organizations. The three groups were born in the same municipality (La Matanza), they comprised poor and unemployed people, they had no formal links with either established political parties or with labor unions and in the mid-1990s they had similar membership profiles.[21] Members of MTD La Matanza, however, neither blocked roads nor received workfare benefits from the government. Today MTD La Matanza is insignificant, both in terms of membership and political power, compared with the other Piqueteros organizations: while it has 50 members (*Segundo Enfoque* October 2004), FTV has 125,000 members and CCCD 70,000 members. Comparing the evolution over time of MTD La Matanza with respect to FTV and CCCD is the closest we can get to a natural experiment. And the outcome of this comparison is clear: access to workfare funds was fundamental for the exponential growth of an organization.[22]

The following comments by Néstor Pitrola, leader of Polo Obrero, can also be interpreted as evidence supporting our claim, although it is quite speculative:

> Regarding social programs, we resisted them at the beginning. Our strategy was to obtain a subsidy for all unemployed people, and we still have that strategy. But after a political assessment, we decided to begin demanding workfare benefits as another step in our fight. And that is the way we consider it today.[23]

A subsidy for all unemployed people, as the organization demands, is not an excludable good. Since this policy benefits all unemployed workers, it erodes the individual incentive to participate in protests and, therefore, diminishes the prospects of successful collective action. In our view, Pitrola realized that exclusively demanding universal unemployment insurance raised the free-rider problem, and he therefore chose to also demand workfare benefits (an excludable good) in order to gain members and political power.

Table 8.2 presents data on membership and control over workfare benefits for the five major Piqueteros organizations (Table 8A.1 includes figures for other smaller organizations). The figures in both Table 8.2 and Table 8A.1 were drawn from daily Argentine newspapers and figures reported to the media by the Piqueteros organizations.

The data have several interesting features. First, the correlation between the number of workfare beneficiaries controlled by the organization and membership is positive, large (0.86) and statistically significant at the 1 per cent level (the correlation is 0.9 when including organizations in Table 8A.1). Organizations which control more workfare have more members. Second, the evolution over time of both variables also appears to be positively correlated. Between 2002 and 2004, the number of beneficiaries controlled by the Piqueteros organizations

Table 8.2   Membership and Control of Workfare Benefits across the Five Largest Piqueteros Organizations, 2002–2004

Piquetero organization	Number of workfare beneficiaries controlled by organization	Number of members	Ratio workfare/ members	Year
FTV	75,000	125,000	0.60	2004
	75,000	120,000	0.63	2003
	45,000	80,000	0.56	2002
CCCD	50,000	70,000	0.71	2004
	42,000	70,000	0.60	2003
	45,000	50,000	0.90	2002
Polo Obrero	20,000	25,000	0.80	2004
	23,000	29,000	0.79	2003
	20,000	35,000	0.57	2002
Coordinadora	na	na	na	2004
Aníbal Verón	5,000	30,000	0.17	2003
	9,000	15,000	0.60	2002
MIJD	7,000	60,000	0.12	2004
	9,000	60,000	0.15	2003
	9,000	30,000	0.30	2002

Source: All figures were reported by the leaders of the Piqueteros organizations to the media (*Clarín* 26 September 2002; *Clarín* 1 December 2003; *La Nación* 23 November 2002; *La Nación* 28 June 2004). Data collected for other organizations are in Appendix 8A.1.

increased from 119,000 to 152,000 and their membership also increased from 195,000 to 280,000.[24] Third, in most organizations approximately two-thirds of the members receive a workfare benefit; a field study conducted by journalists put the figure at three-quarters (*Clarín* 26 September 2002). This evidence suggests that the majority of members joined the organizations with the objective of accessing workfare benefits. Even the leaders of the Piqueteros organizations recognize that without workfare only half of their members would continue participating in the organization and only 10 or 15 per cent would continue blocking roads (*Clarín* 26 September 2002).

LONGITUDINAL ANALYSIS OF COLLECTIVE EVENTS

In this section we study the relative importance of workfare, system strain and other factors in accounting for the occurrence of road blockades across provinces and over time. According to the classical model, worse social conditions lead to more protests, while in the approach we follow, worse conditions contribute to the formation of a latent group but not necessarily to collective action. Workfare is, according to our view, the major factor explaining the development of insurgency.

More precisely, we predict the following relationship between road blockades organized by the Piqueteros and workfare: First, we expect no demonstrations when workfare does not exist. We also expect no protests when workfare benefits are accessible to all needy individuals, except if political bosses impose high costs upon beneficiaries.[25] Finally, when the number of workfare beneficiaries represents a small share of the needy population (such as from 1993 to 2001) and some local political bosses extort recipients, we expect that increases in funds allocated to workfare have a positive effect on demonstrations for two main reasons. First, more workfare participants today mean more ex-participants a few months later seeking to re-apply. Second, the larger the number of participants, the larger the number of people who realize (and presumably react to) the shady conditions imposed by local political bosses. These people join the Piqueteros organizations as an alternative channel to access workfare, and the organizations use these individuals to conduct new blockades, because blocking roads is an effective method to obtain more funds from the government and meet the demands of their new members.

Figure 8.1 plots the number of workfare beneficiaries and road blockades from 1993 to 2004. The first prediction is confirmed by the fact that the Piqueteros organizations did not exist before workfare was implemented (1993). Second, the number of workfare beneficiaries and road blockades appears to be positively correlated during 1993–2001 and, as expected, we observe a reduction in movement activity during 2003 and 2004, after workfare universalization in May 2002.

We proceed to econometrically assess the validity of the second prediction by studying a panel across provinces during 1994–2001.[26] The relation between road blockades and workfare is modeled as:[27]

$$Road\ Blockade_{it} = \beta_0 + \beta_1\ Workfare_{it} + \beta_2\ System\ Strain_{it} + \beta_3\ X_{it} + \varepsilon_{it} \quad (8.1)$$

where *Road Blockade*$_{it}$ is the monthly average number of events in province i in year t, *Workfare* is the monthly average number of workfare beneficiaries, *System Strain* is a vector including measures of deprivation (income inequality,

Figure 8.1   Workfare Beneficiaries and Road Blockades, 1993–2004

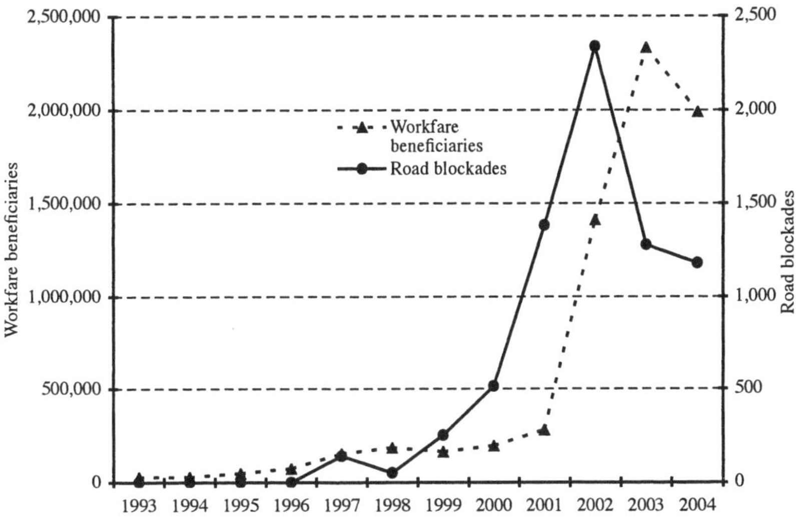

Note: Participants in both federal and provincial workfare programs are included, except in 2004, where only federal beneficiaries are included.

poverty and unemployment), and X is a vector of political variables (measures of corruption and stability in the structure of power) which, according to our hypothesis, have played a role in the development of insurgency.

We use data from several sources: *Road Blockade* figures are from the Centro de Estudios Nueva Mayoría and were collected from nine national daily newspapers.[28] For the purpose of this study, the dataset has two limitations: First, it starts in January 1997, but there were a few events in 1996. Second, it does not allow us to distinguish between road blockades conducted by Piqueteros and blockades conducted by other organizations. While the Piqueteros have arguably conducted most of the road blockades, other organizations such as labor unions have also used this form of protest. We collected data on road blockades during 1996 from *La Nación* digital reports and found that only six blockades were reported during that year. Also, Blanc et al. (2004) show that 74 per cent of all road blockades which occurred during the first half of 2004 were effectively conducted by Piqueteros organizations. To be consistent, and since results are not sensitive to including blockades in 1996, all figures and tables reported in the text are based on Nueva Mayoría.

Workfare is the sum of federal and provincial workfare beneficiaries. Data on federal beneficiaries came from the Argentine Ministry of Labor (1998,

Table 8.3   Means and Standard Deviations

Variable	Mean	S.D.
Road blockades (monthly average)	1.060	4.248
Workfare beneficiaries (monthly average in thousands)	6.149	12.315
Income inequality (Gini coefficient)	0.466	0.030
Poor and unemployed (in thousands)	40.051	93.289
Corruption perception (percentage)	19.975	5.584
Congress support (% congressmen same party as govt)	47.313	3.457
Governor's party is Peronism	0.609	0.489
Governor's party is UCR	0.168	0.375
Governor's party is Alianza	0.082	0.274
Governor's party is local party	0.141	0.349

Note: Number of observations is 184. The unit of observation is a province-year.

2001, 2002), and provincial beneficiaries are from the Argentine Ministry of the Economy (2001, 2002, 2004).

We use *Income Inequality* (measured by the Gini coefficient) and *Poor and Unemployed* (defined as the number of unemployed individuals between 18 and 65 who are below the poverty line, according to per capita household income) to assess the effect of social strain factors. These variables are obtained from the Permanent Household Survey (EPH).

We control for *Corruption Perception* (defined as the percentage of people who consider corruption to be the main problem) using data from Gallup. According to the classical model, more discontent leads to collective protests. In our perspective, clientelism in the allocation of workfare benefits and extortion of workfare participants increase aggrieved people's willingness to search for alternative means of accessing benefits. To the extent that these factors are partially captured by the above measure, we expect a positive effect on the likelihood of protests.

Finally, we include a proxy for stability in the power structure (*Congress Support*), defined as the percentage of congressmen who are of the same party as the government, and a set of indicators for the *Party of the Governor* to capture ideological preferences of protesters.[29] Our accounts of the development of insurgency suggest that only the first factor played an important role.[30] Table 8.3 presents basic statistics for the sample we study below.[31]

Column 1 in Table 8.4 presents the random effects estimates where the log of *Road Blockade* is regressed on *Workfare*, the two measures of social strain and year effects.[32] The correlation between resources and protests is positive, as expected, and significant. Contrary to the classical model, both measures of social strain are statistically insignificantly correlated with events.

In column 2 we add the remaining covariates. *Corruption Perception* is positively associated with protests and *Congress Support* is negatively associated, as expected. The party indicators are statistically insignificant. Both measures of social strain remain statistically insignificant, and the relation between resources and protests remains positive and significant.

In column 3 we allow unobserved time-constant effects to be correlated with the explanatory variables to control for omitted variable bias in the random effects model, and present fixed effects estimates. The correlation coefficient between *Workfare* and *Road Blockades* becomes smaller but remains positive and statistically significant at the 1 per cent level. The magnitude of the estimate suggests that an additional road blockade per year is likely to occur when the government increases the number of workfare beneficiaries by 2,500 (computed with all variables held at their means). Contrary to the deprivation hypothesis, providing more resources to aggrieved people increases insurgency. Furthermore, the effects of income inequality, poverty and unemployment are statistically insignificant. Worsening social conditions do not appear to be a robust explanation for the growth in protests. Finally, the estimates suggest that increases in corruption perceptions and instability in the power structure are significant factors explaining the development of insurgency.

Overall these results appear to be very consistent with narrative accounts about what actually happened in Argentina. In the mid-1990s, a few years after the government began distributing a limited number of workfare benefits, D'Elia and Alderete were leading informal groups of no more than a few hundred individuals. When they realized, together with other shrewd political entrepreneurs, that workfare benefits constitute material selective incentives and provide resources to the group, blockades began to occur. The government, lacking legitimacy due to its clientelistic practices, reacted to protests by providing more workfare benefits, contributing to an escalating cycle in demonstrations and workfare. By 2001, the number of workfare beneficiaries was ten times larger than in 1993 and membership in the Piqueteros organizations reached six digits.

In December 2001 President De la Rua resigned. Duhalde took office and increased the number of workfare beneficiaries to more than 2 million, making the program virtually universal. According to our hypothesis, we expect a decrease in the number of road blockades and a gradual reduction in Piqueteros membership, since accessing benefits through established institutions becomes easier for eligible individuals and blocking roads unnecessary. But at the same time, the Piqueteros organizations have already been formed and, as far as they continue controlling workfare, they have the resources to attract members and conduct demonstrations to maintain or even increase external funding.

Table 8.4   Regressions for Log Road Blockades, 1994–2001

Variable	(1) Random effects	(2) Random effects	(3) Fixed effects
Workfare	0.0271***	0.0277***	0.0228***
	(0.0039)	(0.0039)	(0.0052)
Poor and unemployed	0.0004	0.0005	0.0017
	(0.0005)	(0.005)	(0.0014)
Income inequality	0.9436	0.7934	−1.5236
	(0.7302)	(0.7206)	(1.8433)
Corruption perception	–	0.0180***	0.0278***
		(0.0047)	(0.0062)
Congress support	–	−0.0710***	−0.0872***
		(0.0072)	(0.0146)
Governor Peronist	–	−0.1070	−0.0510
		(0.0725)	(0.1425)
Governor UCR	–	−0.0094	−0.1189
		(0.0813)	(0.2282)
Governor local party	–	−0.0064	−0.1113
		(0.0937)	(0.1941)
Year dummies	Yes	Yes	Yes
Province fixed effects	No	No	Yes
Chi^2	553***	562***	
R^2			0.71

Note: Number of observations is 184. The unit of observation is a province-year. Robust standard errors in parentheses. The omitted category is Governor Alianza.
***p < .001 (two-tailed tests).

While it is not the purpose of this study to evaluate recent events, we observe a significant reduction in the number of road blockades – from 2,336 in 2002 to 1,181 in 2004. An alternative, although not mutually exclusive explanation for the recent reduction of protests, is the political alignment between current President Néstor Kirchner and some leaders of the Piqueteros, most notably D'Elia.

CONCLUSION

This chapter argues that access to material benefits has been a major factor motivating people to join the Piqueteros. These organizations were able to emerge and attract large numbers of poor and unemployed people thanks to the possibility of obtaining excludable external resources (workfare benefits) from the government. Workfare also contributed by fostering networking among aggrieved people. We agree that social strain played a role in the development of insurgency, but, contrary to previous research, we view this factor as underlying the formation of a latent group. Similarly, instability in the power structure of established political institutions – in particular internal divisions within the governing party – opened windows of opportunity for non-institutionalized groups. In our view it was the implementation of temporary public works programs (workfare), however, which solved the free-riding problem and reduced coordination barriers, both triggering the emergence of the movement and fueling its growth.

Our emphasis on access to material benefits does not imply that other factors (such as collective identities, social incentives, solidarity, psychological benefits or changes in collective perceptions of the prospects of insurgency) have not played a role in the emergence of the Piquetero movement. According to secondary sources, however, most of these factors appear to have been either irrelevant or not fundamental. First, collective identities, instead of having played a causal role in the emergence of the movement, are actually being framed by the Piqueteros (Gordillo 2003). Second, Davolos and Perelman (2004) suggest that participating in a road blockade does not increase reputation among workers. Third, and contrary to what has been found with other movements (McAdam 1999), we find no evidence that a shared cognition among poor people (i.e., oppressive conditions are subject to change) was crucial to the subsequent generation of insurgency (see Appendix 8A.2). We suspect that psychological benefits, such as feelings of dignity, efficacy and empowerment, contributed to the growth of the movement, since their members have usually been deprived of such feelings (for anecdotal evidence see Auyero 2003). But these are all highly speculative arguments; more research is needed to assess their importance.

This chapter analyzes different sources of information and provides new empirical evidence. First, using the Piquetero organization as the unit of analysis, we find a large and positive correlation between control over workfare benefits and membership, both across organizations and within organizations over time. Furthermore, comparing the evolution of three groups that were originally very similar shows that the one which did not control workfare benefits (MTD La Matanza) remained small and politically insignificant while the other two grew exponentially (FTV and CCCD). Third, using longitudinal data at the provincial level we find that, in a patronage environment where workfare funds are available only to a small fraction of the needy population, an increase in the monetary resource pool is likely to generate more protests, and the universalization of access has the contrary effect on mobilizations.

Our final words are to encourage more research on social movements in the less developed world. In several Latin American countries, for example, social movements have become important political actors during the last decades. Comparative studies would enhance our knowledge on the factors that have contributed to their growth, and considering that several years have passed since the emergence of the movements, we are in a position to start assessing their effects on development.

NOTES

1. We categorize the Piqueteros as a social movement following McAdam and Snow's definition: 'A collectivity acting with some degree of organization and continuity outside of institutional channels for the purpose of promoting or resisting change in the group, society, or world order of which it is a part' (1997, xviii). Recently, some Piqueteros leaders have become increasingly linked with institutional actors – such as the close relation between Luis D'Elia and President Néstor Kirchner – suggesting that some organizations are operating inside political institutions, and hence should be conceptually considered interest groups. The focus of this chapter, however, is on the emergence and growth of the movement.
2. Some studies do not distinguish between the emergence of a non-traditional form of demonstration: the *piquete* (road blockade), from the emergence of a new social movement: the *Piqueteros* (which we define, following the popular usage of the term, as organizations of poor and unemployed people not linked together by previous work experience). The few road blockades which occurred in the early 1990s were organized by recently fired workers with long experience working in the same firm (usually a public company in the process of privatization).
3. Eisinger (1973) and Tilly (1978) argue that the frequency of protests bears a curvilinear relationship with political openness. Democratization, by increasing the space of toleration, promotes the formation of social movements. This view appears more consistent with the case we are studying than arguing that the movement emerged as a reaction to limited democracy.
4. The first attempt to create a movement of unemployed people in Argentina occurred in 1897, when anarchist activists mobilized 5,000 unemployed people in Buenos Aires to protest social conditions (Godio 2000). The protest was repressed by the police; the movement did not receive any resources from the government and had disappeared by the end of that year.
5. Walker (1983) argues that the origin and maintenance of voluntary associations in the United States depend more upon their leaders' ability to secure funds from outside their membership rather than relying on material selective incentives. As we show below, both factors appear to be fundamental to explaining the emergence and growth of the Piqueteros.
6. Ronconi (2002) describes workfare programs in Argentina. Most of the authors who view workfare as a government reaction to the emergence of the Piqueteros point to the implementation of the Programa Trabajar, ignoring prior workfare programs.
7. The monthly benefit ranged from $150 to $350, depending on the program and the year. The legal minimum wage during the late 1990s was constant at $200 per month.
8. We searched Argentina's two largest newspapers (*La Nación* and *Clarín*) and found that

75 per cent of all the reports referring to workfare mention the existence of corruption and misallocation of workfare funds.

9. According to Oviedo (2001), the formation of what is now one of the largest Piqueteros organizations was triggered when Juan Carlos Alderete (its actual leader) accused Buenos Aires governor Eduardo Duhalde of coercing workfare beneficiaries into participating in a political demonstration supporting his party for the next election.

10. Even Rodolfo Díaz, the former secretary of labor who implemented workfare in 1993, recognized in 1995 that the government needed to improve the transparency in the allocation of workfare benefits (Díaz 1995, 131).

11. The first road blockades occurred in late 1991 when workers from YPF and Somisa (another state-owned company) blocked routes in Salta and Buenos Aires in protest against the privatization of the company.

12. Journalists interviewed the rank-and-file of the three largest Piqueteros organizations and found that members who receive a workfare benefit must contribute approximately $5 per month to the organization (*Clarín* 26 September 2002). The monthly fee ranges from $2.5 to $10 in Neuquén and Río Negro, according to what the Piqueteros reported to a regional newspaper (*Diario Río Negro* 22 December 2003).

13. The Ministry of Labor sent 500 auditors to several blockades to analyze why people participate in demonstrations. They found that the Piqueteros organizations require their members receiving workfare to participate in road blockades under threat of losing their benefit. These organizations use a ranking to allocate workfare benefits among their members based on how many times they participate in protests and in internal meetings of the organization (*La Nación* 9 August 2001). Similar evidence was reported by journalists after conducting a field study (*Clarín* 26 September 2002).

14. Peronism is a labor-based party. For a recent study on Peronism see Levitsky (2003).

15. In Buenos Aires, the largest province in Argentina, there were 62 organizations in 2004, according to the provincial Ministry of Human Development (*La Nación* 14 March 2004).

16. The Coordinadora was recently dissolved after several founding organizations left the group. The main organizations which remain are Movimiento de Trabajadores Desocupados (MTD) Aníbal Verón, MTD Solano and MTD Teresa Rodríguez.

17. The group that later became the FTV was called Cooperativa el Tambo, and it is the only group whose origins date back to the 1980s, when it was involved in a struggle with the provincial government over access to public land in greater Buenos Aires.

18. The FTV joined the Central de Trabajadores Argentinos in 1998, and the CCCD and the MIJD joined the Corriente Clasista Combativa in 1998 and 1996 respectively.

19. The creation of the Polo Obrero was impelled by the Partido Obrero, a leftist political party which historically represented employed workers. Polo Obrero began organizing unemployed people in 2001.

20. Authors' translation from the MTD Solano website: www.solano.mtd.org.ar.

21. There are no data about membership for any of these three groups in the mid-1990s. According to Oviedo (2001) and Svampa and Pereyra (2003), MTD La Matanza was among the largest groups of unemployed and poor individuals at that time.

22. Selection bias is a potential problem, since members of MTD La Matanza may be less interested in gaining power than the other two organizations, and a difference in preferences can help to explain their different evolution. A desire for power, however, is not a sufficient condition to obtain it. Access to workfare appears to be the most adequate explanation for the strikingly different levels of growth experienced by these organizations.

23. Cited in Svampa and Pereyra (2003, 41); authors' translation.

24. These figures do not capture the true magnitude of the positive correlation over time between membership and control over workfare benefits, since they are restricted to the period 2002 to 2004. Regrettably, we could not find any measure of these variables during 1996–2001, but as the Piqueteros' leaders suggest, they had very few members (presumably less than 100) before gaining access to workfare.

25. Individuals may opt to join a Piquetero organization even when access to the program is

universal, provided that the cost of joining (participation in road blockades) is lower than the expected benefit (avoiding extortion by the government). Another reason is that these organizations can set different eligibility requirements, allowing people who are ineligible according to the government criteria to access workfare benefits.

26. A better geographical unit of analysis is the municipality, since most workfare projects were implemented at this level, but data are not available. We exclude the year 1993 because there is no information about how workfare was distributed across provinces during that year.

27. In Franceschelli and Ronconi (2006) we control for potential simultaneity between workfare and road blockades and find that two-stage least squares estimates of the effect of workfare on demonstrations are positive and significant, although smaller than the OLS counterparts.

28. The data can be downloaded from http://nuevamayoria.com. They were collected by triangulating reports from: *Ámbito Financiero, Clarín, Crónica, Diario Popular, El Cronista, La Nación, La Prensa, La Razón* and *Página 12*.

29. During the period analyzed, Argentina had governors from the UCR, Alianza, Peronist and local parties. The ideology of these parties ranges from the left to the right side of the ideological spectrum.

30. For a review about the importance of political opportunities in the emergence of other social movements see Meyer (2004).

31. Argentina is politically organized in 23 provinces and a federal district (City of Buenos Aires). However, we treat the province of Buenos Aires and the City of Buenos Aires as the same unit, because many road blockades organized by movements located in greater Buenos Aires took place in the city or on the bridge which separates both jurisdictions (Puente Pueyredón).

32. Since event counts are non-negative and discrete they do not satisfy the normality assumption in OLS. Therefore, we logged the counts after adding 1.0 to each observation and use this transformed measure as the dependent variable. For methods of estimation in collective event analysis see Halaby (2004).

BIBLIOGRAPHY

Argentine Ministry of the Economy (2001), 'Informe sobre los programas de empleo provinciales' [Report on Provincial Employment Programs], Buenos Aires, Working Paper No. GP/09.

―― (2002) 'Informe sobre los programas de empleo de ejecución provincial 2001' [Report on Implementation of Provincial Employment Programs 2001], Buenos Aires, Working Paper No. GP/13.

―― (2004) 'Informe sobre los programas de empleo de ejecución provincial 2003'[Report on Implementation of Provincial Employment Programs 2003], Buenos Aires, Working Paper No. GP/15.

Argentine Ministry of Labor (1998), 'Informe de Coyuntura Laboral' [Report on Workfare], Buenos Aires.

――(2001), *Panorama de la Seguridad Social* [Social Security Perspectives], Buenos Aires, Argentina.

――(2002), *Panorama de la Seguridad Social* [Social Security Perspectives], Buenos Aires, Argentina.

Auyero, Javier (2003), *Contentious Lives: Two Argentine Women, Two Protests, and the Quest for Recognition*, Durham, NC: Duke University Press.

Blanc, Ana, Juan Fal, Julieta Gurvit, Andrea Paz, Tomás Raffo and Cecilia Vitto (2004), 'Protestas sociales en la Argentina contemporánea' [Social Protests in Contemporary Argentina], Instituto de Estudios y Formación, Central de Trabajadores Argentina.

Camarero, Hernán, Pablo Pozzi and Alejandro Schneider (1998), 'Unrest and Repression in Argentina', *New Politics*, **7** (1), 16–24.

Chatterton, Paul and Natasha Gordon (2004), 'To the Streets!', *City*, (8), 116–25.

Chong, Dennis (1991), *Collective Action and the Civil Rights Movement*, Chicago, IL: University of Chicago Press.

Colmegna, Paula (2003), 'The Unemployed Piqueteros of Argentina', *Theomai Journal*, (7), 1–11.

Conti, Rodrigo and Iván Schneider Mansilla (2003), *Piqueteros: una mirada histórica* [*Piqueteros: An Historic Perspective*], Buenos Aires: Astralib.

Davolos, Patricia and Laura Perelman (2004), 'Acción colectiva y representaciones sociales' [Collective Action and Social Representation], Amsterdam, International Institute of Social History, Labour Again Publications on Latin America.

Delamata, Gabriela (2004), 'The Organizations of Unemployed Workers in Greater Buenos Aires', Berkeley, University of California – Berkeley, Center for Latin American Studies Working Paper No. 8.

Díaz, Rodolfo (1995), *¿Prosperidad o ilusión?* [*Prosperity or Illusion?*], Buenos Aires: Editorial Ábaco.

Eisinger, Peter K. (1973), 'The Conditions of Protest Behavior in American Cities', *American Political Science Review*, **67** (1), 11–28.

Espinoza Schiappacasse, Andrea (2004), 'Piqueteras: Construyendo el movimiento desde el anonimato' [Constructing a Movement from the Anonymity], 27 December, at http://sepiensa.net.

Farinetti, Marina (1999), '¿Qué queda del "movimiento obrero"?' [What is Left of the Labor Movement?], *Trabajo y Sociedad*, **1** (1).

Ferrara, Francisco (2003), *Más allá del corte de rutas* [*Beyond Road Blockades*], Buenos Aires: La Rosa Blindada.

Franceschelli, Ignacio (2004), 'Cortes de Ruta y Planes de Empleo: Una Historia Poco Romántica del Movimiento Piquetero' [Road Blockades and Employment Programs: A Not Very Romantic Perspective on the Piquetero Movement], Undergraduate thesis, Universidad de San Andrés, Buenos Aires, Argentina.

Franceschelli, Ignacio and Lucas Ronconi (2006), 'The Causal Effect of External Resources on Mobilization', unpublished paper.

Galafassi, Guido (2003), 'Social Movements, Conflicts and a Perspective of Inclusive Democracy in Argentina', *Democracy and Nature*, **9** (3), 393–9.

Godio, Julio (2000), *Historia del movimiento obrero argentino* [*History of Argentina's Working Class*], Buenos Aires: Ediciones Corregidor.

Gordillo, Paula (2003), 'De la subordinación al antagonismo' [From Subordination to Antagonism], in Maria Susana Bonetto, Marcelo Casarin and María Teresa Piñero (eds), *Escenarios y Nuevas Construcciones Identitarias en América Latina* [*New Identity Construction in Latin America*], Córdoba, Argentina: Universidad Nacional de Córdoba, pp. 173–84.

Halaby, Charles (2004), 'Panel Models in Sociological Research: Theory and Practice', *Annual Review of Sociology*, **30**, 507–44.

Isman, Raúl (2004), *Los Piquetes de La Matanza* [*The Piquetes of La Matanza*], Buenos Aires: Ediciones Nuevos Tiempos.

Kohan, Aníbal (2002), *¡A las calles!* [*To the Streets!*], Buenos Aires: Ediciones Colihue.

Korol, Claudia (2004), 'Tiempo de guerras y emanciaciones en las tierras del petroleo' [War and Emancipation in the Oil Territories], *La Jiribilla*, No. 174 (September), Havana, Cuba.

Laufer, Rubén and Claudio Spiguel (1999), 'Las "puebladas" argentinas a partir del "santiagueñazo" de 1993' [Popular Uprisings after the "santiagueñazo"], in M. Lopez Amaya (ed.), *Lucha Popular, democracia, neoliberalismo* [*Popular Struggle, Democracy, and Neoliberalism*], Caracas, Venezuela: Nueva Sociedad, pp. 15–44.

Levitsky, Steven (2003), *Transforming Labor-Based Parties in Latin America*, New York: Cambridge University Press.

Lucha Internacionalista (2002), 'Sigue la revolución argentina' [The Argentine Revolution Continues], *Revista mensual*, No. 32.

McAdam, Doug (1999), *Political Process and the Development of Black Insurgency, 1930–1970*, Chicago: University of Chicago Press.

McAdam, Doug and David Snow (1997), *Social Movements: Readings on their Emergence, Mobilization and Dynamics*, Los Angeles, CA: Roxbury.

Meyer, David (2004), 'Protest and Political Opportunities', *Annual Review of Sociology*, **30**, 125–45.

Olson, Mancur (1965), *The Logic of Collective Action*, Cambridge, MA: Harvard University Press.

Oviedo, Luis (2001), *Una historia del movimiento Piquetero* [*A History of the Piquetero Movement*], Buenos Aires: Ediciones Rumbos.

Pozzi, Pablo (2000), 'Popular Upheaval and Capitalist Transformation in Argentina', *Latin American Perspectives*, **27** (5), 63–87.

Ronconi, Lucas (2002), 'El Programa Trabajar' [The Work Program], Buenos Aires, Argentina, Centro de Estudios para el Desarrollo Institucional, Working Paper No. 63.

Ronconi, Lucas and Ignacio Franceschelli (2003), 'Nuevos Movimientos Sociales en Argentina' [New Social Movements in Argentina], paper presented at the Sixth National Political Science Congress, Rosario, Argentina, 8 November.

Ronconi, Lucas, Juan Sanguinetti and Sandra Fachelli (2006), 'Poverty and Employability Effects of Workfare Programs in Argentina', Poverty and Economic Policy Research Network (www.pep-net.org), Working Paper No. 2006-14.

Scribano, Adrián (1999), 'Argentina cortada' [Argentina Blockaded], in M. Lopez Amaya (ed.), *Lucha Popular, democracia, neoliberalismo* [*Popular Struggle, Democracy and Neoliberalism*], Caracas, Venezuela: Nueva Sociedad, pp. 45–72.

Svampa, Maristella and Sebastián Pereyra (2003), *Entre la ruta y el barrio* [*Between the Road and the Neighborhood*], Buenos Aires: Editorial Biblos.

Tilly, Charles (1978), *From Mobilization to Revolution*, Boston: Addison-Wesley.

Tommasi, Mariano (2002), 'Federalism in Argentina and the Reforms of the 1990s', Stanford, CA, Stanford Center for International Development Working Paper No. 147.

Walker, Jack (1983), 'The Origins and Maintenance of Interest Groups in America', *American Political Science Review*, **77** (2), 390–406.

Wilson, John (1973), *Introduction to Social Movements*, New York: Basic Books.

APPENDIX

Appendix 8A.1   Membership and Control of Workfare Benefits across Some Piqueteros Organizations

Piquetero organization designation	Number of workfare beneficiaries controlled by organization	Number of members	Ratio workfare/ members	Month–year	Source
Barrios de Pie	7,000	60,000	0.12	06–04	b
	6,000	na		11–02	b
	na	4,000		07–02	c
Teresa Rodríguez	5,000	na		11–02	b
Frente de Trabajadores Combativos	2,800	7,000	0.40	06–04	b
Coordinadora de	na	5,000		02–05	e
Unidad Barrial	1,140	4,680	0.24	06–04	b
MTD Solano	150	350	0.43	11–01	f
	na	7,000	0.17	01–05	e
MTD Aníbal Verón	5,000	30,000	0.17	12–03	a
Movimiento Sin Trabajo	na	95,000		12–04	h
Teresa Vive	5,000	na		11–02	b
Movimiento Territorial	na	5,000		12–04	h
de Liberación	4,000	na		11–02	b
Futradeyo	na	650		12–04	h
UTD Mosconi – Salta	na	2,000		02–04	g
	na	7,000		07–02	c
MTD – Río Negro	800	1,200	0.67	12–03	d
CCC – Río Negro	230	500	0.46	12–03	d
Barrios de Pie – Río Negro	400	600	0.67	12–03	d
Polo Obrero – Río Negro	230	250	0.92	12–03	d
Teresa Vive – Río Negro	262	500	0.52	12–03	d

Note: In all cases the figures were provided by members of the respective Piquetero organization either to the media or to researchers. The month–year column indicates the point in time to which the data on membership and control of workfare refer. The table includes all figures we found after searching online. Figures for the five major organizations are in Table 8.2.

Source:
a.   *Clarín* 1 December 2003.
b.   *La Nación* 23 November 2002, 28 June 2004.
c.   *Lucha Internacionalista* July 2002.
d.   *Rio Negro* 22 December 2003.
e.   *Segundo Enfoque* February 2005.
f.   Chatterton and Gordon (2004).
g.   Korol (2004).
h.   Espinoza Schiappacasse (2004).

Appendix 8A.2   Shared Cognitions and the Development of Insurgency

McAdam (1999) presents evidence that, in the mid-1940s, African-Americans were more optimistic regarding future opportunities for advancement than the rest of the U.S. population. He interprets the data as supportive evidence that a shared cognition within the black community (i.e., oppressive conditions are subject to change) was crucial to the subsequent generation of insurgency. Information extracted from the Encuesta de Desarrollo Social suggests the opposite in the Piqueteros' case. The survey was conducted during August 1997, at a time when the Piqueteros were still a minor group. Poor and unemployed people reported slightly *less* optimism about their future than the average citizen. The table below shows that 44.5 per cent of those individuals located in the bottom quintile of the income distribution considered that their economic situation in 20 years was going to be better, while the figures for the other socioeconomic groups ranged between 46 and 48 per cent (the difference between the poorest and richest quintile is significant at the 1 per cent level). If we restrict the analysis to unemployed people located in the bottom quintile of the income distribution, their rate of optimism is even lower (43 per cent).

How Do You Expect Your Economic Situation to Be in Twenty Years (per cent)

	Poorest quintile	2nd quintile	3rd quintile	4th quintile	Richest quintile
Better	44.5	45.9	47.5	47.1	46.0
Same	24.5	24.0	23.8	24.5	25.3
Worse	18.7	18.5	16.9	16.8	17.5
Do not know	12.3	11.7	11.8	11.6	11.2

Index

accountability 56–8, 62–3
Acemoglu, Daron 22, 68, 86
administrative subordination 101, 102,
    103, 106
Agarwal, Bina 209, 223
Agrawal, Arun 204, 205
Akai, Nobu 127
Akhmedov, Akhmed 74
Alderete, Juan Carlos 234, 243, 247
Alesina, Alberto 4, 7, 64, 151
Almond, Gabriel 148
America *see* United States
Andhra Pradesh *see* joint forest
    management and participation,
    India
Angelsen, Arild 188
anti-institutionalism 22, 23
Arabari experience 205
Ardagna, Silvia 4
Argentina
    fiscal decentralization 36–7, 106–7
    local politicians 107
    political system 31, 32
Argentina, workfare and the Piqueteros
    background 228–30
    collective events, longitudinal analysis
        240–45
    conclusion 245–6
    government and the workfare
        235–6
    Piqueteros control of workfare
        benefits 236–9, 251
    Piqueteros, emergence of 230–31
    Piqueteros, membership 236–9,
        251
    workfare beneficiaries 231–5
    workfare in patronage-based system
        235–6
Aron, Janine 4, 7, 86

Asia
    democratization 73
    presidential democracies 25
Asian values 72
assimilative capacity 147–8, 154, 161
authoritarian political systems 73, 76
    categorization 29–30
    and economic growth 79, 80
authoritarian transition 33
autocracies 73, 75, 76

Bagehot, Walter 141
Baland, Jean-Marie 201
Balooni, Kulbhushan 205, 206
Bangladesh
    democracy and poverty reduction
        48–9, 57, 58
    evolution of democracy 49
Bardhan, Pranab 102, 201
Barenstein, Mathis 127
Barro, Robert J. 8, 75, 96, 109
Bates, Robert 4, 6
Bathla, Seema 202, 203
Beck, Thorsten 108
Behera, Bhagirath 205
Bertelsmann Transformation Index (BTI)
    141–2
Besley, Timothy 46, 59
bicameralism 28, 40
Blanc, Ana 240
Blanchard, Olivier 102, 103, 106, 107
Block, Carolyn Rebecca 154
Borooah, Vani 204
Bossert, Thomas J. 106
Botswana 37, 80
Bourguignon, François 43
Bratton, Michael 58, 66
Brazil
    federalism 36–7